"Tamm and Luyet know what they're talking about and they know how to teach it. *Radical Collaboration* is a road map for creating collaborative, high performance organizations. I've seen this approach make authentic and positive differences in people's lives."

—*Don Pomraning, former Senior Manager of Organizational Development,*
*Boeing Commercial Aircraft Group*

"Finally, a practical, insightful and comprehensive road map to creating successful relationships. Adopt these principles and watch your connections with others improve overnight. A must-read for all of us in these turbulent times."

—*Greg Hicks, author of* LeaderShock . . . and How to Triumph over It

"Successful relationships are the key to success in business, sports and just about any life endeavor. The skills discussed by Tamm and Luyet are easy to implement and more importantly, they work. Try them and you'll not only be more productive, but live a life that is more fulfilled and much happier."

—*Robert J. Kriegel, Ph.D., author of* If It Ain't Broke . . . BREAK IT! *and*
How to Succeed in Business Without Working So Damn Hard

"At last a practical manual on how to develop collaborative capital and improve the quality of one's personal and professional relationships. Tamm and Luyet are experienced guides and have provided us with the tools and road map to skillfully navigate our interior landscapes and create successful collaborative outcomes."

—*Michael Rossiter, Vice President, Chubb, PLC*

"My favorite line in this book is, 'If your relationship doesn't bump up against conflict every once in a while, you're either in complete denial or overly medicated.' With this in mind, the authors present their interest-based model for resolving differences in an easy-to-read no-nonsense style, which includes how to develop a contingency plan if your attempt at finding a solution goes south. Well worth reading!"

—*Harriet Chaney, Director of Management Development,*
*Mountain States Employers Council, Inc.*

"*Radical Collaboration* offers a refreshingly practical approach for building collaborative skills, for individuals and within organizations. Jim Tamm and Ron Luyet are the two brightest new stars in the business consulting field today."

—*Helen Palmer, author of* The Enneagram in Love and Work: Understanding
Your Intimate and Business Relationships

# RADICAL
## COLLABORATION

Five Essential Skills to
**OVERCOME DEFENSIVENESS**
and Build Successful Relationships

# JAMES W. TAMM
# and RONALD J. LUYET

## COLLINS BUSINESS
*An Imprint of HarperCollins Publishers*

A hardcover edition of this book was published by HarperBusiness,
an imprint of HarperCollins Publishers, in 2004.

HarperCollins books may be purchased for educational, business, or sales promotional
use. For information, please write: Special Markets Department, HarperCollins Publishers, 10 East 53rd Street, New York, NY 10022.

First Collins paperback edition published 2005

Designed by Nancy Singer Olaguera

**Library of Congress Cataloging-in-Publication Data of the hardcover edition has been
applied for.**

ISBN-10: 0-06-074251-8    ISBN-13: 978-0-06-074251-5 (pbk.)

08 09  ❖/RRD  10 9 8 7 6 5

**RADICAL** (rad'i k'l) *adj.* of or from the root: fundamental, favoring basic change, as in the social structure.

**COLLABORATION** (ko·lab'o ra'shun) *n.* to work or act jointly, to labor together.

To seven men who inspired us in different ways,

at different times, to become who we are:

Will Schutz

Roy Tamm

Carl Rogers

Patrick Williams

Roger Fisher

Herman Levy

Martin Haslett

# CONTENTS

# ACKNOWLEDGMENTS

**Being only occasional** authors, we never know when we will have another opportunity to thank so many people who have played an instrumental role in the development of our work in general, as well as this book specifically.

We start with our families and thank them for all the time we weren't available to them. We've learned from our children, Ryan, Janelle, Nola, and Francie, the true value of a good relationship. Kathy Tamm, a gifted psychotherapist and courageous wife (of Jim) and mother (of Ryan and Janelle), has been the most ardent supporter of our work. If the world could tap into her power of persuasion, energy, and belief in what we do, there would be no need for the words *economic downturn*. We especially thank her for her encouragement (i.e., pushing, prodding, and holding our feet to the fire), as well as collaborating with us to articulate the concepts in chapter 9 and the notion that defensiveness is related to the body-mind connection.

We wish to thank Business Consultants Network, Inc., and Shogo Saito, chairman of Business Consultants, Inc., for graciously giving us permission to quote from the works of Will Schutz and FIRO theory, including material used in their workshop titled The Human Element.

Roy and Florence Tamm are the finest living example of a wildly successful collaborative relationship. As a couple they have been a wonderful guiding light for family, friends, and community for more than sixty years.

Dr. Gary Chapin, P. Michael Hunt, Vance Kennedy, and the late Dr. Patrick Williams have gathered with Jim every January for almost thirty-five years for several days of intense personal growth. The collective wisdom of that group has been powerful guidance. The group is a living reflection of the value of truth, choice, and awareness in action and has been a marvelous place to try out new ways of living and theories of collaboration.

Steve Barber, senior partner in the consulting firm of Barber & Gonzales; Janet Walden, CEO of the Center for Collaborative Solutions; John Glaser, superintendent of Napa Valley Unified School District; Les Chisholm, Sacramento regional director of the California Public Employment Relations Board (PERB); and Kathleen Stanbrough, executive director of the Sacramento Mediation Center, are probably more responsible than anyone else for the exponential growth of the interest-based approach to problem solving in the public sector. They lead a small band of skillful entrepreneurial revolutionaries infiltrating the public sector. They took great ideas and gave them wings. It was the ride of a lifetime to be on the same airplane.

Mark Smith, a gifted and generous mentor, and the late Jan Abbot were also instrumental in the success of the California labor-management relationship project that is the basis of much of this book. They also both played a positive role in Jim's decision to leave the law and start a new chapter in his life by going into consulting.

Anita Martinez, San Francisco regional director of the California PERB; Jerilyn Gelt, labor relations specialist at PERB; Fred D'Orazio, chief administrative law judge at PERB; and Ron Blubaugh, former chief administrative law judge at PERB, not only offered Jim tremendous encouragement and support, they also covered his real workload while he was off having fun settling strikes. The support and friendship they gave Jim made twenty-five years at PERB worth twenty-five years of his life.

Ailish Schutz and Jerry Miller were the heart and soul of Will Schutz Associates when we first sought to partner with them. They fully embraced the concept of a collaborative relationship with us, allowing us the opportunity to spread this work internationally, and have offered continuous encouragement and support for this book project.

Marian Pastor, Dorothea Hamilton, James Cusack, Kathy Tamm, and Jo Saia, all staff of the Institute for Personal Change, have for twenty-five years been Ron's colleagues and friends. They have made major contributions to our understanding of human behavior and the psychology of unconscious programming that is reflected in this book. Norm Brice and Dick Gould of California State University, Chico, were also a positive influence on Ron's life direction.

A number of key individuals not only encouraged us but also added great individual efforts to spread the concepts throughout the world. Dr. Jorge Diaz, president of Quidam International in Boston and Mexico City; Sune Almkvist of Kommunikator A&W AB in Bornby, Sweden; Susanne Gorander, Leif Cervin, Christian Rudquist, Marianne Lidgren, principal consultants and partners at Right Sinova AB in Stockholm, Sweden; Keijo Halinen of GDC Group Oy of Finland, and Alain Duluc, senior manager of CEGOS Corporation in Paris, were primarily responsible for the growth of this work in Mexico, Scandinavia, and Europe.

Al Beck, professor of management at the U.S. Department of Defense, Defense Systems Management College; Don Pomraning, former senior manager of organization development for Boeing's Commercial Aircraft Group and corporate development leader, Idaho Power Corp.; Sandra Sell Lee, organizational development consultant and executive coach for Boeing's Business Operations and Process Management Group; and Gary Copeland of Copeland Consulting, LLC, were all early supporters of the work in the United States. Their support made it much easier to hang in there during the early lean growth years. The early support of Peggy and Conrad Smith also served as the foundation for the development of much of our collaborative work. Don White and Thomy Barton are exceptional organizational consultants who have continuously deepened our understanding of the concepts of truthfulness, accountability, and friendship.

David Murphy, superintendent of the Davis Unified School District, has through the years generously offered us opportunities to present our ideas to his various school staffs. Michael Rossiter has given us an opportunity to present self-knowledge-oriented training experiences to major corporations around the world.

We have had the privilege to work with several organizations giving us an opportunity to field test many of the *Radical Collaboration* practices: the Corporate Development Department at Idaho Power Corp., including Don Pomraning, Anne Smith, Vikkey Soderman, Kevin Wartman, and Dave Armstrong; the Management Development Department at Mt. States Employers Council including Robin Zwisler, Harriet Chaney, and other members of the department who exemplify a collaborative working environment; the Alliance Management Team at Eli Lilly and Company, who have adopted *Radical Collaboration* practices and have been willing to share their practical experiences with us; David Le Sage and then Jan Moore at NASA, as well as the many men and women on various NASA teams, who for the past twenty years have been engaging in interpersonal exploration as well as exploring the galaxy.

Judy Teng, dean of contract and continuing education at City College of San Francisco, not only offered encouragement but also opened the doors of China and Peking University for Jim and introduced him to the joy of one of the most interesting places on earth, the Beijing Flea Market at Panjaiyuan, where it's possible to rapidly test out any theory on negotiation or collaboration.

The wisdom and friendship of Eileen Roach, Donna Jennelle, Phil Bliss, Jack Downing, and Cheryl Duvall have added immeasurably to a more compassionate understanding of the human condition.

Barbara Courtney's relentless support and encouragement for writing this book fed the seeds of fantasy long before it really seemed like a possibility. Paul Hamilton's initial editing of our book proposal forced us to be more articulate. Paul used more red ink than Arnold Schwarzenegger will use on all of his California budgets.

Jerry Miller, Rod Taylor, Marianne Lidgren, Celeste Blackman, Ailish Schutz, Roy and Florence Tamm, Gary Chapin, Vance Kennedy, Kathy Tamm, and Kathleen Stanbrough all offered helpful comments after reading early drafts of the manuscript.

We thank Dick Thompson, not only for his efforts to popularize FIRO theory, but also for his willingness to take a leap of faith and partner with us to offer FIRO Element B assessments for readers.

The encouragement and support of our agent, Jimmy Vines, of the Vines Agency Inc. in New York, was extraordinary. In addition to breaking the mold for literary agents by answering practically every phone call or returning it within ten minutes, he also delivered on every promise he made, including bringing this project to Harper-Collins. The help of Leah Spiro, our editor at HarperCollins, was also extraordinary. In a supportive but firm way, she challenged us to be articulate. Readers who are unfamiliar with some of the more complex concepts we present in this book, such as FIRO theory, have Leah to thank if they can understand the concepts after reading the book. If they don't understand them, they still have us to blame.

Almost last, but certainly not least by any possible measurement, we want to thank Professor Mayte Barba, director of Business Administration Studies at Universidad Tec de Monterrey in Cuernavaca,

Mexico, for three things. First, for her helpful research showing the dramatic effectiveness of the Beyond Conflict–Accountable Collaboration program in reducing defensiveness; second, for her great assistance regarding self-esteem, the subject of her doctoral studies; and finally, for her efforts to inspire and pass these concepts on to the next generation of entrepreneurs in Latin America.

Finally for the source of all that was written.

## Trademarks

FIRO Element B: Behavior; FIRO Element F: Feelings; FIRO Element S: Self; FIRO Element O: Organizational Climate; FIRO Element J: Job; FIRO Element W: Work Relations; FIRO Element C: Close Relations; Elements of Awareness; Trustworthy Leader Survey; and Concordance are all trademarks of Business Consultants Network, Inc. The Human Element is a registered trademark of Business Consultants Network, Inc. FIRO and FIRO B are registered trademarks of Consulting Psychologists Press, Inc. Teflon is a registered trademark of Dupont. Velcro is a trademark of Velcro Industries. Beyond Conflict and Beyond Conflict: Accountable Collaboration, Radiant Transit Exercise, and Radical Collaboration are all trademarks of James W. Tamm and Ronald J. Luyet.

# PREFACE

*Radical Collaboration* **teaches** practical methods to significantly improve your skills for building collaborative relationships. The training and research reported in this book present a clear case that collaborative skills can be learned quickly and easily. This book is based on research that documents dramatic improvements in both individual skills and organizational culture that can have a powerful impact on effectiveness. Many participants began with working relationships that were ineffective, adversarial, and nontrusting. Their relationships were transformed into effective, cooperative, and trusting partnerships. For example, research[1] based upon data supplied by the State of California Public Employment Relations Board, where Jim was a senior administrative law judge and San Francisco regional director, showed:

- Almost one hundred organizations reduced their conflict[2] by an average rate of 67 percent.
- The ten most troubled organizations at the start of the project reduced their conflict by an average rate of 85 percent over three years.

Research conducted by Professor Mayte Barba, a director of Business Administration Studies at Universidad Tec de Monterrey in Cuernavaca, Mexico,[3] showed:

- Over a six-year period, individuals from nine countries reported they reduced their own defensiveness in conflicts by half and were 45 percent more effective at getting their interests met in conflicts using the skills in this book.

- Participants also reported significant gains in their ability to build and maintain climates of trust.

Research conducted at the University of California, Berkeley, Institute of Industrial Relations,[4] showed:

- Prior to the training, 70 percent of participants characterized their working relationship as adversarial. After sixteen months, less than 1 percent said it was adversarial.
- Individuals also reported significant gains in raising trust levels and reducing the impact of adversarial attitudes in relationships.

The long-term sustainability of the benefits reported in this research demonstrates that these skills are not just another flavor of the month. This research is outlined in more detail in appendix 1.

The book is also based upon a heavily researched theory of interpersonal relationships and team compatibility called FIRO theory. FIRO stands for Fundamental Interpersonal Relations Orientation and was created by Dr. Will Schutz[5] when the U.S. Navy asked him to conduct research on understanding and predicting how groups work together, particularly in stressful situations. The research provided a wealth of information about how to improve the effectiveness of teams. In his research,[6] for example, if randomly selected new teams were successful 50 percent of the time, using FIRO theory to focus on team compatibility increased that success rate to 75 percent. In today's business environment that is so dependent on ever-changing project teams, that is a remarkable increase in effectiveness. In chapters 7 and 8 you'll have the opportunity to take the FIRO Element B assessment online and learn the application of this research to your relationships.

We also base this book on our collective seventy years of firsthand experience helping people turn conflict into collaboration, on what we've learned from generous sharing by workshop participants over the past fifteen years, and the teaching and writing of Will Schutz and Roger Fisher.[7] Knowing that these collaborative skills can be learned quickly, we give readers five essential skills that are necessary for successfully building long-term relationships. By learning the skills offered in this book, *you* can become more effective at building collaborative relationships. Because teams, businesses, and organizations live or die based upon the effectiveness of relationships, learning these skills will result in a dramatic and measurable impact on the bottom line.

*Radical Collaboration* is divided into two main areas, the first focusing on the internal and the second on the external. Chapters 1 to 9 focus on the interpersonal skills essential for collaborative relationships. Chapters 10 to 17 focus on collaborative problem-solving strategies and methodologies that are necessary to succeed with the outside world.

We hope this book will give readers a clear picture of the terrain they must navigate and the skills they need to acquire on their way to building wildly successful collaborative relationships.

*Jim W. Tamm*
*Ron J. Luyet*

# RADICAL
## COLLABORATION

# INTRODUCTION: THE FIVE ESSENTIALS

**They weren't even** talking to each other, much less listening. The relationship had been shattered. A rogue union member was attempting to puncture the tires of fellow employees' cars as they tried to cross a union picket line. Certain managers were covertly plotting retaliation against union leaders. At the medium-sized California school district,[1] almost twenty-one thousand students were receiving little or no education. Bitterness in the labor-management relationship had brought effective education to a halt. Substitute teachers were little more than babysitters. Community members were distraught at being treated like pawns in a war of conflicting press releases and accusations, while precious education dollars were squandered on litigation. After several weeks, and with the help of a mediator, the labor dispute was eventually settled, but only after a great deal of pain for everyone involved.

Now time-travel ahead two years to the district's next labor-management contract negotiation. This time the negotiators were not only talking to each other, they were actually listening. They weren't sitting across from each other pounding their fists on a table. Rather, they were sitting interspersed among each other in comfortable chairs arranged in a semicircle facing a flip chart. If observers didn't know who the players were, they would not have been able to tell who represented the union and who represented management. Negotiators took turns facilitating the negotiating session. They were all working together to improve the educational system, as well as the quality of life for the educators. They all worked hard to satisfy the interests of everyone involved. They were committed to both telling and hearing the truth. They didn't get defensive, and when, on occasion, someone ruffled somebody else's feathers, they took time to talk about their relationship.

Impossible? Not at all; we've seen it happen. What made the difference? They learned how to create a successful collaborative relationship. They realized that the only way they could solve their problems was by building an effective relationship.

Today nobody succeeds alone. If you don't have the skills to build relationships, you'd better win the lotto, because you'll never thrive in any organization, and you probably won't even survive in most businesses. These are simple facts of modern life! The inventor or entrepreneur who creates an idea, then single-handedly markets a product successfully, is a thing of the past. The world has become far too complex and interrelated for individuals to succeed without collaborative skills. Even fierce competitors of the past are finding it not only desirable but absolutely essential to form alliances and to collaborate on projects.

Who would have thought that IBM and Apple, or Microsoft and Oracle, would ever collaborate on projects; or that labor unions and management would become keenly collaborative to help a business (or a school district) thrive, or that the United States and Russia would collaborate by sharing intelligence information to track down members of the Taliban in Afghanistan?

## COLLABORATIVE CAPITAL

Companies are beginning to recognize that the ability to build and maintain relationships is an essential set of skills. They recognize that the collaborative capital of their employees, which is the collective ability of their employees to build effective collaborative relationships, is as important as their intellectual capital and their financial capital.

Research has shown that IQ and technical expertise do not fully account for the performance difference between exceptional employees and average performers.[2] One factor that does make a significant difference is the collaborative networks that exceptional employees develop. These collaborative networks enable top employees to tap into the collective wisdom of a much larger brain trust. Consultant

Steven Kelner has been doing competency evaluations on the collaborative skills of managers for over fifteen years. He reports a dramatic increase over the past five years in the interest of companies regarding collaborative skills.[3]

One international company we worked with started teaching relationship-building skills to their key managers when they recognized that from 50 to 75 percent of their future products would come from collaborative alliances with smaller entrepreneurial companies. These smaller companies are more creative and can react faster, but they don't have resources for testing products extensively nor for bringing them to market. It was a real eye-opener for the larger company to learn that many smaller companies would not consider working with them because of a reputation for being untrustworthy and not at all collaborative. They had already lost opportunities for many potentially profitable products. They recognized that if three-quarters of their future products would arise from alliances, and nobody wanted to do business with them because of poor collaboration skills, their company was not long for the world. Shortly thereafter the company began investing heavily in developing collaborative skills.

By contrast, a defense contractor client was able to resolve a dispute involving hundreds of millions of dollars because the key leaders of the disputing organizations trusted each other, had reputations for telling the truth, and were able to maintain a successful collaborative relationship.

## DISCRETIONARY EMOTIONAL ENERGY OR ENTHUSIASM

Collaborative relationships are valuable to an organization not only because they produce better processes and better results, but also because they increase the amount of discretionary emotional energy that employees will devote to the organizational effort. *Discretionary emotional energy* is a term coined by consultant and author Stan Slap[4] to describe the passion, excitement, enthusiasm, and dedication that individuals choose to give freely to those causes, projects, relationships, and organizations in which they truly believe. Discretionary emotional energy cannot be mandated, and attempts to do so will inevitably lead to either outright rebellion or passive-aggressive undermining behavior. It is personal buy-in that can't be bought.

---

**BOX I-1**

Discretionary emotional energy is the passion, excitement, enthusiasm, and dedication that individuals choose to give freely to those causes, projects, relationships, and organizations in which they truly believe. It can't be mandated, and attempts to do so will inevitably lead to either outright rebellion or passive-aggressive undermining behavior.

---

Discretionary emotional energy in a business setting exists when employees are excited about making suggestions for making their jobs more effective and profitable. For example, in San Juan Unified School District in Sacramento, California, the food service department was losing the district so much money the district was considering contracting with outside vendors to run the program. The union, together with employees, tapped into the employees' enthusiasm, or discretionary emotional energy, and devised a successful plan to run the food service program themselves. This saved enough money to continue providing the same level of service to students.

Don White[5] was a manager in a Procter & Gamble plant where the company had been working with employees to be more self-accountable, truthful, and self-aware. Don describes what happened:

> We had been working for about six months using these principles when I noticed a distinct change in the climate among employees. Productivity, safety awareness, appearance, and morale (in a word, aliveness) were all up at the same time. I had never experienced this before and thought long and hard about the cause. I finally decided that the main difference was that people were actually working on work instead of working on one another.

---

**BOX I-2**

Productivity, safety awareness, appearance, and morale (in a word, aliveness) were all up at the same time . . . I finally decided that the main difference was that people were actually working on work instead of working on one another.

*Don White, P&G*

---

A practice called "work to rule" provides an example of employees using discretionary energy against a company. Employees use the work-to-rule tactic by following the company work rules exactly and meticulously, which almost always decreases productivity. Then, when confronted about their unproductive behavior, employees innocently reply, "Gee, we were just following the company rules."

At a General Electric Co. lighting systems plant in Hendersonville, North Carolina, employees on the assembly line were annoyed by an autocratic new supervisor. Company policy was that if employees suspected a mistake or quality flaws in their own work, they could stop the assembly line long enough to either correct the mistake or remove the flawed product from the line. In response to a thoughtless action by the new supervisor, employees all of a sudden became very conscious of potential quality flaws. They stopped the line at the slightest concern (some would say imaginary concerns). The assembly line came to a grinding halt and production was zero for an entire day.

When the new supervisor criticized them for their tactics, telling them not to be so conscientious, they followed his directions precisely. They weren't nearly as conscientious and let all possible quality flaws pass down the assembly line, creating a nightmare for the quality inspectors at the end of the line.

In both situations the employees said they were just following orders of the new supervisor. Their negative attitude effectively sabotaged the supervisor, destroying productivity for two days. The supervisor's authority was undermined for months to come, simply because he lacked skills to build an effective working relationship with his employees.

## COLLABORATION IS NECESSARY FOR TEAMWORK

Strong collaborative skills increase natural enthusiasm not just among individuals, but also among team members and between departments, customers, suppliers, and partners. Collaborative skills leverage the effectiveness of all relationships. Collaborative relationships support healthy environments in contrast to the toxic effect of conflicted relationships.

Organizations today are advocating more flexibility in people's roles, acceptance of change at a faster pace, more shared decision making and creative problem solving, and more trust from teams who must constantly be redefining their task. Many organizations also expect this without excessive internal competition and are unwilling to support individuals and teams in positive ways of building effective relationships and managing the inevitable conflict that will arise.

## WHERE COLLABORATION BEGINS

Collaborative strategies, however, are not simply another business methodology that can be imposed like a new cost-accounting scheme. Many companies learned this the hard way when they tried to create teams without first teaching employees the skills necessary for effective teamwork.

---

**BOX I-3**

Collaborative strategies, however, are not simply another business methodology that can be imposed like a new cost-accounting scheme. Many companies learned this the hard way when they tried to create teams without first teaching employees the skills necessary for effective teamwork.

---

Many companies had developed all their employees for years by encouraging them to excel at becoming "star" individual contributors. Now, with a change of policy like a flick of a switch, they were supposed to think, feel, and act like a team, where their greatest contribution now might be to support someone else's success.

---

**BOX I-4**

Without collaborative skills, a team is just a group of individuals who each follow their own agenda.

---

True collaboration begins inside the individual, not the organization. It begins with an intentional attitude we describe as being in the Green Zone (as opposed to the Red Zone). Collaboration begins within the individual and then works its way out into the organization. Until individuals operate in the Green Zone, an organization won't be able to tap into the excitement, aliveness, and power of collaborative relationships. When individuals are operating in the Green Zone, collaboration is a catalyst for innovation and for higher levels of problem solving.

---
**BOX I-5**
True collaboration begins inside the individual, not the organization.

---

Individuals in the Green Zone convey an authentic, nondefensive presence. The Green Zone gives individuals the attitude and a state of mind that allows them to focus their energy and skills on creative problem solving. In an atmosphere free of intrigue, mistrust, and betrayal, individuals have greater opportunities to realize the full potential of their circumstances.

## THE FIVE ESSENTIAL SKILLS

A long-term, successful relationship is unlikely without the five skills presented below:

**Essential Skill #1: Collaborative Intention:** Individuals stay in the Green Zone, maintain an authentic, nondefensive presence, and make a personal commitment to mutual success in their relationships.

**Essential Skill #2: Truthfulness:** Individuals commit to both telling the truth and listening to the truth. They also create a climate of openness that allows all people in the relationship to feel safe enough to discuss concerns, solve problems, and deal directly with difficult issues.

**Essential Skill #3: Self-Accountability:** Individuals take responsibility for the circumstances of their lives, the choices they make either through action or failing to act, and the intended or unforeseen consequences of their actions. They would rather find a solution than find someone to blame.

**Essential Skill #4: Self-Awareness and Awareness of Others:** Individuals commit to knowing themselves deeply and are willing to explore difficult interpersonal issues. They seek to understand the concerns, intentions, and motivations of others, as well as the culture and context of their circumstances.

**Essential Skill #5: Problem-Solving and Negotiating:** Individuals use problem-solving methods that promote a cooperative atmosphere. They avoid fostering subtle or unconscious competition.

---

**BOX I-6**

Five Essential Skills for Successful Collaborative Relationships

1. Collaborative Intention

2. Truthfulness

3. Self-Accountability

4. Self-Awareness and Awareness of Others

5. Problem-Solving and Negotiating

---

Some people maintain that it is impossible to be truthful, accountable, aware, and collaborative unless you are in a safe environment. They feel it is too dangerous to always tell the truth and to boldly take responsibility for all of their actions. We argue instead that it is precisely these behaviors that create safe environments. The more individuals stay in the Green Zone, tell the truth, are accountable for the consequences of their choices, strive to increase self-awareness, and communicate their good intentions, the greater the chances for successful collaboration.

---

**BOX I-7**

The right attitude, telling the truth, self-awareness, being accountable, and skillful problem solving make a difference, regardless of the nationality, culture, size, or nature of the organization.

---

Our international colleagues in Japan recognized this in a big way fifteen years ago when they first started working with Dr. Will Schutz, one of the pioneers of the human potential movement. Since then our colleagues have delivered courses in over a thousand Japanese companies focusing on increasing truthfulness, self-accountability, and self-awareness.[6]

Our Japanese partners are not alone in this realization. Our colleagues around the world are reaping the same benefits. In "The People Puzzle,"[7] Maxi Trope outlines his use of these concepts to improve the performance of the Norwegian Djuice Dragons sailing crew as they competed in the 2001 to 2002 Volvo Round-the-World Ocean Race. The story gives an excellent example of creating strong motivation, commitment, and strength (i.e., high team efficiency) in a competitive environment where members of the team constantly have to live on or beyond the boundaries of their comfort zones. Trope writes:

> The ability of team members and organizations to handle stress, challenges, failures, and changes in their environment depends on the self-awareness and self-esteem of the team members and their ability to work together compatibly as a team. When things are tough and challenging, the single most important success factor is self-determination, meaning that the team member feels that he or she has the ability to cope with, and take responsibility for, his/her own situation and to maintain trust between team members.

In "Doing a Freys,"[8] Marie Larssen and Anna-Karin Neuman describe how collaborative skills were an essential part of a radical change at Freys Hotels in Stockholm, Sweden. All management levels were abolished, and the hotel staff took over complete responsibility for running two hotels. The first year that the staff ran the hotels revenue increased by 28 percent.

The California AfterSchool Partnership is an example of a public sector collaborative venture. It is managed by the Center for Collaborative Solutions, which is funded by federal and state after-school funds and by private foundations. Due to its collaborative efforts with a diverse group of stakeholders, the partnership is at the forefront of ensuring the success of after-school programs in California.

At Eli Lilly, Dave Haase has responsibility for managing alliances with Lilly's manufacturing partners. Haase reports that when they are training people who work in alliances, they first use difficult case simulations that teams are rarely able to resolve. Then they teach them the Red Zone/Green Zone concepts and attitudes and have them redo the same case. The teams usually do much better. Then they teach the teams the Interest-Based Problem Solving method and ask the teams to work through the same case a third time using a Green Zone mindset and the Interest-Based methodology. According to Dave, most teams are then able to reach a successful solution to the original case study which seemed unsolvable at the beginning.

---

**BOX I-8**

Seagram's had little interest in spending money to train emerging leaders about self-awareness and accountability. After we ran a few pilot projects helping the new leaders become more self-aware, accountable, and truthful, it was obvious to the CEO that our key people had started dealing more directly with each other and were cutting through the typical political BS. I didn't have trouble getting my training budget approved after that.

*Rod Taylor, Senior Vice-President, Seagram's Wine and Spirits*

---

*Radical Collaboration* does not attempt to convey a lot of information about when to collaborate. Many good books already offer that information. Instead *Radical Collaboration* teaches methods to significantly improve your own collaborative skills, so that if and when you choose to build a collaborative relationship, you know how to.

---

**BOX I-9**

*Radical Collaboration* teaches methods to significantly improve your own collaborative skills, so that if and when you choose to build a collaborative relationship, you know how to.

---

As you read through the rest of this book we invite you to reflect on how the presence of these five essential skills supports collaboration in your life, or how the lack of these skills may undermine your potential for successful collaborative relationships. Remember, successful collaborative relationships work from the inside out. Collaboration starts inside of you first, then moves out into individual relationships, teams, and organizations. To the extent you fail to integrate the personal mastery skills of chapters 1–9, the collaborative strategies in chapters 10–17 will be undermined in the long run. If your heart and your head are not in alignment, or if you are inauthentic or defensive, collaborative strategies will become just another flavor of the day.

# COLLABORATIVE INTENTION

Chapter 1 is about your own attitude and the effect it can have on relationships. Do you live in a defensive, adversarial Red Zone, or a more collaborative, nondefensive Green Zone? Chapter 2 explores whether you are defensive by tracing the history of your own defensiveness. You create a personalized early-warning system to tip you off if you start to get defensive. Then you can create an action plan for overcoming your defensiveness. In Chapter 3, you are given a tool for better understanding what's really happening when your buttons get pushed and your emotions get triggered.

# CHAPTER 1
# ATTITUDE AND INTENTION
## Staying in the Green Zone

**Where do you** spend most of your life, in the Red Zone or the Green Zone? It's a choice. Most people don't recognize that this is a choice between two fundamental attitudes as they enter into relationships and conflicted situations with others. It's a choice that will fundamentally affect everything else you do and how you approach collaboration. Early in relationships, your attitude will either support collaboration or undermine it. Your attitude will determine how you perceive the world, whether situations are safe or threatening, and influence how you respond to those situations. The terms Red Zone and Green Zone summarize two alternative mind-sets and intentions. We must first understand our attitudes and then, if necessary, change them.

---

**BOX 1-1**

We invite you to reflect on this question:
Do you build your relationships
from the Red Zone or the Green Zone?

---

The Green Zone reflects an authentic, nondefensive presence. In the Green Zone, people's actions in a relationship are not driven by fearful motives, nor are they determined by an unconscious competitive spirit. Individuals in the Green Zone seek connection from a centered place according to deeply held values and character, rather than tactical or strategic thinking. Their outer self and their inner self are congruent, meaning their conscious actions are in harmony with any unconscious motivations. When conflict arises, they seek to understand and to grow, for they desire mutual gains rather than victory. They seek to get their interests met rather than simply trying to defeat the other side. From the Green Zone, people do not perceive potential conflict as threatening, for they have tools and coping methods that allow them to deal with difficult situations in a less reactive way. Green Zone attitudes foster collaborative actions and are more receptive to overtures for collaboration from others. Green Zone attitudes also give people additional skills for responding effectively to those who don't want to be collaborative or don't know how to be collaborative. Individuals in the Green Zone are more effective when called upon to deal with others in the Red Zone.

In his book *Good to Great*,[1] Jim Collins writes that his research team evaluated more than fourteen hundred companies to identify those that had progressed from good companies to sustained greatness and to determine the factors necessary for the transformation. Collins deliberately avoided the hypothesis that a company's greatness is a reflection of the CEO. The results of the study, however, proved otherwise. The leaders of each "great" organization have two things in common. First, they are fiercely ambitious for the long-term success of the company. Second, their personalities fit the Green Zone mold, namely, each CEO exhibits a compelling modesty and humility. They aren't boastful or egocentric. They demonstrate understanding rather than bravado, and they reveal a nondefensive authenticity.

In contrast to the authentic confidence of the Green Zone, individuals in the Red Zone exhibit defensiveness and fear. They often appear to be aggressive, so others usually fail to perceive that their attitudes and behavior are driven by underlying fears. Their motivation, however, is often to defeat the other side in order to defend themselves, to win regardless of the cost, and to make the other side feel wrong so that they can feel right.[2]

---

**BOX 1-2**

It's not enough that we win; everyone else must lose.

*Red Zone statement of Larry Ellison, CEO of Oracle,*
*discussing his bid for PeopleSoft*

These Red Zone protective mechanisms lack a generosity of spirit and heart. More often than not, they arise from fears that produce short-term thinking rather than long-term planning. Conflicts feel warlike rather than like problems to be resolved creatively. Forgiveness is foreign, and apologies are begrudging rather than heartfelt. Individuals in the Red Zone focus only on the best outcome for themselves with little or no regard for the interests of others. Positions are often stated in very strong terms, and the other side's views may be only a secondary consideration, if a consideration at all. Individuals in the Red Zone continually argue the validity of their own position and the fallacies of the other side's position, and they will often take disagreement more personally than warranted.

---

**BOX 1-3**

**A Person in the Green Zone**

- Takes responsibility for the circumstances of his or her life
- Seeks to respond nondefensively
- Is not easily threatened psychologically
- Attempts to build mutual success
- Seeks solutions rather than blame
- Uses persuasion rather than force
- Can be firm, but not rigid, about his or her interests
- Thinks both short term and long term
- Is interested in other points of view
- Welcomes feedback
- Sees conflict as a natural part of the human condition
- Talks calmly and directly about difficult issues
- Accepts responsibility for consequences of his or her actions
- Continuously seeks deeper levels of understanding
- Communicates a caring attitude
- Seeks excellence rather than victory
- Listens well

**BOX 1-4**

**A Person in the Red Zone**

- Blames others for the circumstances of his or her life
- Feels threatened and wronged
- Responds defensively
- Triggers defensiveness in others
- Is rigid, reactive, and righteous
- Uses shame, blame, and accusations
- Is unaware of the climate of antagonism he or she creates
- Has low awareness of blind spots
- Does not seek or value feedback
- Sees others as the problem or enemy
- Sees conflict as a battle and seeks to win at any cost
- Does not let go or forgive
- Communicates high levels of disapproval and contempt
- Focuses on short-term advantage and gain
- Feels victimized by different points of view
- Is black/white, right/wrong in thinking
- Does not listen effectively

We're not suggesting that the difference between the Green Zone and the Red Zone is all-or-nothing; a saintly collaborator vs. the devil. There are many hues between Red and Green. There are occasions in life when we really are threatened or in danger and some Red Zone attitudes may then be appropriate and useful. We find, however, that these emergency responses are not appropriate for most work relationships, collegial decision making, family circumstances, creative problem solving, or other collaborative situations.

Individuals who are successful at collaborative relationships remain in the Green Zone and may occasionally move to the Red Zone in dangerous situations. People who remain in the Red Zone and only occasionally move into the Green Zone are not generally successful at building long-term relationships.

> **BOX 1-5**
>
> We coach our leaders to periodically pull away from the content of a meeting and just listen to the language people are using. If the language reflects the Green Zone, then the leader gets involved again in the content of the meeting. If the leader hears Red Zone attitudes, then they call a time-out and challenge the group to find a way to move back into the Green Zone.
>
> *Dave Haase, Alliance Manager, Manufacturing, Eli Lilly and Company*

## BIOLOGICAL FACTORS

Red Zone responses are complex because they are biologically based and may be encouraged by our competitive and argumentative culture. Daniel Goleman, author of *Emotional Intelligence*,[3] explains that becoming emotionally charged and unbalanced in response to triggering events can be likened to an emotional hijacking.

Recall a recent time that you "lost it," blew up, or ran away from a conflicted situation. As you think about that situation, see if you can acknowledge the magnified or unjustified overresponse. Such moments are classic examples of being in the Red Zone. It is this "stressed" response we want you to understand, so that in difficult situations your own physiological reactions do not undermine or hijack your conscious intentions and long-range collaborative interests.

A simplified version of what can happen is that physiological reactions can dominate the brain and the resulting behavior. Research suggests that threatening and nonthreatening events activate different circuits in the brain. Evolutionary psychologists contend this makes excellent sense, because a more direct neural pathway ensures that we respond more rapidly to present and remembered threats. Emotional memories can, however, be faulty, for they may be reactivated by imagination and by faulty perceptions. In addition, emotional memories are often dated and irrelevant, especially in the fluid social world we inhabit. The brain scans experience from the past, comparing current perceptions with stored memories. The process is associative. So, when a current event activates memories of similar situations in the past, the brain can incorrectly call it a "match." The neural pathway for emotional memories responds before perceptions reach the higher brain centers, where evaluation occurs. Thus we may react to present events with emotions that were imprinted long ago.

As adults in stressful or conflicted situations, our emotional memory process may associate current events with childhood experiences that occurred before we were equipped to deal with them in a balanced manner.[4] Fundamental emotional fears of being ignored, humiliated, rejected, or helpless may threaten us as much as meeting a tiger in the woods. Our emergency reaction, however, may arise from the past rather than from current circumstances.

"Fight, flight, or freeze" responses were important in human evolution. Those options are still available, and we may wish to consciously choose them for emergencies. But the emotional memory circuits in the brain may hijack people's capacity to be emotionally and intellectually appropriate in potentially collaborative situations. People's feelings and their reasoning capacity both get distorted. That is why when people are really emotionally upset, they may say they can't think straight and would be correct. They do not think straight in this activated Red Zone state because the old survival instincts take over and sabotage their ability to create collaborative relationships.

For example, Brian was an executive who grew up with an alcoholic father. At the first sign of unpredictability by a business associate, Brian would quickly and unconsciously slide into the Red Zone. He would become overly aggressive, raise his voice, and become accusatory. He wasn't reacting to the current facts or situation as much as he was reacting to his history. He unconsciously and incorrectly associated any unpredictable behavior with the danger he felt as a teenager whenever his father was drinking.

We may react to pleasant or unpleasant sensations without being conscious of a connection to memories. But such memories can lead to full-blown emotional states of overreacting to the situation or unconsciously operating out of fear. We believe our emotions are self-generated and freely chosen. We can fail to see that they often arise from unconscious evolutionary biological survival needs for a feeling of safety rather than from conscious decisions.

## CULTURAL FACTORS

The Red Zone is also compounded by cultural factors, especially in a society that values aggressive intellectual inquiry. Deborah Tannen, in her book *The Argument Culture*,[5] presents a powerful case that many cultures approach problem solving as if they were going to war. Approaching situations like warriors in battle leads to the assumption that intellectual inquiry and problem solving are games of attack, counterattack, and self-defense. According to Tannen, the primary tool in most relationships reflecting this adversarial attitude is "the argument." Criticizing used as a weapon replaces critical thinking. Problem solving is seen as a battle or a game in which winning or losing is the main concern. When people approach conflicted situations with these underlying attitudes, it triggers Red Zone biological survival responses, which then reinforce Red Zone attitudes and strategies. Opposition may be appropriate at times if kept in balance. The danger is that people may approach any issue, problem, or person in an adversarial way.

How often have you found yourself preparing your response to a person's comment even before you've heard the entire comment? We tend to search immediately for logical weaknesses and flaws in our "opponent's" point of view. Our goal is not to listen carefully and fully understand, but rather to refute the other's arguments even before hearing all of them.

---

**BOX 1-6**

Anyone who has watched a presidential debate will recognize that the desired outcome is not about truth. Both candidates seek to win votes, not to find a reasonable solution to difficult issues.

---

Culturally programmed contentiousness and unconscious use of fight-or-flight reactions do not promote collaborative problem solving or relationship building. Truth is found less often through opposition than through joint inquiry. Argumentative attitudes sabotage real dialogue and preclude the exploring, discussing, investigating, listening, and exchanging of ideas that lead to solutions. So as we strive sincerely to stay in the Green Zone, it is useful to be aware of the biological and cultural forces that may stand in our way.

## SELF-TALK

It is possible to track when we are in the Red Zone or Green Zone by our reactions. One way is to notice the "self-talk" going on in our own head.

Self-talk refers to the almost constant inner voice we have in our heads that makes a running commentary about everything in our life. The tone and texture of this self-talk can provide a particularly revealing picture of our own self-concept and deeper unconscious beliefs about the world.

When self-talk takes the form of inner hostile critiquing of our self or others, it can be a strong indication of being stuck in the Red Zone. A Red Zone self-talk example might be "That is a stupid idea. They are so wrong." The Green Zone equivalent might be "That is very different from how I see it. I wonder why they see it that way."

---

**BOX 1-7**

Red Zone self-talk:      "That's a stupid idea.  They are so wrong!"

Green Zone self-talk:    "That's very different from how I see it.  I wonder why they see it that way."

---

Physical sensations also reflect which zone we are in. In the Red Zone we might feel numb, cold, frantic, clammy, excessively hot, charged up, or jumpy. In the Green Zone we would feel more centered, calm, alive, alert, and attentive. In the Red Zone we might be aggressive, adversarial, positional, dogmatic, and focused only on the short term. In the Green Zone we will tend to be assertive yet cooperative, open to outside influence, and committed to the long term. Examples of reactive self-talk in boxes 1-8 and 1-9 provide a comparison of the qualitative differences between the two attitudes.

---

**BOX 1-8**

**Red Zone Reactive Self-Talk**

| | |
|---|---|
| This shouldn't happen. | They don't care. |
| I can't handle this. | Only a madman would see it that way. |
| This is too much. | How dare they. |
| This is unfair. | They have no right. |
| I should not have to deal with this. | That's stupid. |
| This is about my survival. | They are bad and evil. |
| They are out to get me. | |

---

**BOX 1-9**

**Green Zone Accountable Self-Talk**

I don't like this but I can handle it.

This is curious.

I can deal with this.

I need more information.

This is not about "me."

I am not the proposal, idea, or suggestion.

I can take care of myself.

I can listen.

They have a right to a different viewpoint.

I can support myself.

That's different.

What do I want to happen next?

---

## ORGANIZATIONAL ENVIRONMENTS

The organizational culture or environment is created by the collective attitudes and reactions of the individuals in the organization. Groups with a critical mass of individuals in the Red Zone will create hostile and unproductive environments. Groups with a solid majority of individuals in the Green Zone will create more collaborative attitudes and productive environments. Boxes 1-10 and 1-11 reflect the differences between the two environments.

---

**BOX 1-10**

**Red Zone Environments Are Marked By**

- Low trust
- High blame
- Alienation
- Undertone of threats and fear
- Anxiety
- Guardedness
- Hyperrivalry
- Hostility
- Withholding
- Denial
- Hostile arguments

- Risk avoidance
- Cheating
- Greed
- An attitude of entitlement
- Deadness
- Cynicism
- Suspicion
- Sarcasm
- A tendency for people to hide mistakes
- Work experienced as painful
- Dependence on external motivation

---

**BOX 1-11**

**Green Zone Environments Are Marked By**

- High trust
- Dialogue
- Excitement
- Honesty
- Friendship
- Laughter
- Mutual support
- Sincerity
- Optimism
- Cooperation
- Friendly competition

- Shared vision
- Flexibility
- Risk taking
- A tendency to learn from mistakes
- Facing difficult truths
- Taking a broad perspective
- Openness to feedback
- Sense of contribution
- Work experienced as pleasure
- Internal motivation
- Ethical behavior

---

The long-term consequences of a Red Zone culture can be devastating to an organization, a team, or a business. Pain and fear take a grip on individuals, and creativity and overall effectiveness decrease. In their classic book *Corporate Culture and Performance*,[6] John Kotter and James Heskett reported on the role that corporate culture plays on the success or failure of major corporations. The well-researched empirical study, covering more than two hundred blue chip enterprises in twenty-two industries, measured standard performance benchmarks. Using cultural values, behavioral patterns, and shared attitudes, Kotter and Heskett compared what they called Enhancing Cultures (reflecting a Green Zone environment) with Nonenhancing Cultures (reflecting a Red Zone environment). Over an eleven-year peoriod the differences were quite dramatic. For example:

| Over an 11-year period | Enhancing Cultures (Green Zone) | Nonenhancing Cultures (Red Zone) |
|---|---|---|
| Net income improved | 756% | 1% |
| Stock price grew | 901% | 74% |
| Work force expanded | 282% | 36% |
| Revenue increased | 682% | 166% |

It is virtually impossible for Red Zone environments to produce and sustain long-term, high-performing, collaborative relationships. In one of the largest and most current statistically representative surveys on the attitudes of U.S. workers, Watson Wyatt's Work USA 2002 survey *Weathering the Storm: A Study of Employee Attitudes and Opinions* (additional information about this study can be obtained at www.watsonwyatt.com), researchers found that companies with high trust levels outperformed companies with low trust levels by 186 percent in total returns to shareholders, defined as the appreciation in stock price over three years plus dividends.

Box 1-12 identifies the likely consequences for individuals engaging in sustained Red Zone behavior.

---

**BOX 1-12**

**Long-Term Consequences of Red Zone Behavior**

| | | | |
|---|---|---|---|
| Loneliness | Emptiness | Pain | Hostility |
| Depression | Deadness | No intimacy | Aggression |
| Anxiety | Self-centeredness | Codependency | Violence |
| Fanaticism | Poor health | Self-destruction | No enjoyment |

---

Exercise 1-1

## Red Zone–Green Zone Feedback

The first step in creating a job environment that nurtures collaboration is to gain awareness about your own attitudes. Box 1-13 is a vehicle for getting feedback about how you conduct your relationships. It is a checklist of both Red Zone and Green Zone descriptors. One way to gain new awareness in relationships is to ask colleagues for some feedback by asking them to pick ten words or phrases out of the fifty in box 1-13 that they most generally associate with you.

When they're done, thank them. Ask questions to better understand their point of view. *Do not,* however, try to rebut any feedback, change their minds, justify behavior, or argue with them. They are giving a gift of their perceptions. Treat it accordingly. Having a better understanding about how you show up in relationships will be helpful in explorations of your collaborative skills later in the book.

If asking for feedback seems a little too risky or threatening, you might fill out the checklist yourself by trying to put yourself in another person's mind. Then, using a self-critical eye, pick ten words or phrases that you think a colleague would use to describe you.

**BOX 1-13**

**Red Zone–Green Zone Feedback Checklist**

___Fair
___Friendly
___Cooperative
___Overly competitive
___Seeks mutual success
___Righteous
___Listens well
___Guarded
___Appreciative
___Seeks understanding
___Respectful
___Shaming, blaming, and accusing
___Avoids conflict
___Does not seek feedback
___Sees conflict as a battle
___Seeks to win at any cost
___Hard to read
___Thinks long term
___Anxious
___Calm and direct about difficult issues
___Thinks short term
___Responds defensively
___Dependable
___Black/white, right/wrong thinking
___Hard on others

___Nondefensive
___Easily threatened
___Can be threatening
___Safe to talk to
___Firm but not rigid about interests
___Open
___Feels threatened
___Supports others
___Seeks solutions rather than blame
___Values-driven
___Wants to be right
___Judgmental
___Has low awareness of blind spots
___Does not listen effectively
___Welcomes feedback
___Unforgiving
___Communicates well
___Closed down
___Communicates contempt
___Caring attitude
___Seeks other points of view
___Uses persuasion rather than force
___Rigid and reactive
___Keeps his or her word
___Too passive

## CHAPTER SUMMARY

Conscious and unconscious attitudes early in a relationship will either support or undermine collaboration. Most people don't recognize that attitudes reflect choices. People's attitudes are impacted by biological and cultural factors as well as their personal history, but it's still a choice each individual makes. Choice requires self-awareness and awareness of others to be effective.

The Red Zone and Green Zone concepts represent two opposite sets of attitudes and intentions. Individuals in the Green Zone convey an authentic nondefensive presence, while those in the Red Zone convey defensiveness and fear. Individuals who typically operate from the Green Zone and only occasionally move to the Red Zone in emergency situations are more successful in collaborative relationships. Conversely people who typically operate from the Red Zone and only occasionally move into the Green Zone are less successful at building or maintaining long-term relationships.

# CHAPTER 2
# HEY, BUZZ OFF! . . .
## I Am Not Defensive!

**Remaining nondefensive is** the single most important thing you can do to increase your effectiveness when working to turn conflict into collaboration. Defensiveness fans the flames of conflict and divisiveness. We're consistently reminded how important an authentic nondefensive presence can be.

---

**BOX 2-1**

Maintaining an authentic nondefensive presence is the single most important thing you can do to increase your effectiveness when working to turn conflict into collaboration.

---

The main reason people get into relationship trouble is because they get defensive. As a judge, Jim rarely had to deal with pure legal issues. Parties usually ended up in litigation because one or both sides became fearful and defensive. When people get defensive, their thinking becomes rigid, and they are lousy problem solvers. Defensiveness not only impacts their own problem-solving skills, it also invites everyone else to get defensive, rigid, and ineffectual as well. When the room is filled with defensive, rigid-thinking, ineffective problem solvers, the result is disaster!

---

**BOX 2-2**

Defensiveness is a poison pill to good relationships. In conflict, defensiveness is like blood in the water to a shark. A little here, a little there, and in no time the situation has degenerated into a feeding frenzy.

---

Defensiveness, ultimately, is not about protecting ourselves from other people. People get defensive because they don't want to experience uncomfortable feelings within themselves. Getting defensive will temporarily block the feelings that they don't want to experience. Psychologist Gary Chapin calls defensiveness "secrets we unknowingly keep from ourselves."[1] For example, if we (Ron or Jim) are leading a workshop or giving a speech and we fear we are not doing a competent job, that fear can create considerable discomfort. Instead of letting ourselves feel and explore this discomfort, we may unconsciously behave in ways that allow us to avoid, dismiss, or diminish it. This usually involves blaming someone else.

During a workshop, for example, we may start making excuses about how the participants didn't really want to be in the workshop or tell ourselves that they were all required to attend, which explains why the workshop isn't going well. Or we may imagine that the audience just wanted to get away from work for a while to dine out in some wonderful San Francisco restaurant at the company's expense. By behaving this way we may unconsciously create the illusion that the problems are the fault of others. We thus avoid feeling our own fear that we are not doing a competent job.

---

**BOX 2-3**

Defensiveness is secrets we unknowingly keep from ourselves.

*Dr. Gary Chapin*

---

To summarize: We fear that we may not be doing a good job. The fear causes discomfort that we don't want to feel. So, we behave in a way that lets us avoid feeling that discomfort. We get defensive and blame others in order to protect ourselves from experiencing our own uncomfortable feelings and thoughts.

---

**BOX 2-4**

Defensiveness is always based on a fear.

---

Defensiveness is always based on a fear. Always, always, always! If someone is acting like a defensive jerk, it can be helpful to know that he or she undoubtedly feels threatened or afraid. When people feel insignificant, incompetent, or unlikable, they may act in ways to avoid those uncomfortable feelings. They may act out toward others, become sleepy, intellectualize issues, overeat, flood others with information, talk too fast, trivialize issues with humor, abuse alcohol or drugs, or act in dozens of other ways to avoid or suppress their own discomfort. By exploring skillfully enough and deeply enough, it is possible to learn more about the underlying unresolved feelings and fears and take action to reduce them. Being able to create an atmosphere that reduces other people's overreactions as well as your own is a great asset in building collaboration.

---

**BOX 2-5**

Defensiveness does not defend us from others. It arises to protect us from experiencing our own uncomfortable feelings. The prescription for dealing with your own defensiveness is to let yourself experience those feelings. Do not avoid them.

---

The prescription for dealing with your own defensive fears, then, is to let yourself experience them. Do not avoid or deny them by moving away from them, but rather move toward them, bringing them fully into your consciousness and acknowledging them. While this is counterintuitive, it is the most effective way known to cope with fears and to reduce defensiveness.

Remember that defenses are biologically based and usually charged with physical energy in the body, so defensiveness can sometimes be detected from physiological cues. These may include more rapid breathing, an increase in pulse rate, feeling too hot, too cold, or restless. Other individuals might experience the opposite effect, feeling fatigue or drowsiness, inattention, and poor concentration. There are diverse ways to avoid experiencing uncomfortable feelings.

Defensiveness is so difficult to deal with because defenses operate independently of our conscious thinking processes. They are by nature autonomous and unconscious. People are not consciously aware that their behavior is a strategy to defend themselves from feeling some of their own unwanted feelings. If they had that awareness, they would act differently because unconscious defensive attitudes and behavior are never in their best interest.

We are not saying, however, that people should never defend themselves. The world has seen all too clearly that at times defense from attack is appropriate. This is true at both an international level and an interpersonal level. Not everyone can be trusted to take each other's interests into account. When people legitimately defend themselves from attack, however, they should do so from a place of centered self-awareness, rather than from a reality distorted by unconscious defensive fears.

Another problem with getting defensive is that it provides only temporary relief. Because defensive behavior occurs as a way to avoid uncomfortable feelings, it only works as long as the individual is engaging in distorted thinking. The defense is not dealing with the deeper problem, that fearful, vulnerable place inside you that may reduce your effectiveness in dealing with any substantive issue. Rather, your defensive strategy is trying to hide that vulnerability from your consciousness in order to avoid discomfort. It will never resolve the underlying anxiety. The real issues are obscured and the process becomes an exercise in self-deception, an internal trick people play on themselves. Anyone doubting the power of self-deception should view a few of the early rounds of the *American Idol* television talent search.

---

**BOX 2-6**

Defensiveness provides only temporary relief. It's like covering dog poop with whipped cream. It may look and smell better for a short time, but it doesn't deal with the underlying issue or clean up the mess.

---

## WHERE DEFENSES COME FROM

Defense systems, however, are not evil. Human defenses arose from evolutionary development. Individual defenses emerged from each person's history. They helped people cope with the stress of growing up in a world where they had little control over their lives. Individuals created certain behaviors to defend themselves from fears such as feeling insignificant, incompetent, unlikable, or helpless. These defenses became the shelters that protected them from unwelcome feelings. Without defenses, coping with childhood and adolescence would have been exceedingly difficult if not impossible.

The problem is that defense mechanisms can assume a life of their own and unduly control adult lives. People exhibit their defenses with the same lack of awareness that they show when they open a door, ride a bicycle, go swimming, or climb a flight of stairs. They don't think to themselves, "Let's see, this next step is higher than the last one, so I need to raise my foot about ten inches higher, so that it will be high enough to land on the top of the next step." Instead the behavior has become part of them, something automatic, and most of the time they aren't even conscious of what they are doing.

Acting out their defenses, people may continue to behave in ways that might have been useful in their childhood but are no longer helpful as adults. They commonly fail to recognize that their defensive attitudes and behaviors stem from outmoded fears. They can instill hair-trigger responses rather than fostering an open and sincere attitude of inquiry toward any situation.

At one time or another, most people have had less than optimal childhood experiences that have led to defensive behaviors and automatic thinking patterns. These early childhood experiences leave their imprints on developing nervous systems. People tend to create new stories to justify old behaviors. In one experiment, researchers told hypnotized subjects that when they saw a certain phrase in a questionnaire they would later be asked to fill out, they would go to an umbrella stand in the room and open an umbrella. They were also told that they would not recall being told to do that. Then the hypnotic state was terminated and one at a time they were given the questionnaire to fill out. Sure enough, when they saw the magic phrase, each subject got up from the desk, walked across the room to the umbrella stand, removed an umbrella, opened it, then closed it and placed it back in the umbrella stand. Then they each returned to their table and completed the questionnaire as though nothing unusual had just occurred.

The most interesting part of this experiment comes from their responses when the subjects were asked why they opened an umbrella during the middle of answering the questionnaire. Each person offered a reason. Not one person said they didn't know why they engaged in the odd behavior. Having no conscious recollection of the hypnotic suggestion, each subject produced a "sensible" reason. Some said they were worried it was going to rain; some expressed an urge to just get up and stretch; others said they were simply curious to see if the umbrellas would work. Everyone made up a reason that offered some logical explanation for the irrational behavior. We are all meaning-seeking creatures. We want our behaviors to make sense to us, and to others, so we attribute meaning to our actions even when we don't understand them.

Take a moment to reflect back on your childhood, thinking of it as an eighteen-year-long hypnotic induction. Think of the behaviors that you adopted and the messages that you learned and have since forgotten. You might realize how defenses that were helpful to you in childhood may have taken on a life of their own and may no longer be helpful to you as an adult. Situations make people fearful and they don't want to experience those fears, so they adopt attitudes and behaviors that help them not feel the fears. But their avoidant behavior can become a familiar and comfortable pattern that is inappropriate, although they may not even realize they are acting defensively.

---

**BOX 2-7**

If you think of your childhood as an eighteen-year-long hypnotic induction, you'll have a better idea about how behaviors that were helpful to us as children may have taken on a life of their own and may not be helpful to us as adults.

---

When you were a child, for example, if your parents were always fighting, their arguments could cause you great pain. You couldn't stop them from fighting and you couldn't move out on your own. Perhaps one way that you could defend yourself from that pain, however, was to stop listening well, for if you didn't hear it, the fighting wouldn't be as painful. So, maybe you just tuned out and learned not to listen. This is an effective survival strategy for a child in those circumstances. It is not an effective strategy for an adult. If you learned this defensive strategy of not listening well during conflicts and use it as an adult, you've simply grown up to be a lousy listener. What helped you as a child makes you ineffective as an adult.

Maybe you couldn't block out the noise of your parents fighting, so perhaps you learned a different defense system. Instead of not hearing the words, you may have numbed your emotions, so you wouldn't feel so much pain. You shut down your emotions and chose not to feel anything intense. If you carry that strategy into adulthood, you will experience a limited range of emotions. You may feel less pain, anger, and sadness, but you will also experience less joy, love, and excitement because you are not as alive as you might be. Because you learned to defend yourself this way as a child, you now experience a very narrow range of emotions as an adult.

Or perhaps you learned to get sick as a defense, so you would get attention and not feel ignored. Maybe you learned to become sarcastic or withdrawn or to be passive-aggressive. The personal favorite of one of our colleagues is to become confused. If that colleague is getting feedback from a group of friends that he really trusts, and he is the only one in the group who doesn't understand that feedback, that's a sure sign that he's getting defensive. The feedback causes him discomfort that he doesn't want to feel, so he behaves in a way that allows him to avoid the uncomfortable feelings. He gets confused and doesn't understand the feedback. If he doesn't understand the feedback, he doesn't have to deal with the uncomfortable feelings it brings up.

Another colleague's personal favorite pattern is to withdraw into silence. When faced with criticism that creates uncomfortable feelings, she may simply tune out as a way of breaking contact rather than staying conscious of the uncomfortable feelings and dealing with them more directly. Her pattern is not an effective strategy for problem solving; however, it provides some comfort through the illusion that being out of contact equals being out of danger. While the strategy doesn't make sense intellectually, it is operating at an unconscious level.

It's easy to see how and why these defenses are created by difficult childhoods that include alcoholic or abusive parents, multiple divorces, or early deaths of a parent. But defenses are also learned in perfectly normal, everyday, average, nontraumatic childhoods.

---

**BOX 2-8**

Defensiveness distorts our reality, causing us to spend more energy on self-preservation than on problem solving.

---

## HOW DEFENSES CAUSE PROBLEMS

Defensiveness gets people into trouble by distorting reality, primarily through projection. Projection is when someone tends to see their own fears and feelings in other people rather than within themselves. If an individual has unconscious feelings, he or she might project them onto another person. They attribute their own feelings to the other person, not based upon objective reality, but from their own distortions. It could look like this: I have unresolved fears about my own competence, so I project them onto you, and I begin to believe that you think I'm not competent. I then start reacting to you as though my projection were true. I may feel judged by you and may start trying to convince you that I am competent. Although it appears that I'm trying to convince you of my competence, I'm really attempting to convince myself, because I'm the one who is unconvinced. However, because I am unaware of this, I will tend to feel victimized by you and blame you.

Frances was a competent engineer. She grew up, however, with a mother who constantly told her that she wasn't good enough, that nobody in the family was smart. Frances carried that message with her into adulthood. It was always on her mind that she wasn't good enough. She projected that belief onto her supervisor and was constantly worried that she was disappointing her supervisor. Contrary to Frances's belief, her supervisor saw Frances as one of her most talented engineers. The supervisor's only disappointment was that Frances would not take a stronger leadership role in the office. The combination of old messages from her mother and her projection of her own fears onto her supervisor had taken over Frances's life and was undermining her career.

We often see projection at work in our mediation of conflicts. In one case a supervisor had a dispute with an employee. The supervisor was deceitful and manipulative, but of course he didn't see that in himself. Instead he saw those qualities in the employee, even though there was absolutely no evidence of that in the behavior of the employee. The supervisor projected his own unconscious deceitful motives onto the employee.

---

**BOX 2-9**

When our defenses take over our adult lives, we don't have defenses, *they have us*!

---

Regardless of whether the distorted lens is rose-colored or a dark and smoky one that creates a sinister outlook in every situation, it becomes a burden on any good relationship.

## LOOKING AT YOUR OWN DEFENSES

The first step toward not acting defensively is to become aware of when you are getting defensive. Increasing your self-awareness about your defense systems also increases the accuracy of your perceptions of others. Events are less likely to be seen through a distorted lens. As people increase their self-awareness, they are also better able to see how others perceive them.

Defenses are created during events in your history. So we now invite you to engage in some emotional archaeology, i.e., uncovering your emotional history, to help you discover the roots of your own defensiveness. Spend ten to fifteen minutes drawing what we call a Conflict Lifeline. This provides a visual history of the conflicts and difficult relationships in your life, from birth to the present. The Conflict Lifeline is a tool for gaining more awareness about where your defenses may have come from. Specific instructions for the Conflict Lifeline begin on page 38.

As you draw your Conflict Lifeline, focus on instances when you felt the most distressed. Use words, pictures, symbols, or any other ways to depict those events in your life. As you draw, reexperience the emotions connected with the events. Don't worry about what the Conflict Lifeline looks like, for the purpose is to generate insight, not great art. You don't have to show it to anyone else if you don't want to. Visualizing the significant conflicts in your life will help you spot defensive patterns that you may have learned over a lifetime to defend yourself from uncomfortable feelings and situations.

Here are a few examples of Conflict Lifelines.[2]

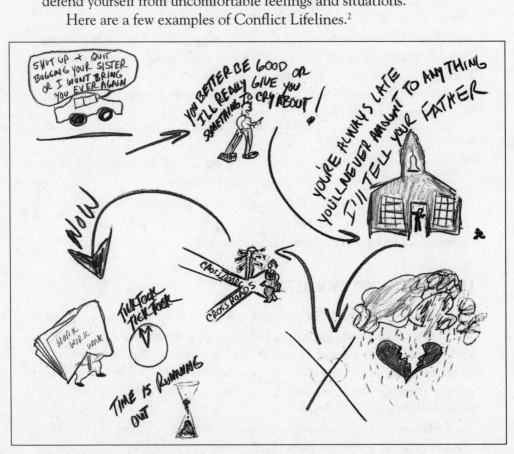

Conflict Lifeline example #1

Lifeline example #1 was drawn by a psychology student. In the upper left corner a father is yelling "Shut up and quit bugging your sister or I won't ever bring you again." Then, "You better be good or I'll really give you something to cry about." At school there was a threat to tell the father. Next is a broken heart leading to a broken marriage. That leads to a crossroads involving too much work and time running out, reflected by the hourglass and the ticking clock.

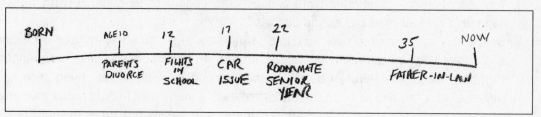

Conflict Lifeline example #2

Lifeline example #2 is our no-frills favorite from an engineer. Born, parents divorce, fights in school, car issue, roommate issue, father-in-law, and then now.

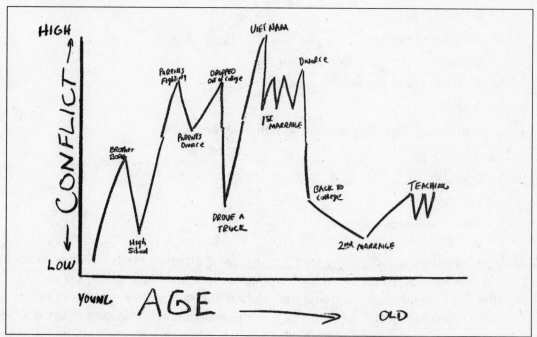

Conflict Lifeline example #3

Lifeline example #3 is from an MBA student. The chart depicts "Age" from young to old and "Conflict" from low to high. The issues range from low conflict in high school, when driving a truck and in a second marriage, to high conflict with parents fighting, Vietnam, and a divorce.

---

Exercise 2-1

## Conflict Lifeline

1. You can make this as simple (with a paper and pencil) or as creative (with flip-chart paper and colored markers) as you choose.

2. Before you start drawing, take a couple of minutes to sit quietly with your eyes closed and reflect back on the relationships, situations, and conflicts you have experienced in your life. Absorb the flavor of those experiences and let yourself feel them once again. Notice what it felt like to be in the middle of each experience. To help focus your awareness, pay particular attention to conflict situations at the various times in your life with:

> Parents
>
> Siblings
>
> Neighbors
>
> Extended relatives
>
> Spouses/ex-spouses
>
> Children
>
> Authority (including teachers, police, military)
>
> Friends
>
> Institutions (including schools, government, hospitals)
>
> Bosses
>
> Coworkers
>
> Employees
>
> Any other sources of conflict

3. Then, whenever you are ready, start drawing, using pictures, words, symbols, or anything else that will help you depict these instances in your life. Make it look any way you like.

4. After you have completed drawing your lifeline, take a few more minutes to reflect back on what you have just drawn. Notice how the situation was managed. What did "they" do? How did you respond? Notice what feelings came up and any patterns of behavior that you were able to spot. Pay particular attention to any underlying messages about your own significance, competence, or likability. Consider how these messages may still be affecting your current adult behavior, particularly in the workplace.

---

When you are done drawing your Conflict Lifeline, try another exercise to get a better felt sense of the impact these experiences may have had on you. Take one of the earlier childhood scenes in your Conflict Lifeline and do the visualization exercise listed below. Read the visualization and the follow-up questions through first to get a sense of what you will be doing, then do the visualization and answer the questions.

------------------------------------------------------------

Exercise 2-2

## Lifeline Visualization

Reflect back on a time in your Conflict Lifeline when you were a child and less able to fend for yourself, a time when you were shamed, laughed at, ridiculed, or bullied. Take your time. Let yourself get a felt sense in your body as well as in your mind. When you have a vivid recollection of that experience, notice what you are feeling and thinking. Notice what is happening in your body. Then answer the following questions:

### Questions

1. *What were you feeling emotionally?* Were you aware of feeling scared, confused, ashamed, helpless, hopeless, humiliated, or full of dread?

2. *What was happening in your body?* Were you feeling expansion or contraction, a tight chest, shallow breathing, increased heartbeat, hot or cold, wanting to fight back or a sense of rubber legs or impending collapse, wanting to run, or stiff as in "scared stiff"? Was your vision or hearing altered in any way?

3. *What were you thinking?* Were you confused, trying to make sense of why this was happening to you or what you did to bring this on, or did you freeze with no thoughts at all? What do you remember thinking about yourself or about others? Were you taking the insult personally?

4. *What was happening to your energy?* Were you feeling aroused, activated, energized—or dead, zombified, numb, frozen? How long did the change in energy last? What happened afterward? Did you get help or fight back, or did you shut down?

5. *What are you thinking and feeling now as you look back on this scene?*

6. *Have there been other similar situations or scenes in your past life?* Look for repeating patterns or themes.

------------------------------------------------------------

When you feel complete in experiencing the visualization, breathe, stretch, and take as much time as you need before answering the questions. When you are ready, answer the questions in detail. Your answers will be important to your understanding of how you have learned to process stressful situations, both consciously and unconsciously.

Everybody has been subjected to traumatic situations. What's important is for you to begin to learn and recognize what happens to you mentally and physically during moments of stress. During these times most people report an increase in heartbeat and breathing, and a feeling of panic or anxiety as feelings of being overwhelmed increase. Some people respond with an agitated "fight" type of response. Others mobilize with a "flight" response of wanting to run away. Still others constrict with a numbing "freeze" response. The body's nervous system is being activated in an attempt to instinctively protect itself.[3]

Now look at the symptoms you reported in the scene you reexperienced in your visualization. Were your reactions more fight, flight, or freeze? When children are laughed at, humiliated, shamed, frightened, or bullied, and there is no way out, you can imagine how their nervous system would be activated.

Imagine one hypothetical example, a young boy named Billy, frightened by a scary situation—perhaps an overbearing, punishing parent, or a group of bullies. Billy is being yelled at and shamed. The child's heartbeat accelerates; his intake of breath is swift before he holds his breath. His shoulders shoot up, eyes wide with fear as the threat approaches menacingly. The physical energy in Billy's body has no place to go. There is no adequate discharge of this energy. The energy can get stuffed over a lifetime when there are many episodes of a person not being allowed to adequately speak up or stand up for himself. When Billy is not allowed adequate expression or emotional development, damage is done.

When people have been traumatized or have received distorted messages in childhood (e.g., "you aren't very important," "you can't do anything right," or "you're unlovable"), people carry these messages into their adult lives like their skin. Without awareness people can continue to live out the scripts written for them early in their upbringing.

For example, if your mother was a rigid, stern disciplinarian and you have a boss who is a demanding female, you might easily act out the undischarged, pent-up emotional charge from your childhood. You may project your mother's traits onto your boss with little provocation or understanding. In stressful situations people's nervous systems shift into high gear, into a highly energized state to meet the demands of the situation. When they can meet the challenge head-on and carry the energy all the way through from start to finish, they can be fine. It's when they are helpless, like Billy, or in other charged situations when they fear they are helpless again (i.e., the old memories come up unconsciously and without their awareness), that they get flooded and stuck in the old patterns all over again. They can become the masters of their own fate only by bringing more awareness into their lives.

Now that you have a better sense of what was happening inside your body, and what you were thinking and feeling, look back to your Conflict Lifeline to see if you can determine what defenses you may have used to help you cope with those situations. How did you behave so that you would not have to feel helpless, ignored, humiliated, rejected, or other uncomfortable feelings that you did not want to feel?

For example, the woman who drew Conflict Lifeline example #1 noticed that she had a pattern of going numb emotionally, becoming silent, and withdrawing physically whenever she was threatened. That was her way of avoiding her own uncomfortable feelings. In reviewing her Conflict Lifeline, she recalled first avoiding her feelings when her father yelled at her, and she carried that defensive behavior into school when teachers frightened her, and later into her marriage and at work. Instead of dealing with conflicts directly, she would go numb, refuse to talk about it, and withdraw from her husband or colleagues, which was one of the factors leading to a divorce and career difficulties.

The Conflict Lifeline doesn't have to be great art to be a helpful exploration of the origins of defensiveness. Reflecting on Conflict Lifeline example #2, the engineer realized he had a habit of feeling victimized by his circumstances and playing "poor me."

The man drawing Conflict Lifeline example #3 behaved almost the opposite of the first two people. His pattern was to act out and become very aggressive and sarcastic whenever he became fearful. He noticed that during times of low stress—for example, during high school, while driving a truck, and during his second marriage—he didn't feel overly aggressive and was rarely sarcastic. However, when he was feeling stress, his aggression and sarcasm helped him to avoid feeling his fear.

Looking back on your own Conflict Lifeline, did you run away or tend to attack? Did you become passive-aggressive, get sick or confused, go shopping, get drunk, get sarcastic, or withdraw into silence? Did you become overly nice and refuse to even admit that you were in a difficult situation? Pay particular attention to any patterns you can see. Try to give your defensive behaviors a descriptive name.

## CREATING AN EARLY WARNING SYSTEM

When you finish your review, take a few minutes to reflect how helpful it could be to be able recognize when you are becoming defensive and reverting to these earlier learned reactions. If you have your own Personal Early Warning System, something to alert you as soon as you start getting defensive, you can act to reduce your defensiveness before it causes you any damage. This requires two things. First, you need to be aware of when you are starting to get defensive. Second, you need to have an action plan to reduce the impact of your defensive reactions. This action plan should be devised ahead of time so that you can implement it automatically and don't have to be thinking something through at a time when your thinking is impaired.

---

**BOX 2-10**

Your *Personal Early Warning System* can alert you when you are starting to get defensive. Then you can act to reduce your defensiveness before it causes you any damage.

---

Most people don't realize that they are getting defensive until it's too late to do much about it. Once they are firmly hooked by their defensive behavior, it is difficult for them to remain effective in a relationship. They don't have enough awareness of what their defensiveness looks like to be able to tell when they are starting to become defensive. The Signs of Defensiveness exercises below will help you increase your awareness about your own special defensive patterns. You will put a name to them and know what they look like. By naming your favorite defense mechanisms you can better recognize when you are getting defensive. This will create your own Personal Early Warning System to tip you off that you are becoming defensive. At that point you will be able to take action to reduce the impact of your defensiveness. You'll have an opportunity to create your own action plan a little later in the chapter.

---

Exercise 2-3

## Signs of Defensiveness

1. Review the Signs of Defensiveness in box 2-11 and put a check mark by each sign that applies to you. The list is not meant to be exhaustive. It's simply a list of possible defensive behaviors that were collected by our colleagues and from participants over the years. If you notice any defensive behaviors in yourself that are not listed, feel free to give them a name and add them to the list.

2. When you finish putting check marks by all signs that apply to you, go back over the list and circle the top three items. The top three are the ones that you are so good at doing that you could probably teach them at the university level. They are the ones you know well because you use them so often.

3. If you have trouble finding any signs that apply to you, we suggest that you go directly to number 12 (denial) and circle it right at the start. (Another strategy might be to ask your spouse or colleagues for some help with this exercise. Spouses and colleagues seem remarkably willing to help out here and are remarkably accurate as well.) If you would like to share any new signs of defensiveness that you believe should be on the list, please e-mail them to us.

---

**BOX 2-11**

### Signs of Defensiveness

_____ 1. Loss of humor

_____ 2. Taking offense

_____ 3. High charge or energy in the body

_____ 4. Sudden drop in IQ

_____ 5. Wanting to be right ("No question about it")

_____ 6. Wanting the last word

_____ 7. Flooding with information to prove a point

_____ 8. Endless explaining and rationalizing

_____ 9. Playing "poor me"

_____10. Teaching or preaching

_____11. Rigidity

_____12. Denial

_____13. Withdrawal into deadly silence

_____14. Cynicism (victim)

_____15. Sarcasm

_____16. Making fun of others (being highly critical)

_____17. Terminal uniqueness (I'm so special; rules don't apply to me)

_____18. "It's just my personality; it's just how I am"

_____19. Not wanting to negotiate

_____20. Blaming

_____21. Sudden onset of illness or accident

_____22. Confusion

_____23. Suddenly tired or sleepy

_____24. Intellectualizing

_____25. Acting crazy (the temporary-insanity defense)

_____26. Eccentricity

_____27. Being too nice

_____28. Selective deafness

_____29. Attacking (the best defense is a good offense)

_____30. Holding a grudge

_____31. Trivializing with humor

_____32. Inappropriate laughter or giggling

_____33. Sour grapes!

_____34. "I'm aware of that; leave me alone" (defense of awareness)

_____35. Becoming addicted to alcohol, drugs, people, shopping, working, gambling, chocolate, workshops

_____36. Personalizing everything

_____37. All-or-nothing thinking

_____38. Catastrophizing

_____39. Fast breathing/heartbeat

_____40. Cold, clammy skin

_____41. Hot, sweaty skin

_____42. Mind reading

_____43. Jumping to conclusions

_____44. Magnifying everything

_____45. Minimizing everything

_____46. Emotional rigidity (if I feel it, it must be true)

_____47. Tight stomach

_____48. Speaking too fast

_____49. Becoming physically immobile

_____50. Obsessive thinking

Looking at the top three signs of defensiveness that you circled, you now have names for your top three defensive behaviors. We urge you to become familiar with these behaviors. Become articulate about them. Make them your friends. They are no longer your enemies; they are now your allies. They are your Personal Early Warning System that you are becoming fearful about something and beginning to get defensive.

It is much easier for most of us to spot our defensive behavioral responses than it is to identify the underlying feelings that we don't want to feel. Because the whole point of defensive behavior is to help us avoid feeling something we don't want to feel, we can often recognize our defensive behavior before we are aware of the underlying feelings we are trying to avoid.

A person may not understand that he is starting to feel unlikable when he is in the middle of a conversation with his older brother, or that he doesn't want to feel that he is unlikable. He may, however, realize that he has once again started to react to his brother in a sarcastic manner. If he knows that one of his personal early warning signs of becoming defensive is to react with sarcasm, he can work backward to better understand his underlying feelings. The thought process might go like this:

> I notice that I'm getting sarcastic as I talk with my brother. I also know that getting sarcastic is one of my warning signs that I'm getting defensive. So that tells me I'm probably getting defensive now for some reason. I'd better try to tune in to what I'm feeling right now so I can better understand why I'm getting defensive.

People may not recognize their feelings as clearly or as quickly as they can see their behavior, so they can use their behavior to tip them off that they're having feelings that would be helpful for them to explore.

## CREATING A DEFENSIVENESS ACTION PLAN

So far you've looked at your history and you've identified a Personal Early Warning System that you may be getting defensive. Now you have a choice about how to react. You can try to ignore the information you are faced with or blame yourself for getting defensive, or instead you can experience compassion for yourself and start exploring the feelings. Successfully reducing your defensiveness involves increasing your self-awareness and having compassion for yourself. Beating yourself up because you find yourself getting defensive is not an effective strategy for reducing your defensiveness. It's a little like beating on a turtle's shell to get it to stick its neck out. Exploring your fear requires greater safety, not self-aggression. You cannot intimidate yourself or others into a feeling of safety.

---

**BOX 2-14**

Successfully reducing your defensiveness involves increasing your self-awareness and having compassion for your underlying feelings.

---

So now what do you do when your early warning system tells you that you're getting defensive? Here are some general ideas that are helpful. Review them all and then take some time to develop your own Defensiveness Action Plan.

### 1. Take Responsibility for Yourself

Acknowledging that you are becoming defensive is a good first step. By doing so you increase your awareness that you are unconsciously fearful and you can start exploring what that is about. You may want to go a step further and acknowledge your defensiveness to those you are dealing with, for this can create greater depth in the relationship. Do you remember our colleague whose IQ suddenly drops and who gets confused when confronted with information that is discomforting for him? For example, one time he was getting feedback from colleagues that he could have improved his last customer presentation by better clarifying the company's pricing structure. He didn't want to hear this feedback because it reflected upon his competency and he would have felt bad about that. So his defense mechanism kicked in to help him not feel those uncomfortable feelings. He got confused and didn't understand the feedback from his colleagues. Because the feedback didn't make sense to him, he could easily have dismissed what they were telling him. Instead, he paid attention to his early warning system and realized that he was becoming defensive. He stopped the conversation to announce, "I seem to be getting a little defensive here, and I don't understand the feedback you're giving me. I'm not sure what that's about yet, but I want to understand what you're telling me. Can you go back over what you said a little slower because I want to understand it."

By doing this he acknowledged his defensiveness both to himself and to his colleagues, and he asked for their help in dealing with it. It may not always be appropriate to ask for that help, but if you are dealing with people that you trust, it not only offsets the damage caused by the defensiveness, it can actually create greater intimacy and a stronger relationship.

### 2. Slow Down

Remember that defensiveness has physiological aspects. People are usually flooded with adrenaline and charged with energy, so slowing down physically and relaxing can be helpful. Going for a short walk, going to the restroom and splashing some water on your face, or taking a time-out and rescheduling the rest of the meeting are all possible ways to slow down and help become more centered. Others don't even need to be aware of this centering strategy if it doesn't seem appropriate to tell them. Simply take a couple of deep breaths without making a big deal about it to anyone else, and it will be a calming and centering experience.

### 3. Confront Your Negative Self-Talk

Negative self-talk is the internal dialogue that goes on in your head as you are watching actual events. If someone is giving a speech and sees an audience member get up and walk out, the speaker can have a dialogue going on in his head about what's happening. It can make him much more defensive if the negative self-talk sounds like "Darn, I'll bet she's unhappy. I hope she's not the conference organizer. I'll bet she hates what I'm saying. She'll probably give me a bad evaluation. I'll bet I never get invited back to this group again."

If the speaker is conscious that he is engaging in such negative self-talk, he can confront it and actively change it into a more supportive frame of mind. Perhaps it would sound like this: "I wonder why she's leaving. Maybe I can check with her later. Everyone else seems to be fully engaged and enjoying the material. Things are going very well right now." With this more positive self-talk the speaker can stay centered and present with the rest of the audience and let her go for now. The speaker's defensiveness will not turn into a vicious downward spiral.

### 4. CYA

People often make incorrect assumptions about the meaning of CYA. It stands for Check Your Assumptions, not cover your ass. In most mediations, someone (often both parties) has made incorrect assumptions. A common one is "the other side is behaving that way because they don't like me." Often, however, it is simply that the interests of the conflicting parties are different.

---

**BOX 2-15**

**CYA**

People often make incorrect assumptions about the meaning of CYA. It stands for Check Your Assumptions.

---

Everyone has to make many assumptions daily to get by. There is nothing wrong with making assumptions, and it would be impossible to live a normal life without making them. The problem is the rigidity with which they are held. If people are conscious that they are making assumptions, they can then check them out to see if they are correct or incorrect. People then tend to get less defensive than when they automatically believe the assumptions are true.

> **BOX 2-16**
> The biggest problem with assumptions is the rigidity with which we hold them.

### 5. Detach

There are two good reasons to adopt an attitude of detachment. First, it can be helpful to prevent acting out inappropriately. For example, if you recognize that you tend to flood others with information or become too aggressive when you are getting defensive, you can acknowledge these tendencies to yourself and choose not to act out with that behavior. You can instead go deeper with conscious awareness, trying to understand the root causes, and ask yourself, "What am I trying to override?" You can choose to experience the discomfort you are trying to avoid, asking yourself not to act in a defensive way, even though the behavior may offer you some temporary relief. That is detaching from a desire to act out.

A second way is to detach from overidentification with the outcome of the situation. How often have you seen someone submit a report or offer a solution to a problem during a meeting, then feel personally rejected when the report or solution is rejected? One of the great advantages that humans have is our ability to identify with other individuals and objects. That can also be a great disadvantage when people overidentify with those same objects or individuals. It is possible to remain passionate about an idea and yet remain detached enough from it to not take a rejection personally. The key is to not get your ego involved with it. This engaged yet detached mind-set is the ability and willingness to step back and see things more objectively by disconnecting our deepest sense of identity and self-worth from the specific situation and outcome, while still remaining caring and concerned.

For example, Beth, one of the managers Ron was coaching, had one of her projects canceled. Beth's immediate reaction was outrage. She felt rejected and thought that she was being told her contribution had no value, and that she personally had no value. It took time and much discussion for her to see that she was not "the project." She was able to see that from time to time projects get canceled regardless of the effort put into them. While it was useful for her to advocate and do all in her power to persuade people to support the project, if at the end of the day the project was still canceled, it was then in her interest both personally and professionally to let go of her identification with the project. Admittedly, it is difficult to both care deeply but also not overly connect our self-worth and self-identity to the outcome or results. She did not have to "forfeit" her positive feelings and evaluation of herself just because something did not turn out the way she hoped.

In this case, Beth learned to change her self-talk. When she was overidentified with the project, her self-talk sounded like "I can't stand this; they don't appreciate me. They are saying I have no worth. They don't want the project and that means they don't want me." After gaining some perspective, her self-talk sounded like "I don't like this and I don't agree with the decision. However, I did my best to have it go the way I wanted, and now I am curious how this happened so I can be more effective next time. I am not the project and this is not a vote on my worth as a human being."[4]

After a few weeks Beth had another great insight. She reported that she realized her interpersonal energy produced by her overattachment to the project was not seen as passion by others, but was perceived as arrogance and self-righteousness. She was able to see how this perception might actually have contributed to the demise of her project.

Spanish matadors have a phrase describing the detachment necessary for dealing with the onslaught of the beast: *ver llegar*. Hemingway spoke of the phrase in *Death in the Afternoon*, stating, "To calmly watch the bull come is the most necessary and primarily difficult thing in bullfighting." It is to calmly detach from the situation enough to see what is happening and maneuver appropriately. So it is when one faces a charging "other" (such as a boss, teammate, employee, colleague, or spouse). By focusing on your intentions, it is possible to watch and listen and allow the charging energy to flow around you like a wave but not define who you are in the moment.

## 6. Start Over

The approach we suggest is not a model of perfection. It is a recovery model. So, when your Personal Early Warning System tells you that you might be getting defensive, acknowledge that to yourself, take some action to reduce your defensiveness, and then start over. Everyone gets defensive occasionally. It's not the end of the world. You will usually be better served by letting it go and focusing on the future than by blaming yourself for your defensiveness in the past.

**BOX 2-17**

*When You Get Defensive*

1. Take responsibility for yourself

2. Slow down

3. Confront your negative self-talk

4. CYA (check your assumptions)

5. Detach

6. Start over

---

Exercise 2–4

# Defensiveness Action Plan

After you review the preceding suggestions, we recommend that you take a few minutes right now to think about what specific action you could take considering your particular circumstances and your own specific defensive behaviors. Use box 2-19 as a planning tool. By doing this now you will have an action plan already prepared when your Personal Early Warning System signals your defensiveness. You will know ahead of time what specific actions you will take to increase your effectiveness when you are getting defensive. For example, if you start noticing that you are flooding someone with information, that behavior is a signal you should instead be quieter and put more energy into effective listening. Or if your favorite defense is to get passive-aggressive, you can instead put energy into being more direct about what you are feeling. The purpose of the action plan is to make your options more conscious and available during times when you normally tend to operate from unconscious defensiveness. Then the job is to keep practicing during each opportunity presented to you.

List your top three signs of defensiveness (from page 44 ) in part A of the action plan. Then decide upon two specific action steps you will take as soon as you notice yourself engaging in your top defensive behaviors. It is important that you create specific action steps such as "I will tell the person I am with that I'm starting to notice my own defensiveness" or "I will take two deep breaths" or "I will stay quiet for at least fifteen seconds." Vague or generalized action steps, such as "I will stay centered and open to all possibilities" or "I will remain nondefensive," will offer you little help. To illustrate how this works, here's a real example.

Karen is talking to her boss, John, about an idea she had regarding a company project. As she is talking, John turns and reaches for his coffee cup. Karen's immediate reaction in her mind is "Oh damn, he must not want to hear this. He probably thinks it's really stupid." Karen starts talking faster, flooding her boss with information because she fears he will soon start ignoring her. She loses her train of thought, repeats herself, and talks in circles.

John, who simply wanted a sip of coffee, has no idea that he triggered Karen's fear when he turned his back to her while she was talking. He simply wonders why Karen, who is usually very articulate, seems to have dropped thirty IQ points and is rambling in circles.

Karen, who had many childhood instances of feeling overwhelmed when she was ignored and humiliated, found her defenses activated and responded by talking very fast. She projected her childhood fears onto John. She first became aware that something was happening in her body. When her boss turned away to get his coffee, Karen felt her stomach sink and she lost her confidence. In response, Karen jumped into one of her defensive reactions. She started talking very fast, flooding him with information. The more defensive she became, the more confused and inarticulate she felt.

It became a vicious cycle. The more confused and less articulate Karen became, the less John was interested in what she was saying. The less he was interested in what Karen was saying, the more she was convinced that her defensive projection was correct. Thus Karen's defensive projection encouraged exactly the reaction in her boss that she most feared. Our strongest defensive traits can become self-fulfilling prophecies.

Karen was driving full steam ahead with the gas pedal to the floorboard and her eyes firmly fixed on the rearview mirror of her childhood. Karen's history is commanding her future. Karen's way out of this vicious cycle is to challenge her projection by coming into the moment with new energy and fresh thinking instead of continuing with distorted thinking.

Karen knows from her Conflict Lifeline exercise and visualizations about some of her childhood experiences that when she becomes defensive her top three signs of defensiveness are *Flooding with Information, High Charge of Energy in her Body,* and a *Sudden Drop of IQ.* Karen also has identified two steps in her action plan. One deals with the energy in her body and the other deals with the story she invents in her mind. She will get her erratic energy under control through a simple centering technique, which is described below. She also replaces the negative story in her mind with a more positive reminder that is more in line with her present reality.

Karen's Defensiveness Action Plan looks like this:

---

**BOX 2-18**

**Karen's Defensiveness Action Plan**

A.  When my Personal Early Warning System tells me I'm starting to get defensive, i.e., I notice myself using any of my top three defensive behaviors listed below:

    1. Flooding people with information

    2. High charge of energy in my body

    3. Sudden drop in my IQ

B.  I will take the following actions:

    1. I will slow myself down by breathing deeply and bringing my energy from my head down through my belly and into the ground beneath me, grounding my energy.

    2. I will remind myself that the people I'm talking to probably do want to hear what I have to say.

---

When Karen caught herself in her defensive pattern, she consciously slowed herself down, breathing deeply. She focused her attention on her belly, allowing her energy to drop down first into her belly, then down through her legs and feet into the ground. She created a mental image of her energy connecting her solidly to the ground as she continued to talk. She reminded herself that John wasn't her father or brothers, who used to ignore and humiliate her. She reminded herself that her boss did want to hear her ideas about the project, and then she again started talking to John, who was drinking his coffee, understanding Karen better and enjoying the discussion they were having.

Karen addressed her situation in two significant ways, in both her mind and her body, in what she was thinking and what she was aware of physically within her body. Without this conscious awareness of both the stories of her mind and the erratic out-of-control energy of her body she may be doomed to re-enact her stressful or traumatic early childhood situations over and over again. As the good Dr. Freud said, we keep working on it in an attempt to finally get it right.

---

Now you create your own Defensiveness Action Plan. List your top three signs of defensiveness in part A. Then in part B, create two specific action steps tailored to deal with your particular defenses.

---

**BOX 2-19**

**Defensiveness Action Plan Worksheet**

A.  When my Personal Early Warning System tells me I'm starting to get defensive, i.e., I notice myself using any of my top three defensive behaviors listed below:

1.  _____

2.  _____

3.  _____

B. I will take the following actions:

1.  _____

_____

2.  _____

_____

---

**BOX 2-20**

The key to our growth and breaking negative ties binding us to our past is conscious awareness.

---

## CHAPTER SUMMARY

Maintaining a nondefensive presence is one of the most effective things people can do when trying to build collaboration. Defensiveness does not protect us from others. It arises to defend us from experiencing uncomfortable feelings that we don't want to feel. Something happens to trigger feelings or fears within us that we don't want to feel, so we behave in ways that let us not feel those disturbing feelings. Most of the time we are unaware of the reasons we are behaving that way. We don't realize that we are protecting ourselves or avoiding uncomfortable feelings. Defensiveness distorts reality and reduces our effectiveness when trying to resolve conflicts or to build collaborative relationships. It causes us to put more energy into self-preservation than we put into problem solving. We all have favorite ways of defending ourselves, usually a combination of behaviors affecting both our mind and our body.

By exploring our top three defensive behaviors, we each can create a Personal Early Warning System to tip us off when we are getting defensive. By developing a Defensiveness Action Plan tailored to our top three defenses, we can increase our personal effectiveness when our warning system tells us we are becoming defensive.

# CHAPTER 3
# UNHOOKING YOUR BUTTONS

un·hook: to free from a habit or dependency.

**Imagine you are** in an important meeting. You feel comfortable, well-informed, creative, and collaborative. Suddenly someone across the table from you says something, and for no apparent reason a strong electrical shock surges up through the table and right into your body. It sends such a jolt through your body that you lose your train of thought and you start sweating. Then, as you start to get angry, you realize that nobody else at the table seemed to feel this jolt of electricity.

You don't say anything about it, but just when you start to regain your composure, someone raises the same subject that caused the earlier jolt, and sure enough you get another jolt of electricity. Now you're not just shocked, you're really mad. You may even start yelling at the other people, accusing them of shocking you. Now, of course, the other people at the table, who have no idea about the jolt of electricity, are all looking at you as if you were from another planet. They may not say it out loud, but everyone is probably thinking that you've gone a little crazy and that you are overreacting to what was said.

You don't feel that you are overreacting, however, because through their words, ideas, tone of voice, or maybe body language, someone is shocking your system just as though they had their hand on a button with your name on it. That person has said or done something that pushes a tender and vulnerable spot deep inside you. It's a spot that can cause you pain or fear or other uncomfortable feelings whenever it is touched or exposed. It typically also triggers a strong reaction from you when you are reminded of that spot. This is what we mean by the phrase *getting your button pushed*.

One of the tricky things, however, is that you are probably not even conscious that a button is being pushed or that you are having a reaction that may seem unreasonable or out of proportion to others. People are often not aware of their own buttons, so they react unconsciously and sometimes irrationally when their buttons get pushed. Getting their buttons pushed makes people horribly ineffective in relationships or in problem solving.

When their buttons get pushed, people typically get dumber rather than smarter. By our informal calculations there is about a twenty-point drop in IQ. Unfortunately this is often accompanied by an equal but opposite conviction that we have become more perceptive rather than dumber.

People aren't getting their buttons pushed every time that they have a strong emotional reaction to something. Strong reactions can often be appropriate. What we're talking about is when a reaction is over the edge from what is appropriate: when it is an overreaction. Occasionally a pushed button is reflected by a significant underreaction (i.e., where the individual froze and did nothing). When looking back on the situation, the person might ask himself, "Where did that reaction come from?"

You can be pretty sure that someone pushed your button if, when describing the incident, you want to end with the sentence "and therefore they must suffer!" It's a little like the difference between Teflon and Velcro. If some annoying action of the other person slips off you like Teflon, you probably don't have a button that's getting pushed. If, however, the incident sticks in your throat or heart or gut like Velcro, then you've probably got some unresolved fears or pain that will create a button just waiting to be triggered.

---

**BOX 3-1**

The difference between a small annoyance and a "button" is like the difference between Teflon and Velcro. If it slips off you like Teflon, it's not a button getting pushed. If, however, the incident sticks in your throat, heart, or gut like Velcro, then you've probably got some unresolved fears or pain that is a button just waiting to be triggered.

---

## MANAGING YOUR BUTTONS

There are two main ways to manage your reactive buttons. The first way is to gain a better understanding about what is going on inside you, to become more aware of your buttons. Then you realize that the feelings that accompany them come from a tender spot inside you, a vulnerability that you carry around with you, rather than from what somebody else just did to you. Having this awareness is a way to start unhooking your buttons.

The second way to keep from getting your buttons pushed is to try to get the rest of the world to quit pushing your buttons so that you will never have to feel those vulnerable spots. Maybe you'll have more luck at this method than we have. Our experience is that most of the people we spend time with are remarkably unwilling to change their behavior simply to avoid pushing our buttons. So our advice is to put energy into gaining self-awareness about your buttons, rather than trying to prevent the rest of the world from pushing those buttons.

Unhooking your buttons refers to unhooking the electrical wires from a button that you push, for example, a doorbell. It may take the shape of simply minimizing the intensity of your response when a button is pushed. It may not be possible to unhook all your buttons. Some deep wounds or strongly formed reactive spots may never completely go away. But we can compassionately and firmly take responsibility for them. This capacity to step back and notice our patterns and automatic tendencies is critical in becoming a nondefensive problem solver.

---

**BOX 3-2**

**Two Ways to Manage Your Buttons**

1.  Gain self-awareness about why you have the button.
2.  Try to get the rest of the world to always avoid pushing your buttons.

Guess which method works best!

---

## THREE STEPS TO UNHOOKING YOUR BUTTONS

One of the most effective ways to gain awareness about your buttons is to explore what feelings arise and what stories you tell yourself when your buttons get pushed. Since our buttons are mostly in our unconscious, this takes self-exploration and detective work to get to the root of the button. Here is a three-step process to help you gain self-awareness by exploring your buttons.[1]

1. Think of a situation when your button got pushed by something that another person did to you. Remember, this is an instance that

triggered an overreaction on your part. Describe the facts as you understood them, including any feelings that came up for you.

> Bob was supposed to drive by my house and pick me up this morning at 8 a.m. He was an hour late. I was furious that he was such an inconsiderate jerk and didn't show up on time or even bother to call to say he would be late.

2. Explore the story that you are telling yourself about what this other person must be thinking about you in order to treat you this way. This often involves some variation of a belief on your part that the other person must think you are insignificant, incompetent, or unlikable.

> It must not have mattered to Bob that I was waiting for an hour. He must not think I'm very significant. If I were important to him, he wouldn't have kept me waiting.

3. Now explore any underlying fear or vulnerable places inside you that may get triggered by that story, or the perceived judgments of the other person. Usually it will involve the mirror image of the story you have made up about what the other person thinks of you. It may trigger a strong reaction in you when someone else thinks you may be insignificant or incompetent or unlikable if you fear it is true.

> Why would it bother me so much that Bob treats me like I'm not very significant? Maybe it's because some part of me feels insignificant. I don't like being reminded of that feeling, so I get angry at Bob for making me feel that way.

This is not to suggest that you shouldn't take action to correct Bob's behavior. A discussion with Bob about his being late is certainly appropriate. However, it can be helpful to realize that the pain or upset feelings you are experiencing come from the vulnerable part of you that may not feel significant, rather than from what Bob actually did to you. If you didn't have a vulnerable part inside you that feared being insignificant, it probably wouldn't bother you so much that Bob may think you are insignificant. If you didn't have that little part of you that doubts your own significance, you might still have to deal with the problem of Bob picking you up late, but you wouldn't have such an emotional charge. It would just be another problem to solve. This awareness can reduce some of the emotional charge you may feel toward the other person and allow you to move more quickly out of blaming and into problem solving.

Another example might be helpful. During one of our workshops for new consultants, the participants took turns making presentations to the class. One participant, Chris, had particularly poor listening skills. Just about everyone in the workshop agreed that Chris had lousy listening skills. Chris's poor listening really incensed Jane, another participant in the course. When Jane made a presentation and Chris wouldn't pay attention, Jane's anger was obvious to everyone in the room. While Chris's poor listening was a slight distraction for other participants, it really pushed Jane's button.

Jane's willingness to explore her button getting pushed is summarized below:

1. The facts and feelings:

*I went to a lot of trouble to prepare a good presentation and Chris didn't seem to pay any attention. I don't think he heard a word I said. It made me so angry for him to disrespect me like that. He's such an idiot; I wouldn't ever want to work with him.*

2. Exploring the story and/or judgments:

*The story I tell myself is that Chris must be thinking that I'm not worth listening to. He must not believe I have anything important to say. If he respected me as a trainer, he wouldn't be ignoring me the way he does. He would be paying closer attention to what I have to say if he thought I was a competent trainer.*

3. Exploring the pain or fear:

*I guess not being listened to or taken seriously has bothered me for quite a while. I probably have a part of me that worries that I'm really not worth being listened to. I know I'm a new consultant and I have some doubts about my competency. I hate feeling incompetent, so when Chris reminds me of those feelings, I hate him too.*

Knowing that the real charge or pain was coming from inside her helped Jane let go of her anger toward Chris. Jane realized that Chris wasn't "causing" the pain within her. Rather the pain was coming from that vulnerable place inside Jane that questioned her own competency. Gaining this understanding about herself didn't make Chris a better listener, but at least Jane could be in the room with Chris and not take his poor listening skills personally. Jane still wouldn't choose to ever hire Chris or partner with him, but she didn't have to have him publicly humiliated just to feel better either.

This self-discovery can often be the end of the process. Just gaining a better understanding of your underlying feelings can help you unhook your buttons and defuse the anger. For example:

> I get it. I'm not really mad at Dave because he's doing something to me. I'm angry at him because he reminds me of my older brother. My brother never seemed to like me, and I guess I still worry about whether I am likable. It doesn't feel good when Dave reminds me of those feelings.

Just knowing that it isn't Dave that is the issue can help you let go of the anger toward Dave.

Although it's not always necessary, if you do want to take it a step further and talk about the issue with the person who triggers you, you will be able to do so using a very different tone. We'll be talking more about that in chapter 4, when we review some tools for telling more of your truth. In chapter 9 (Breaking Free of the Past One Thought at a Time) we offer additional tools for dealing with these vulnerable feelings.

---

**BOX 3-3**

Your buttons are buried only from your consciousness, not from your life.

---

Remember, the fear or pain underlying your button is usually unconscious. That's why it's so hard to discover. It takes a lot of persistent detective work that is also compassionate toward that vulnerable spot deep within you. This unconscious material is having a profound impact on your behavior and your relationships, even if it is out of your awareness. The issues are buried only from your consciousness, not from your life. It's like driving a car on the freeway. You can do it better with your eyes open than with your eyes closed. In the long run you are better off bringing the unconscious material to the surface and dealing with it, even though it may be uncomfortable. An effective way of exploring unconscious material is one button at a time.

---

**BOX 3-4**

**Unhooking Your Buttons Worksheet**
Think of a time when someone pushed your button.

1. The facts and feelings are _____

_____

_____

2. The story I tell myself about what they must think of me to treat me this way is

_____

_____

_____

3. The pain or fear within me might be _____

_____

_____

(Hint: Usually it is a fear of experiencing uncomfortable feelings and/or the pain of some self-judgment.)

---

## CHAPTER SUMMARY

When we get our buttons pushed, it feels as if someone were doing something to us. In fact, they are just putting us in touch with a vulnerable place we already have deep within us. Most of us spend a lot of energy trying to get other people to stop pushing our buttons, but the best way to deal with our buttons is to unhook from them. We do that by exploring the painful place within us that feels so vulnerable. Using the Unhooking Your Buttons Worksheet can help you understand both the story you may be inventing about those feelings and the underlying fear and pain that is the source of the button. By gaining self-awareness about the source of the buttons, you can eventually unhook from those buttons.

# PART 2
## 2ND ESSENTIAL SKILL

# TRUTHFULNESS

Truthfulness is a skill that you can learn. It requires two things: the ability to speak the truth and to listen to the truth. Chapter 4 offers tools for being more truthful. Chapter 5 offers ways to become a more effective listener.

# CHAPTER 4
# THE GRAND SIMPLIFIER

Truth is the grand simplifier.
—*Will Schutz*

**Nothing damages** a relationship as quickly as not telling the truth. Just ask Gray Davis, the former governor of California, who was recalled from office just a few months after being reelected to his second term. He was recalled in large part because the voters didn't believe he was telling them the truth. Knowing full well that the state was heading into the worst fiscal crisis in its history, Davis kept that news quiet until after he won reelection. Then when the full impact of the fiscal crisis became known, few voters were willing to give Davis the benefit of the doubt. Presidents Nixon and Clinton also learned the hard way, each creating his most significant crisis not by what he did, but rather because he lied about it, namely Watergate and Monica Lewinsky. Even Martha Stewart's undoing was her lying, not her stock manipulations.

---

**BOX 4-1**

The level of trust in a relationship is determined to a great extent by the amount of truth that is being told.

---

For years we have had workshop participants do a little "endarkenment" exercise (as opposed to an "enlightenment" exercise).[1] Participants are asked to create and prioritize lists of all the things they could do if their job were to destroy trust in a relationship or organization. Not telling the truth almost always ends up at the top of the list. The amount of truth that is being told often determines the level of trust in a relationship.

Will Schutz, one of the true pioneers in the human potential movement, claimed, "Truth is the grand simplifier." It makes everything else easier. People often express their fear about telling the truth. They fear it will hurt other people's feelings or cause a strain in a relationship or invite retribution. The common perception is that telling too much truth gets us into trouble. However, Schutz always believed the opposite: that we get into trouble for not being truthful enough. W. Edwards Deming, a pioneer in the field of quality, also maintained that quality is impossible when people are afraid to tell the truth.

## AWARENESS + HONESTY + OPENNESS = TRUTH

When we talk about telling the truth, we are not talking about some cosmic universal truth. Nor are we talking about indiscriminate opinion giving, which people mistake for telling the truth (e.g., "I told my boss the truth, that he's stupid. He got mad at me"). Indiscriminate opinion giving often gives truth telling a bad name, because it lacks awareness and accountability. Telling the truth is someone's willingness to share what is going on inside him: inside his mind, his heart, and his gut. It is disclosing himself in an accountable manner.

Telling the truth is a combination of awareness, honesty, and openness. A lack of awareness distorts any truth that someone may choose to share. If people are unaware that they are becoming defensive and putting their energy into self-preservation rather than problem solving, they are not likely to be seen by others as truthful and trustworthy. If a manager is unaware of his deep-seated sexist belief that women belong in the home and not the boardroom, how can he possibly build a truthful and trusting collaborative relationship with a female CEO of one of his customers or suppliers?

If people are self-aware and choose to deceive other people about what seems true for them, how can they build successful relationships? If people mislead each other by distorting information, their lack of honesty will eventually weaken the relationship, especially when the information eventually becomes known. When trying to build a collaborative relationship, it is wisest to assume that any dishonesty will eventually come to light and the damage caused at that time will be difficult to repair.

Finally, even if people are self-aware and honest, but choose never to share their thoughts and feelings with others, their lack of openness will create a barrier to creativity and effective problem solving. Collaboration will be seriously undermined. A lack of openness will also be a barrier to depth and intimacy in personal relationships as well. How will others fully understand what is in someone else's head and heart if he or she doesn't share that information?

---

**BOX 4-2**

Telling the truth about yourself requires a combination of *awareness, honesty,* and *openness.*

---

## TOOLS FOR BEING MORE TRUTHFUL

Here are four tools to help readers increase their self-awareness and be more honest and open in their relationships. First Truth First, Congruent Delivery, What I Have to Share, and a reminder about Unhooking Your Buttons are all tools that will help people be more open and honest in their relationships.

------------------------------------------------------------

Tool 4-1

## First Truth First

Individuals can often get befuddled when thinking about telling the truth because the truth can be complex and complicated. The First Truth First tool[2] is a way of prioritizing and simplifying what to say first. For example, look at a situation where a supervisor has concerns about the way someone is treating her employees and yet is also hesitant to say anything because of fear of damaging their relationship. The first truth in that situation might sound like this:

> Bob, I'd like to talk to you about something that is difficult for me to bring up because I value our relationship and I worry that the issue may strain it.

Then the rest of the truth would follow:

> I've been upset with the way you treat my employees, etc.

Using this tool, someone doesn't have to have everything figured out ahead of time. You just need to be aware of what is foremost on your mind at that time. Perhaps the first truth might be:

> I'm feeling pretty confused about this issue and I'm not quite sure what I think about it.

Or perhaps:

> I'm feeling really nervous when I'm with you, because I want to impress you.

Or perhaps:

> My first truth is that I am afraid that I will look incompetent around you, so I don't come directly to you when I have a problem.

A good reminder about First-Truth-First is that people can rarely go wrong by first talking about their intentions for what they next have to say. Misunderstood intentions often create more problems than actual statements. If you can first be clear about your intentions, your statements will be heard differently.

---

**BOX 4-3**

You can rarely go wrong by first talking about your intentions for what you next have to say. Misunderstood intentions often create more problems for us than our actual statements.

---

Tool 4-2

## Congruent Delivery

People notice how you say what you say. They may not know how to name it, but they judge believability on the manner and tone of your communication. This can be a major source of self-sabotage in relationship building.

Picture an executive addressing a group of employees. He is nervous, not making eye contact; he keeps looking at his watch and seems anxious to leave the meeting. He occasionally wipes sweat from his brow even though the auditorium is cool. The words he is speaking to the employees are:

> I'm really happy to be here today among all my good friends so that I can dispel the rumors that we are in financial trouble and may be facing layoffs.

It may be that the executive is simply afraid of public speaking and that he is telling the truth. Regardless of the truth, however, the message that will likely be perceived is that the company is in trouble and employees had better start looking for other jobs.

Picture an angry young man with a sarcastic, sneering look on his face yelling to his girlfriend as he walks away, "Of course I love you!" His credibility is zero. The content of his message "I love you" is destroyed by the inconsistency of tone of voice and body language. Now picture the young man looking adoringly into his girlfriend's face and saying softly, "Of course I love you!" This time the content of his message "I love you" is what is being communicated.

A lot of research demonstrates that credibility is dramatically reduced when tone of voice, body language, and content are out of alignment. The numbers commonly cited regarding the impact of a message are:

> *Content* (the words) accounts for only 7 percent.
>
> *Tone of voice* accounts for 38 percent.
>
> *Body language* accounts for 55 percent.

Fortunately these percentages are not accurate when the content of the message and the delivery of the message are congruent. That is to say, when the content, tone of voice, and body language are all consistent in communicating the same message, then the content will rule and the message is much more believable.

Much of the research about body language has been misunderstood. In 1967, Professor Albert Mehrabian of UCLA conducted the most cited research.[3] His research attempted to determine the impact of inconsistent messages: when the content was not congruent (i.e., in alignment or consistent) with the tone of voice or the facial expressions, posture, or other gestures. While Mehrabian cautioned that his research percentages were only approximate, the evidence was clear that when any nonverbal behavior contradicts what is said in a message, the nonverbal behavior is more likely to determine how the message is understood.

---

**BOX 4-4**

When any nonverbal behavior *contradicts* what is said in a message, the nonverbal behavior is more likely to determine how the message is understood.

Mehrabian believes that particularly in our Western culture, listeners have two main reasons for giving greater weight to tone of voice and body language when they contradict the content of the message.[4] First, people are hesitant to express negative feelings outside of intimate relationships. They might be willing to complain to their spouse, but it would seem rude to share those same negative feelings with a colleague. The second is that we emphasize language skills and neglect any training on nonverbal communications. Thus we are not skilled at concealing our emotions.

Emotions play such a huge role in our social interaction that we can't hide them. They leak out in our communications through tone of voice and body language. When they are inconsistent with the words of the message, they play a larger role in communicating the real message because for most of us they are more difficult to alter. Unless you're an accomplished actor, it's easier to lie with words than with tone of voice and body language because they are more often driven by our unconscious feelings about the message. They are less censored.

This research is significant for people trying to communicate a message they may have some doubts about. Consider, for example, an executive addressing a group of new alliance partners. The executive is trying to communicate that their new partnership will be greatly enhanced by an environment of openness, where each party can feel free to share all of their concerns with the other party. This is an appropriate and helpful message to establish better communication between new partners.

What if, however, the executive is not an open person himself? He also has some concerns that the other party will take a lot of his time with their complaints about his new policies. His unspoken hesitation about a more open environment is likely to leak out into the delivery of his message to his new partners. The Mehrabian research confirms that in this situation the "real" message will be communicated through the executive's tone of voice and body language. The message that people will pick up is:

I need to tell you to be open because that's what I'm supposed to say, but I really don't want to be that open and I don't want it from you either. I want you to keep your complaints to yourselves.

The best way out of this predicament is to use the First-Truth-First tool. This helps speakers be more open about their concerns so that their message is congruent with their tone of voice and body language. The executive we talked about above might say:

I know that creating a more open environment is going to be crucial for our success. I have a few of my own fears about that. I'm a pretty private person so this will be a stretch for me. I'm also a little concerned that I'll get overwhelmed with complaints about all the changes that will be taking place. But I also know that to become as successful as we intend, it is absolutely essential for us to be able to share our concerns, to tell the truth, and to listen to the truth. So I'm asking all of you to stretch a little to become more open with each other, just as I make the same commitment to you.

This message is completely congruent. It communicates openly and honestly the executive's own concerns as well as a sincere desire to create a more open environment. The message will not be undermined by inconsistent tone of voice or body language.

---

**BOX 4-5**

People trying to communicate a message that they have doubts about had better pay particular attention to their body language and tone of voice.

---

What People Believe When the Content of a Message Is
Not Congruent with Tone of Voice and Body Language.

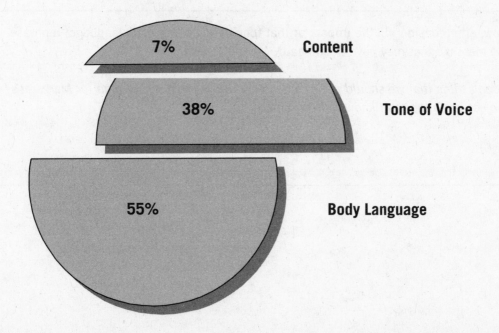

7% Content

38% Tone of Voice

55% Body Language

Exercise 4-1

## Congruent Delivery Exercise

Reflect back on a recent message you delivered where your tone of voice and body language contradicted your message. Review the following example and then complete the worksheet on the next page.

| THE CONTENT (the words) | TONE OF VOICE (including sarcastic, hostile, warm, sincere) | BODY LANGUAGE (including gestures, touching, distance, eye contact, smiles, smirks) |
|---|---|---|
| *I told the office staff that it was important that we put together a promotional plan for the new software that Margaret is developing.* | *I don't think I sounded as interested in that as I did the other projects. I probably sounded bored. I'm sure I sounded more excited about the project Phil and Nancy are working on.* | *I mentioned Margaret's project as I was leaving the room. I didn't make any notes, and I probably looked distracted.* |

Now, after considering the impact of that tone of voice and body language, rephrase the message that may have been heard.

*I don't think that we should put much energy into a promotional plan for Margaret's project, even though I know we're supposed to.*

| THE CONTENT (the words) | TONE OF VOICE (including sarcastic, hostile, warm, sincere) | BODY LANGUAGE (including gestures, touching, distance eye contact, smiles, smirks) |
|---|---|---|
| | | |

Now, after considering the impact of that tone of voice and body language, rephrase the message that may have been heard.

_____

_____

_____

_____

Because so much of our real intention can be communicated by body language and tone of voice, it is particularly important to add clarity about your intentions to your message when using the telephone or e-mail, since they limit body language and tone of voice. The telephone includes tone of voice but not body language. E-mail, which is now the most popular form of business communication, excludes both body language and tone of voice. We've worked with a company that spent hours of meetings in response to two or three cryptic words in an e-mail. It is crucial to include information about your intentions in important e-mail messages.

---

**BOX 4-6**

The most popular form of business communication today, e-mail, cannot communicate body language and tone of voice. Therefore, it is crucial to clearly communicate your intentions in important e-mail messages.

---

Tool 4-3

## What I Have to Share Checklist

Sometimes people may not share information because it never occurs to them that they have information they might choose to share. When asked if they would like to talk about a situation and they say no, it may be that they aren't deliberately withholding the information. They may simply not know what to say. The What I Have to Share checklist is a reminder of the kind of information that is available to share if people choose to.

---

**BOX 4-7**

**What I Have to Share**

1. Thoughts
2. Facts
3. Feelings
4. Physical sensations
5. Intuition
6. Intention
7. What I want

Here's an example:

**Thoughts:** I'm thinking that you might be rejecting my proposals because you don't believe I'll follow through and complete the projects, and that for some reason you may not trust me.

**Facts:** I've noticed that you have rejected the last four proposals that I have submitted to you.

**Feelings:** I'm feeling hurt that you may not trust me and a bit angry that you might not be treating me fairly.

**Physical sensations:** I notice that my stomach gets tight, my breathing speeds up, and I get agitated whenever I think about our relationship.

**Intuition:** My gut tells me there's a problem between us and that you're not telling me something.

**Intention:** I intend to review my work history to see if I may have performed poorly in the past. I also intend be clearer with you about our relationship issues so that we can improve our working relationship.

**What I want:** I want us to have a better working relationship: one where you trust my performance and I feel fairly treated. I'd like you to meet with me and with a person from the Human Resources department on Tuesday to see if we can better understand what's been happening between us.

Any item on the checklist can be a good entry point to get a discussion started. There is no right or wrong place to start, and you may not want to share all segments. We do suggest, however, that sharing more information rather than less information will usually accelerate problem solving and collaboration. Pick an issue where you may want to share more information with someone and use the following worksheet to clarify what you have to share about that issue.

**BOX 4-8**

### What I Have to Share

Thoughts: _____

_____

_____

Facts: _____

_____

_____

Feelings: _____

_____

Physical sensations: _____

_____

_____

Intuition: _____

_____

_____

Intention: _____

_____

_____

What I want: _____

_____

_____

------------------------------------------------------------------

Tool 4-4

# Unhooking Your Buttons

We introduced the Unhooking Your Buttons worksheet back in chapter 3 to help you discover the underlying fear or vulnerable spot inside you that creates your buttons. That tool is not only a method of increasing self-awareness, it can also be a road map for sharing what is going on inside you at a much greater depth. Often just gaining the additional insight about where your button comes from is enough to defuse much of the emotional charge attached to that button. If, however, you are trying to build a relationship, or deepen the level of intimacy in a relationship, it is helpful to use the Unhooking Your Buttons worksheet as a guide for sharing information about yourself and your interaction with the other person.

Let's look back at the situation with Jane and Chris. Remember Jane would become infuriated when she gave a presentation and Chris wouldn't pay close attention to her. Jane used the Unhooking Your Buttons tool to discover that her anger at Chris had more to do with her own fears about her competency and significance than with Chris.

Here's how Jane explored her button:

## 1. The Facts and Feelings

"I went to a lot of trouble to prepare a good presentation and Chris didn't seem to pay any attention. I don't think he heard a word I said. It made me so angry for him to disrespect me like that. He is such an idiot; I wouldn't ever want to work with him."

## 2. Exploring the Story and/or Judgments

"The story I tell myself is that Chris must be thinking that I'm not worth listening to. He must not believe I have anything important to say. If he respected me as a trainer, he wouldn't be ignoring me the way he does. He would be paying closer attention to what I have to say if he thought I was a competent trainer."

## 3. Exploring the pain or fear

"I guess not being listened to or taken seriously has bothered me for quite a while. I probably have a part of me that worries that I'm really not worth being listened to. I know I'm a brand-new consultant without much experience, and I guess I'm worried that Chris may be right. The possibility that I'm not saying anything worthwhile makes me uncomfortable. I hate feeling like that, and so when Chris reminds me of those feelings, I hate him too."

Jane could then talk to Chris about the issues, and the conversation would be much different. Prior to gaining some awareness about the roots of her button, Jane would have sounded like this:

"Chris, you're an arrogant twit because you don't pay attention to anything I say when I'm presenting. You have the listening skills of a tree stump!"

After exploring her own button, Jane sounded like this:

"Chris, when you don't listen to me, I tell myself that you must not respect anything I have to say, and that triggers my fears about my own competency and significance. It's uncomfortable for me when I am reminded of those fears about my self-worth, so I tend to take it out on you."

There is a huge difference between the two statements. The first is about Chris ("You are so arrogant"). The second is about Jane ("Chris, your actions trigger fears in me that I don't like to feel, so I tend to take my anger out on you, even though it's not really about you"). The first may well trigger Chris's defensiveness. The second probably wouldn't because it is self-revealing of Jane, rather than an attack on Chris. The first reduces intimacy and trust. The second builds intimacy and trust. The first damages the relationship, while the second builds the relationship.

It may not always be appropriate to share this new self-awareness about your buttons. You'll have to make a judgment about your level of safety in the relationship. If, however, you are trying to add depth to the relationship, telling this kind of truth will be one of the most effective things you can do.

-------------------------------------------------------------------

## CHAPTER SUMMARY

Not telling the truth is one of the fastest ways to destroy a relationship. The four truth-telling tools in this chapter can help you increase openness and build relationships. Sharing your First Truth First is an easier and more honest way of sharing what is really going on with you. Congruent Delivery of what you share will increase your credibility. The What I Have to Share checklist can help you better understand what information is available to share. Finally, when someone pushes your buttons, gain self-awareness using the Unhooking Your Buttons tool and then share more truthfully your underlying fear or vulnerability. It will make you more trustworthy and will add depth to your relationships.

# CHAPTER 5
# LISTENING
## The Most Often Taught Unused Skill

**There's a lot more** to listening than simply keeping your mouth shut . . . but that's a good start!

We've already talked about some skills for telling the truth. The other side of creating a truthful environment is being able to listen openly and sincerely to others.

---

**BOX 5-1**

There's a lot more to listening than simply keeping your mouth shut . . . but that's a good start!

---

## THE IMPACT OF LISTENING

The impact of good listening is remarkable. It has a positive impact on the speaker, the listener, and the relationship. People consistently report that they increase their level of openness when they feel listened to. They almost always disclose more information than they thought they would at the start of the conversation. So if you want to learn more information at greater depth, the quickest route is not to cross-examine people, but to be quiet and listen to them.

A second impact speakers usually report is that they start paying more attention to what they are saying. When someone is truly listening to them, speakers take their role more seriously. They tend to feel more responsibility for being articulate and coherent if they know someone is paying attention. This means less rambling and fewer diversions off point.

The third positive impact is that speakers also consistently report that they feel more of a connection with the person listening. Participants in our workshops have spoken to the same people while the listeners varied their attention and listening effectiveness. Speakers routinely report that when the listener was not listening well, the speaker began to dislike the listener, felt greater distance, and sometimes even became angry at the listener. When the listener was paying attention and listening effectively, speakers felt more closeness and connection with the listener. Speakers reported that they tended to like the listener better.

---

**BOX 5-2**

Effects of Good Listening

1. Speakers increase their level of openness.

2. Speakers become more articulate and coherent.

3. Speakers tend to like the listener.

---

There is more to listening than just hearing words. A recent workshop participant explained it best when he was describing a powerful "a-ha" experience during one of the homework assignments we give regarding listening skills. He noted that he had attended several "listening classes" and was technically competent with listening behaviors. He could repeat back almost verbatim what the speaker had said. But he felt that it had never made much difference in his relationships. This time he reported that he finally "got it" that the essence of listening was his "attitude and intention," not his ability to be precise with the words. He discovered that if his listening was motivated by only superficial interest or competition, then his "listening" was perceived as insincere or manipulative. When his listening came from genuine interest and sincerity, or from Green Zone attributes, then another whole level of communication and connection opened up.

People have the ability to communicate just as much by good (or bad) listening as by speaking. Effective listening can reduce defensiveness and communicate an increased sense of significance, competence, and likability. Feelings of significance, competence, and likability are three important emotions that dramatically affect collaborative relationships. We'll be returning to these later in chapters 7 and 8.

## THE LISTENER'S OBLIGATIONS

A listener has two main jobs. The first is to create a safe environment for the speaker to be open about something. People generally only share to the extent they feel safe. People will not be willing to share much depth if they fear they may be ignored, humiliated, or rejected. The second job of the listener is to understand what is being communicated in such a way that the speaker feels understood.

---

**BOX 5-3**

Listening is not a competitive sport.

---

### Job #1: Creating a Safe Environment

The best and simplest way to create safety is to pay attention. Stop multitasking. Have you ever been on the phone during an important conversation and in the background you hear the tap tap tap of a keyboard? Of course it could be that the person on the other end of the phone conversation is simply typing notes of the conversation, but that's probably not the conclusion that most of us will draw first. It's distracting and annoying for most people. So, do what you can to eliminate distractions and interruptions to help you focus on the task of listening.

If you aren't in a frame of mind to concentrate on listening, you are better off being open about that yourself and rescheduling the conversation for another time.

> John, I'm way behind on a report that needs to go to the CEO in about two hours. I think I'd be pretty distracted and not able to give you my full attention. Can we get together this afternoon instead?

Sometimes starting with a brief check-in will eliminate a lot of mind reading and potential misunderstanding. If minutes before you walk into the room wanting to talk, your listener has just learned from the company's biggest supplier that the next order will be delayed by two months, it will be helpful to both of you for you to know that. If you know what just happened, you may be willing to cut the listener a little slack for being a bit distracted. A brief check-in can also help all to become a little more aware of their own state of mind.

Once the speaker starts, the best thing the listener can do is to listen with what we call a "tell-me-more" attitude. It is a Green Zone attitude communicating that the listener sincerely wants to hear the whole story and is willing to let it unfold as the speaker wishes. That is an invitation for the speaker to set the pace and direction of the discussion. Many listeners mistakenly believe it is a signal of good listening to continuously try to clarify the message as it unfolds. Listeners, however, can encourage greater depth and intimacy with a tell-me-more attitude than by a cross-examination as though the speaker were in a witness chair. They can usually gather much more information by quietly listening than by grilling speakers for information. Tell-me-more is an attitude to convey, not necessarily the exact script you want to continually use.

Occasionally participants in our workshops get stuck in a repeating loop of tell-me-more. They want to encourage the speaker to continue, so they keep repeating the magic words *Tell-me-more* after every few sentences. The speaker picks up a mechanical application of a tool, rather than a sincere attitude of listening. The result is counterproductive. Use a tell-me-more attitude, but vary the words or phrases you use to communicate it. Different words or phrases you might use to encourage the speaker to continue are *Really? Wow! And? Is that right? I see, Go on, No kidding, Oh?* or *Uh-huh*.

Another way of making it safe for the speaker to share is for the listener to be able to communicate to the speaker that the listener understands the message. This is also the second job of the listener.

## Job #2: Helping the Speaker Feel Understood

The best way to both gain understanding and communicate that understanding back to the speaker is to "summarize and feed back." It is simply occasionally summarizing the message and feeding it back to the speaker to check that your understanding is correct. The key, however, is to feed back both the content and the feelings that underlie the message. Most messages have emotional content. If you don't understand the feelings attached to the words, you haven't understood the message.

Pay attention to the particular words they select to convey the message as well as their body language, such as a worried brow, anxious tapping of a pencil on the table, or pacing back and forth. Pay attention to the tone of voice. Is it slow and soft in a depressed way, or high and sharp as though they are agitated, anxious, or enthusiastic?

There are hundreds of clues about the feelings that are attached to the message. Most of us could tell when our parents were happy and approachable or angry and unapproachable. Most people can tell when their spouse or colleagues are feeling joy, sadness, anger, fear, confusion, etc. What it takes is paying attention to the signs we already know. Most of us miss tell-tale signs not because we lack awareness of the signs. Rather we miss these clues because we don't pay enough attention to the speaker to notice them.

The point is to be able to feed the information back to the speaker to demonstrate comprehension on your part, about both the speaker's words and the underlying feelings. The feedback should communicate the essence of the speaker's message in the listener's own words, not by a parroting back of the speaker's words. It's not a problem if you don't get it right to the speaker's satisfaction the first time because that's the whole point of checking out your understanding. You are creating an opportunity for the speaker to correct any misunderstandings.

The same words can mean different things to different people. Any message has to be translated through the distortions, defenses, and filters of both the speaker and the listener. The odds are actually against a good understanding without some mechanism for checking it out. Remember the old game where participants pass a message around in a circle by repeating it quietly to the person next to them? Then, after it has passed through each person, it is compared to the original message for accuracy. It is usually a funny game because there is so much distortion. After being passed through the distortions of a few people, the message "I'll swing by, maybe at noon, sweetie" could easily sound like "I'll bring a baby baboon from Tahiti." Feeding back for understanding is the only way to tell if you actually do understand.

It is better to demonstrate understanding by feeding back the message in your own words rather than trying to convince the speaker that you understand by claiming, "Yes, I understand." An assertion of understanding is not as convincing as a demonstration of understanding. On top of that, listeners may truly believe they understand when, in fact, they don't. Summarizing and feeding back is the best way to confirm understanding. If listeners don't confirm their understanding with the speaker, they get no credit for their efforts to pay attention and listen.

---

**BOX 5-4**

Listeners who do not confirm their understanding with the speaker get no credit for their efforts to pay attention and listen.

If the speaker talks incessantly, it may be necessary for the listener to interrupt for a moment to summarize and feed back for understanding. It is better to do that than to let the speaker go on for so long that the listener is unable to summarize all he has heard.

Some people are hesitant to demonstrate their understanding of the message because they fear that will imply that they agree with the speaker. Understanding a message, however, does not imply agreement with it. You can still acknowledge that given their assumptions and beliefs, their position makes sense from their point of view. If you fear the speaker will read agreement into your understanding, you can clarify what you mean in Green Zone language:

> I want to understand what you are saying well enough that I can say it back to you. I also want to be clear, however, that my doing so doesn't necessarily mean that I agree with you. I may see things from a different viewpoint.

---

**BOX 5-5**
Understanding the speaker's message does not imply agreement with it.

---

If you communicate not only that you understand the message, but also that you think it is a reasonable belief from the other's point of view, even though you may have a different view, you will be able to change the conversation from adversarial to a common search for how to deal with two different but legitimate beliefs.

> OK, yes, I can see why from your viewpoint you would think that. Your request is more understandable to me now. Let me explain my viewpoint to you. It's different from yours. Once you understand where I'm coming from, then maybe we can work together to find a solution that works for both of us.

No one wants to enter into problem solving with the other side believing that they are not making sense or being reasonable or acting responsibly. Acknowledging the validity of the other's viewpoint will have a big impact on setting a better tone for joint problem solving. It costs nothing and gains a great deal. We say it costs nothing to acknowledge the beliefs of the other person, because they will be clinging to them whether they are acknowledged or not. Generally the more someone resists another's beliefs, the harder the other person will cling to them. By acknowledging the legitimacy of their beliefs from their point of view, it makes it easier for the other person to explore the validity of your beliefs. It also makes it easier for someone to modify their beliefs.

---

**BOX 5-6**

It costs nothing to acknowledge another person's beliefs. They will be clinging to them whether you acknowledge them or not. Generally the more someone resists another's beliefs, the harder the other person will cling to them.

---

## ISSUES THAT UNDERMINE LISTENING

Here are a dozen issues that commonly undermine effective listening.

1. *Preparing your response before you hear what the speaker has to say.* You feel you know what the speaker is going to say, so you may as well use this spare time to prepare your rebuttal. This practice turns a conversation into a contest. Good listening is not a debate. It should not become a competitive sport.

2. *Failing to summarize and feed back for understanding.* Summarizing and feeding back is the best way to set an inviting tone and to check for understanding. Failing to do it regularly passes up an opportunity to increase understanding and build the relationship.

3. *Not paying attention to the person as well as the words.* You should be aware of your own body language and attentiveness. Are you keeping eye contact, invading the other's space by getting too close, or seeming distant by staying too far away?

4. *Asking too many questions.* Questions are not bad or evil, but they are not listening. They tend to send the conversation in a direction you want, rather than where the speaker would naturally go. People sometimes also make covert statements by asking questions. "Are you really sure you want to do that?" can be a transparent disguise for "I don't think you should do that." "You mean you liked that?" probably really means "You couldn't possibly have liked that."

5. *Multitasking or pretending to listen.* Trying to listen and watching a ball game on TV, or surfing the Internet or typing a letter, will almost always be interpreted as not listening even if you hear every word. Try to eliminate as many distractions as possible to create a better listening environment.

6. *Mind reading.* If you don't understand something, say so and ask for clarification. Don't try to fake authenticity. Also try to be aware of assumptions you may be making and check them out.

7. *Prematurely judging the speaker's message through tone of voice or body language that implies "You are wrong."* Remember, we talked about the impact of tone and body language that is out of alignment for speakers. It is also true for listeners. A facial cringe or a sarcastic roll of the eyes sends a clear negative message that you are not interested in really hearing what the speaker is saying.

8. *Toppers, or doing the speaker one better.* Some listeners use any statement by the speaker as a launching platform for topping the speaker. "You liked *Deliverance*? Well, OK, but *Apocalypse Now*, that's a real movie with a message." Implicit in the topper is that the speaker was wrong in his or her assessment.

9. *Inability to deal with silence.* Silence can be golden for some but agony for others. Good listeners need to be able to deal with the ambiguity of silence. If you jump in to fill every empty space, you can be denying the speaker an opportunity to formulate thoughts. If you feel that you're not doing anything while it's quiet, use the time to tune in to how you are doing as a listener. Notice if you feel calm. Are you sincere and willing to really hear what is being communicated? How are you doing at summarizing and feeding back for understanding?

10. *Denying uncomfortable or difficult emotions.* Some listeners try to talk the speaker out of his or her emotions because the listener can't handle them, not because they are difficult for the speaker. Statements like "Things will get better," "You'll get over it," "It's not that bad," or "Things could be worse" can send a message to the speaker that it's not OK to be feeling his or her emotions. It is

much more effective to acknowledge the emotions: "Wow, it sounds like that makes you very sad."

11. *Giving advice.* There is nothing inherently wrong with advice; there is a time for it. But advice is not listening, especially unsolicited advice. Contain your advice to a time when you have a clear agreement with the speaker that advice is what is being sought.

12. *Failing to acknowledge when a conversation is going off track.* Many people don't know what to do when a conversation is going off track. Rather than just let a conversation deteriorate, stop the conversation and have a conversation about the conversation. Talking about what is going wrong in the conversation may get it back on track.

---

Exercise 5-1

## Implications of Better Listening

Using a scale of 0 (poor listening) to 9 (excellent listening), rate yourself on how well you listen in the following relationships. Then, for each relationship that applies, answer the following question: "What consequences might there be if I listened more carefully and sincerely in the relationship?"

| Rating | Consequences of Better Listening |
|---|---|
| _____ | My boss |
| _____ | My peers |
| _____ | Those who work for me |
| _____ | My customers |
| _____ | My suppliers |
| _____ | My mate |
| _____ | My children |

---

## CHAPTER SUMMARY

The listener has two main jobs: creating a safe environment for the speaker to be open and gaining understanding in a way that the speaker feels understood. Adopting a tell-me-more attitude, being attentive to the speaker, and eliminating as many distractions as possible will create safety for speakers.

The most effective way for gaining and communicating understanding of the speaker's message is for the listener to occasionally summarize and feed the message back to the speaker. This allows parties to check for understanding and correct any misunderstandings. The listener should feed back the essence of both the content and the feeling attached to the speaker's message, using the listener's own words. It is much more effective for listeners to demonstrate understanding of the message by summarizing and feeding it back than by simply asserting that they understand what the speaker means.

Good listening will lead to speakers increasing their level of openness and becoming more articulate. When speakers feel heard, they feel more responsibility for a coherent message and tend to ramble less. Speakers also tend to like people better if they are good listeners.

Understanding the message does not imply that the listener agrees with the message. Acknowledging the validity of each other's point of view can change the conversation from adversarial to a joint search for the best way to deal with two different but legitimate beliefs.

Here are twelve keys to effective listening:

1. Hear what the speaker has to say before preparing your response.

2. Continually summarize and feed back for understanding.

3. Pay attention to the person as well as the words.

4. Ask questions judiciously.

5. Don't multitask or pretend to listen.

6. Avoid "mind reading."

7. Beware of prematurely judging the speaker's message through tone of voice or body language that implies "You are wrong."

8. Avoid topping or doing the speaker one better.

9. Be comfortable with silence.

10. Acknowledge uncomfortable or difficult emotions.

11. Give advice judiciously.

12. Acknowledge when a conversation is going off track.

## PART 3
## 3RD ESSENTIAL SKILL

# SELF-ACCOUNTABILITY

Self-accountability is making conscious choices and then taking responsibility for the results. Chapter 6 says that you have more choices than you think. Yet most people believe, mistakenly, that their choices are narrow. You are invited to look at your beliefs about the amount of choice you have and how to take responsibility for the choices you make.

# CHAPTER 6
# MAKING CHOICES AND TAKING RESPONSIBILITY FOR THEM

Man does not simply exist but always decides what his existence will be, what he will become in the next moment.

—*Viktor Frankl*

**It's easy to** say people choose their existence. The statement takes on a deeper meaning, however, when the speaker is referring to his time in the infamous Auschwitz concentration camp, as psychiatrist and author Viktor Frankl was. Frankl's belief was that people have many more choices in their lives than they are aware of. In his book *Man's Search for Meaning*,[1] Frankl urged people to understand that they can choose how they want to "be," and that what they become, within the limits of their circumstances, is what they make of themselves.

People are aware, to varying degrees, that their lives are filled with choices. Some of the more significant choices have to do with the relationships they choose: whom they date and/or marry, whom they work with and for, whom they partner with, and whom they spend their precious time with. These choices define to a great extent the nature and quality of an individual's life. Yet how conscious are people of the choices they make?

No one can prove how much "choice" people really have. The subject has been intensely debated for most of human history. In our own lives we are continually astounded by the powerful, often unperceived impact of circumstances, context, culture, physiology, biology, family history, etc., on our so-called "free" choices. This is the essential problem of an unexamined life: that it will be determined by forces outside conscious awareness.

Everyone lives in a field of past and present influences that may always have considerably more control over us than people think. Nevertheless, we invite you to explore the consequences of believing that you have much more choice than you might think you have. Experiment with making more deliberate choices and accepting responsibility for everything in your life. This does not mean trying to control everything. It means having a mind-set that you are fully responsible for you, no matter what happens. It means being able to surrender with grace and style if that is appropriate. It means being able to assert and take charge if that is appropriate to your deep sense of self and the situation.

Over time, this mind-set of self-accountability will make a noticeable difference. We predict you will find this way of being in the world exciting and enormously rewarding.

Think back on a recent conference, cocktail party, or big family gathering. Think about whom you ended up spending your time with. How did you make those choices? What was your choosing strategy? Were you the chooser, or were you chosen? Did you reach out to the people you really wanted to hang out with or did you stand around the food table hoping they would come to you, or that you could ensnare them as they reached for the guacamole? If someone who was not your first choice wanted to spend time with you, did you consider saying no? Does even the thought of saying no to someone make you break out in a cold sweat?

Little choices like these can be a reflection of how people make bigger choices in their lives. Life choices reflect both a belief system about how much choice individuals really do have, and awareness about their available choices.

---

**BOX 6-1**

Many people forfeit choices, not realizing that not to choose is also a choice. The way people make little decisions is a reflection of how they make bigger decisions in their lives.

---

## WHAT ARE YOUR BELIEFS?

Consider, for a moment, your own beliefs regarding how much choice you have in your life, on a scale of 0 to 9. At the low end, a 0 means you believe your life is predetermined: you simply have to go with what is presented to you. Your parents controlled your childhood.

Teachers controlled your school years. Your employer determines your work life. Your spouse and family determine your current life, responsibilities, and happiness at home. Your future may be in the stars, but you won't know what it is until after it happens and you have the opportunity to look back on it.

At the high end, a 9 means you believe you determine everything. You choose your body and how you think, feel, and behave, including all your relationships, illnesses, and what other people may identify as fate. Your future is entirely under your control and you can fully determine the quality of your life.

At the midrange you may believe in varying degrees that events happen to you that are out of your control; however, you do have some choice about how you respond to those events and how you feel about them. It's a bit like "shit happens, now deal with it." The higher the number, the greater a person's belief that he influences his own destiny.

Select a number on the scale below that represents your belief regarding the amount of choice you have in your life. There is no correct answer.

---

Exercise 6–1

## What Is Your Belief System?

| 0 | 1 | 2 | 3 | 4 | 5 | 6 | 7 | 8 | 9 |
|---|---|---|---|---|---|---|---|---|---|
| No |  |  |  |  |  |  |  |  | Complete |
| Choice |  |  |  |  |  |  |  |  | Choice |

---

We said there was no correct answer. There are, however, consequences to your answer. Your belief system regarding the amount of choice you have in your life has a huge impact on your feelings of empowerment in determining the quality of your life and the quality of your relationships. Many people forfeit choices available to them not realizing that not to choose is also a choice. We are suggesting that people almost always have more choice than they think they have. If you want to feel more empowered in your life, change your belief system, moving up on the scale about how much choice you have in your life.

The one belief having a great impact on people's sense of well-being is the belief that they have some control over their own life. Powerlessness, i.e., the inability to affect outcomes, usually ranks at the top of issues causing stress. In *Social Causes of Psychological Distress*,[2] Mirowsky and Ross point out that research into distress shows great emotional benefits not from having power over others, but rather from having a sense of power over our own lives.

---

**BOX 6-2**

The most effective thing you can do to feel more empowered is to change your belief system, moving up on the scale about how much choice you have in your life.

---

We worked with a company that was housed in a desirable location right on the ocean in Southern California.[3] Employees could take walks along the beach during lunchtime. Quaint little restaurants and outdoor cafés lined the neighboring streets. The building itself was a showcase. It was spacious, comfortable, and expensive. When the dot-com bubble burst in California, profits of this company plummeted like those of many other companies. To cut its budget, the company determined to move the office inland about twenty miles. Not only was the new location much less desirable, the new building was more like a warehouse. In Southern California, commutes are measured by time, not miles. For many of employees on the night shift that meant an additional thirty-minute commute. For some day-shift employees, however, it could amount to an additional sixty minutes each way. This change in location was a big deal for most employees.

The reactions of employees turned out to be a direct reflection of their beliefs regarding the amount of choice they had in their lives. The employees at the low end of the scale who believed they had little choice in their lives looked at this as just another example of the company doing something to them. They felt victimized, depressed at how powerless they were. Life was doing it to them again. Why didn't they ever get a break? Productivity disappeared while small groups of employees sat around talking about how awful it was. Several just gave up, convinced that they would lose their jobs because they couldn't handle the longer commute.

In contrast, employees at the other end of the scale whose beliefs supported a feeling of greater self-determination in their lives reacted differently. They were still upset at the thought of the move, but they organized a response at several different levels. They formed an ad hoc committee to search out other possible less expensive buildings in their current location. Another committee was formed to look into other possible ways to reduce expenses. They felt that if they could find enough savings in other ways, they might talk management into canceling the move. Another group went to work on a carpool program. If they had to have a longer commute, at least they could reduce cost and annoyance by commuting with other employees. Several other employees took it upon themselves to draft new policies regarding telecommuting and flexible workweeks such as 4–10 days or job-sharing opportunities.

---

**BOX 6-3**

The employees' beliefs about the amount of choice available in their lives either *paralyzed* them or *mobilized* them.

---

One group was paralyzed while the other was mobilized. The paralyzed group had a sense of not being in control, of not having any choice in the matter, and it diminished any motivation to seek creative solutions and solve problems. This all stemmed from their beliefs about how much choice they had in their lives. The mobilized group benefited from seeing they had choices that could affect their situation. Their sense of influence over their lives made the undesirable events less demoralizing.

There can be hidden or unconscious payoffs in the choices people make. An important part of being accountable is to seek to understand those payoffs. For example, Steven is a skilled warehouseman who complains all the time about his job. He says he would prefer work involving more contact with the public. The manager, however, wants to keep him organizing shipments in the back warehouse, a job at which Steven is skilled. So Steven begrudgingly accepts his fate and continues to whine about it to his coworkers during their lunchtime bitch sessions.

In a workshop, Steven began exploring the one choice he was making, his choice to do nothing but sit back and complain. Up until then Steven hadn't even been aware that he was in fact making a choice to do nothing. Steven just believed that his boss was in control and that he didn't have any choice in the matter. He was oblivious to the many things he could be doing to take responsibility for his own life. A few of the most obvious that came up in the workshop were that he could press the boss harder for the job change; he could look for other work; he could go back to school to get additional training to improve his skills dealing with the public; he could seek support from his current supervisor and fellow workers. It was impossible for Steven to take responsibility for his current situation as long as he believed he had no choice over the issue, or if he remained unaware of the many choices that were available to him.

In exploring his choice to do nothing, Steven realized that he has several hidden payoffs for not pressing the point with his employer. He is skilled at his current job and realized he has some anxiety about having to learn a new job. The bitch sessions with other employees were also, in a funny way, a pleasant bonding experience with his buddies. Steven also remembered his father's negative attitude about the "front office snobs." Even though his father had been dead for several years, Steven realized that by staying in the warehouse job he unconsciously avoided the disapproving voice of his father. Steven also realized that he was a bit afraid of annoying the manager by pressing the issue.

Finally, in his most important insight about his situation, Steven realized that if he acknowledged his role in not pursuing the new job, he could no longer just sit back and blame it all on the manager. By taking responsibility for the choice that he was making, i.e., to do nothing, the only person Steven could complain about now was himself.

Understanding the choices available to him does not mean Steven has to do anything different. He could continue working in the warehouse and decide not to pursue the front office job. But whatever he decides now, it will be a conscious decision, one for which Steven will take responsibility. Gaining this incredibly simple yet profound insight, that he has choices and should take responsibility for them, has changed Steven's life. He no longer feels powerless in his situation. He may not be able to control the ultimate outcome, but he feels that he has moved from a 3 up to a 7 on the choice scale. He feels that he now has a say in his own destiny rather than being adrift on the sea. Steven is now being accountable for Steven.

---

**BOX 6-4**

A sense of influence over our own lives makes undesirable events less demoralizing.

## BEING ACCOUNTABLE FOR YOUR CHOICES

At each step of building collaboration, developing relationships, dealing with conflict, or leading others, people are surrounded by choices. Accepting full responsibility for those choices and learning from them is critical. This is what self-accountability is all about. The most effective executives and leaders we work with realize it is to their advantage to assume full responsibility for the circumstances of their lives, as well as their reactions to these circumstances. Therefore, without self-judgment or self-blame they focus attention on self-awareness and on understanding their full range of available choices. They make educated and aware choices. When their choices do not result in their desired outcomes, they focus on what happened and what action to take rather than on who is to blame. It also means they are willing to hold others accountable for making their own educated and aware choices.

In our Trustworthy Leader Survey[4] there is an entire section on self-accountability. The survey asks colleagues to consider issues such as whether the leader accepts full responsibility for the consequences and impact of his or her actions, seeks solutions rather than blaming others, says no and sets boundaries when appropriate, uses failures as opportunities for learning and growth, and takes responsibility for managing his or her own mood, attitudes, and behaviors. These all reflect the individual's awareness of the available choices and the amount of responsibility taken for the outcome of these choices.

---

**BOX 6-5**

Self-accountability is being aware of all the choices we make, and taking responsibility for the results of those choices.

---

In seeking to become more self-accountable, the questions shift from "Who did this to me?" or "Who is to blame?" to "What is my part in this situation?" More relevant questions become:

- What choices did I make that helped create this experience?
- By my action or inaction, how have I contributed?
- How has my very interpretation of events caused some of the trouble?
- Is there a hidden or unconscious payoff for my continuing with this problem?

- What could I have done to avoid this problem or make it better?

These are empowering questions that give direction toward improving the situation rather than feeling victimized, blaming others, and waiting for magic.

Taking high accountability for the choices in your life is suggested as a more effective strategy for building collaborative relationships, not as a moral judgment. It will produce better relationships in your life, and we urge you to experiment with it. A strategy of high accountability also allows for the choice of "surrendering gracefully" to circumstances you perceive as outside your direct control rather than feeling that you must "submit" or "rebel" forever.

---

**BOX 6-6**

Taking responsibility for your actions and choices is not a question of right or wrong. It is simply suggested as a more effective strategy for building collaborative relationships.

---

Exercise 6-2

## How Do You Contribute?

Think of an area in your life that is unsatisfactory to you. Think of the three main reasons you give yourself that it is unsatisfactory that are focused on other people and circumstances.

1. _____

   _____

2. _____

   _____

3. _____

   _____

Now, without any self-judgment or self-blame, reflect on how you might be contributing to this situation and how you can be more accountable by answering these questions:

1. By your action or nonaction what choices have you made regarding this situation?

2. By your action or nonaction how are you contributing to this situation?

3. What payoffs might you have for continuing this unsatisfactory situation?

4. What could you do differently to be more accountable?

---

## CHAPTER SUMMARY

People's lives are filled with choices. Those choices define the nature and quality of their lives, yet people are often unconscious about the choices they make, particularly those made through nonaction. People often have hidden or unconscious payoffs for not taking responsibility. It is worthwhile to explore those payoffs in order to make more conscious decisions.

People almost always have more choice than they think they have. The most effective thing people can do to feel more empowered is to change their belief system, increasing their belief about how much choice they have in their life. A belief that people can influence their own lives can mobilize them, while a belief that they have no impact can paralyze them.

Making aware, conscious choices and then taking responsibility for the results of those choices is what self-accountability is all about. Readers are asked to rate themselves on a scale of 0 to 9 regarding how much choice they have in their lives and then consider the implication for moving up the scale.

# SELF-AWARENESS AND AWARENESS OF OTHERS

If you want to improve a relationship or change the culture of an entire organization, the first step is to increase people's self-awareness. Chapter 7 explains a theory of relationships called FIRO (Fundamental Interpersonal Relations Orientation), which can help you understand your relationships. You'll have the opportunity to take the FIRO Element B assessment online and explore the results with a relationship partner. In chapter 8 you will learn how rigid behavior can harm your relationships. Chapter 9 offers useful tools for letting go of the past, reducing your fear, and building a future by breaking free of the past one thought at a time.

# CHAPTER 7
# UNDERSTANDING YOUR OWN BEHAVIOR IN RELATIONSHIPS

**The ability to** make effective choices and live an authentic life depends to a great extent on a capacity to be self-reflective. Self-awareness is the greatest asset people have for living fulfilling lives that provide a sense of direction and influence over what happens to them. If people do not understand their own feelings, fears, values, intentions, and patterns of behaviors, their lives can be like corks bobbing on the ocean. This may provide an interesting journey, but there will definitely be no sense of control over their own destiny. Such travelers will always be a little puzzled about how and why their lives unfold.

Because relationships with others play a significant role in everyone's life (you wouldn't be reading this book if they didn't), it is also helpful to have an awareness of the basic human concerns, motivations, fears, feelings, and the resulting patterns of behaviors of others. Self-awareness alone is like one hand clapping. If empathy and understanding of others are missing, successful relationships are unlikely.

Most success in building collaborative environments in organizations has been built on a foundation of increasing self-awareness. Basic skill building without emotional depth can be helpful; however, in most cases it will not lead to a more collaborative culture in an organization.

A virtual mosaic of tools, psychological systems, and programs is available to help people explore their own levels of awareness. We have found many to be helpful in our work. We firmly believe that any self-exploration will be valuable and helpful, and we encourage readers to pursue any method that captures their interest.

## FIRO THEORY

Since our work is primarily about building collaboration within organizations and increasing the effectiveness of individuals in relationship to others, we prefer to work with a system known as FIRO theory.[1] FIRO stands for Fundamental Interpersonal Relations Orientation. We prefer FIRO theory because it is specifically aimed at interpersonal relationships and is supported by a strong base of scientific research. It is also simple to understand and easy to use. It was created to help the U.S. military increase the effectiveness of combat command teams. The combination of its scientific base and military history makes it much easier to introduce in the corporate world, which is traditionally suspicious of anything psychological or personal-growth oriented.

FIRO theory was created by Dr. Will Schutz when the U.S. Navy asked him to conduct research on understanding and predicting how groups work together, particularly in stressful situations. Dr. Schutz studied teams in battleship Combat Information Centers, who were working together to quickly evaluate information from different sources and then make life-and-death decisions. The research provided a wealth of information about how to improve the effectiveness of teams. In his research, for example, if randomly selected new teams were successful 50 percent of the time, using FIRO theory to focus on team compatibility increased that number to 75 percent. In a business world so dependent on ever-changing project teams, that is a remarkable increase in effectiveness.

---

**BOX 7-1**

The Navy research determined that if randomly selected new teams were successful 50 percent of the time, using FIRO theory to focus on team compatibility increased that number to 75 percent. In a business world so dependent on ever-changing project teams, that is a remarkable increase in effectiveness.

---

Dr. Schutz's original work produced the immensely popular FIRO B psychological testing instrument. Since then his development of FIRO theory has created a whole new generation of psychometric instruments called Elements of Awareness. This includes the FIRO

Element B (*B* for "behavior") instrument, which provides three times as much information as the older FIRO B in a format Dr. Schutz believed was much easier to use. We've included information about the array of newer FIRO-based materials in appendix 2. Any practitioners currently using the older FIRO B may wish to review the difference between the two in the endnote.[2]

## THREE PRIMARY BEHAVIORS INFLUENCING COMPATIBILITY

Dr. Schutz's research determined that three primary behaviors, Inclusion, Control, and Openness,[3] best explain compatibility within relationships. The theory maintains that people orient themselves toward other people according to their preferences regarding these three behaviors. Success in relationships depends on how flexible we can be when presented with circumstances that call for behavior different from our preferences.

Chapters 7 and 8 discuss three levels of FIRO theory:

- How people want to feel in relationships
- Underlying fears that affect our behavior in relationships
- How people behave because of those feelings and fears

This chapter focuses primarily on the three behaviors of Inclusion, Control, and Openness. Chapter 8 focuses on how feelings and fears can lead to rigid behavior.

According to FIRO theory all people want to feel significant, competent, and likable in varying degrees. All people also have some fear of being ignored, humiliated, or rejected. People's beliefs about their significance, competence, and likability, as well as their fears about being ignored, humiliated, or rejected, will have a great effect on the way they behave in relationships. These feeling and fears affect the way people behave around Inclusion (how much they include others, and how much they want others to include them), Control (how much they want to control others, and how much they want others to control them), and Openness (how open they are with others, and how open they want others to be with them).

Boxes 7-2 and 7-3 show how FIRO theory relates feelings and fears to people's behavior.

**BOX 7-2**

**FIRO Theory: Feelings, Fears, and Behavior**

| All people want to feel: | **Significant** | **Competent** | **Likable** |
|---|---|---|---|

| To some extent all people are afraid of being: | **Ignored** | **Humiliated** | **Rejected** |
|---|---|---|---|

| These feelings and fears affect the way people behave regarding: | **Inclusion** | **Control** | **Openness** |
|---|---|---|---|

**BOX 7-3**

**FIRO Theory: How People's Behavior Is Influenced by Their Feelings and Fears**

1. *Inclusion* behavior is directly influenced by how *significant* people feel, and how much they fear being *ignored*.

   If people have poor self-esteem about their own significance and unduly fear being ignored, they can become rigid in their behavior around inclusion. For example, they may include too much or too little and not be able to respond appropriately to their circumstances.

2. *Control* behavior is directly influenced by how *competent* people feel, and how much they fear being *humiliated*.

   If people have poor self-esteem about their own competence and unduly fear being humiliated, they can become rigid in their behavior around control. For example, they may become domineering or overly passive and not be able to respond appropriately to their circumstances.

3. *Openness* behavior is directly influenced by how *likable* people feel and how much they fear being *rejected*.

   If people have poor self-esteem about their own likability, and unduly fear being rejected, they can become rigid in their behavior around openness. For example, they may silently stonewall or they may flood others with too many emotions and not be able to respond appropriately to their circumstances.

Individual behaviors range along a wide spectrum of preferences regarding these dimensions. For example, while some people prefer to include many other people in their lives (high inclusion), other people prefer to live in greater solitude (low inclusion). Individuals have preferences about how much they want to include others as well as how much they want others to include them. One preference is not better than the other. There is no right or wrong or best preference; however, there are consequences to individual preferences.

On a scale of 0 (low) to 9 (high), the preferences of our population are distributed just about equally.[4] This leads to the humbling, yet helpful insight that most people are different from us regarding their behavioral preferences. No matter what your preferences are regarding how much inclusion you want, what degree of control you want, or how open you choose to be, you can be assured that about 90 percent of the rest of the world has different preferences. Understanding this fact alone should lead to a little more compassion about diverse behaviors. As we describe these three dimensions of behavior below, reflect upon your own preferences as well as those of others you interact with regularly. Later in the chapter, on page 128 in Excercise 7-1, you will be given instructions for going online if you choose to get your actual scores instead of your estimates. At the end of the chapter you can complete a reflective exercise about your own preferences regarding Inclusion, Control, and Openness. Then you can compare your preferences with those people you are in a relationship with, to increase your awareness about the relationship. You may also discover areas of rigidity that may be undermining those relationships.

## INCLUSION

Inclusion is how much contact you want with others. Some people cherish solitude. Others like to be around lots of people most of the time. People who prefer low inclusion might spend their spare time reading a book or taking a walk by themselves. Someone who prefers high inclusion might rather go to a party or invite several friends along on the walk. People preferring low inclusion might choose jobs as forest-fire lookouts over jobs as social directors on cruise ships. This doesn't mean they couldn't be successful as social directors, but low-inclusion people would have to move up on the scale to perform well in high-inclusion jobs. Someone preferring high inclusion may still perform well in a more solitary job, such as the fire lookout, but to do well they would have to move down on the scale and be comfortable dealing with more alone time.

The key is to understand your preference and be flexible enough to change your behavior to match your circumstances. For example, when Jim was in his role as a judge, it was appropriate for his behavior to reflect low inclusion. He didn't invite lawyers or witnesses to join him for lunch. When he was mediating a strike, however, he was often surrounded by large groups of bargaining team members, sometimes around the clock. The behavior that was appropriate in his role as a judge was not effective in his role as a mediator. People get into relationship trouble not because of their preferences, but rather because they get rigid and are not flexible in their behavior.

While there are no good, bad, right, wrong, or best preferences, your preferences have consequences. If you prefer high inclusion and want to take your spouse out partying with friends all weekend, but your spouse prefers low inclusion and wants you both to stay home and read or watch a movie, those preferences will be an area of potential conflict. If you understand that your desires stem from different preferences about how much you want to be around other people, and not simply from your spouse wanting to ruin your weekend, you may be able to talk about your differences in a nonjudgmental, nonpejorative way and figure out some accommodation to deal with those differences.

---

**BOX 7-4**

While there are no good, bad, right, wrong, or best preferences, your preferences have consequences.

---

If a boss prefers high inclusion, he may like to hold lots of meetings because he enjoys the contact with the employees. This will fit well with employees who also prefer lots of contact with others. If, however, that same boss is supervising an employee with a strong preference for being alone, the employee may feel overwhelmed by all the meetings.

People often make up stories about another person's preferences. For example, the low-inclusion employee might feel that the boss doesn't trust him and therefore wants lots of meetings to keep an eye on the employee. The boss might start believing that he is not significant to the employee because the employee never stops by the boss's office just to visit and always resists coming to his meetings.

Inclusion behaviors are greatly influenced by our beliefs around the issue of significance (our own and others') and the underlying fear of feeling ignored. We'll discuss how this works when we talk about rigidities in the next chapter.

## CONTROL

Control has to do with how much people want to influence others and how much they want others to influence them. Some people like to take on a lot of responsibility. They like being in charge; they like being the boss and having a great deal of influence about what happens and how it happens. Other people prefer to have less responsibility and work better when given clear directions. Jim has a higher preference for control than Ron. When we plan a vacation for both our families, Jim enjoys looking at all the guidebooks and maps to decide the best places to go and the best route to take. Ron might take a more laid-back approach: "I know I'll have fun anyplace we go, so you do all the preparation and tell me when to be ready to leave."

Once again, there is no right or wrong or best preference to have. The key is not so much what your preference is, but rather whether you can be flexible enough to behave appropriately in whatever your circumstances. For example, if an individual who has a high-control preference is invited out on a sailboat, and that person has no sailing expertise, it will probably make for a more enjoyable day for everyone if the individual flexes down on control.

If two individuals with low-control preferences get rigid in their behavior when trying to plan a meeting, they may never get it done or end up with a meeting planned by default. It might sound like this:

Mike:    Where do you want to hold the next management retreat?

Susanne: I don't care. Where do you want to go?

Mike:    It doesn't matter to me. What do you think we should have on the agenda?

Susanne: I don't care. I'm really open to what you want to do.

Mike:    Me too. I'm really open to what you want to do.

Susanne: So where do you want to go?

Mike:    I don't care. Where do you want to go?

And so on, and so on! If they get rigid in low-control behavior, they may never make it to any meeting.

If two individuals with preferences for high control get rigid in their behavior when trying to plan the same management retreat together, it will probable require skillful negotiations, because they each may have strong feelings about what they want to do and where they want to go. If they both get rigid, they'd better include a mediator in the planning, because it may seem like a constant battle of "my way or the highway!"

Just as with the dimension of Inclusion, there is an almost even distribution of preference across a wide spectrum; so no matter what your preference is, most of the rest of the world is different from you.

Now here is a trick question for you. Where is the best place to be on the scale from low control up to high control if you want to be a good manager? Remember, it's a trick question. Think about it for a minute.

The correct answer is anyplace you want to be, so long as you can be flexible in your behavior to be appropriate to the circumstances you are facing. There will be times as a manager of a newer employee that you will need to be higher in control, giving more direction and clear instructions. If an employee is performing poorly, you may need to flex up, spending more time with that employee and directing strong corrective action. If you are managing self-starting, experienced employees who know what they are doing and want to be left to their own initiative, you will need to flex down on the control scale and support the employees in performing on their own. Our preferences don't cause problems for us; it is our inability to be flexible in circumstances that call for an approach different from our preference that creates a problem.

---

**BOX 7-5**

**Trick Question**

To be a good manager, where is the best place to be?

| Prefer | Prefer | Prefer |
|--------|--------|--------|
| Low | Midrange | High |
| Control | Control | Control |

**Answer:**

Anyplace you want to be, as long as you can be flexible!

Behavior regarding control is greatly influenced by our beliefs around the issue of competence (our own and others') and the underlying fear of feeling humiliated. We'll explore this and rigidities around control in chapter 8.

## OPENNESS

Openness has to do with how much we want to open up about ourselves, and how much we want others to open up or disclose to us. Where inclusion relates to breadth of relationships, openness has to do with depth. It is possible to enjoy being around lots of people all the time (high inclusion) and prefer to keep the sharing rather superficial (low openness). Some people prefer to share their deepest thoughts with a limited number of close friends, if at all. You will not find many low-openness people appearing on *Oprah, Dr. Phil,* or the *Jerry Springer* TV shows. Others are quite comfortable being an open book; what you see is what you get.

When we lead workshops that are filled with high-openness people, we have to pay particular attention to staying on time and moving the participants from one exercise to the next. It's easy to fall behind because at the end of each exercise when we ask participants to talk about the experience, they all have so much to share. If the workshop is filled with low-openness people, we end up doing most of the talking. The low-openness group may be fully engaged in the exercise and getting a lot out of it, but when we debrief an exercise, it might sound like this:

| | |
|---|---|
| Jim and Ron: | Did you like that exercise? |
| Group members: | Yes, that was great. |
| Jim and Ron: | Did you learn anything about yourself or your organization? |
| Group: | Yes, a lot. |
| Jim and Ron: | Would you like to share what you learned? |
| Group: | Nope! |

They might be learning just as much as a high-openness group. They just don't have any particular desire to share what's going on inside them with us or the rest of the group.

As with Inclusion and Control, the distribution of Openness preferences is spread almost evenly over the range of 0 to 9, so about 90 percent of the population will have a preference different from yours.

---

**BOX 7-6**

No matter what your preferences regarding the amount of Inclusion, Control, and Openness you want in your life, research shows that almost 90 percent of the rest of the population will have a different preference.

---

Unlike our beliefs about Inclusion and Control, we do have a strong bias about the advantages of increasing Openness if your goal is to build more effective collaborative relationships. Problem solving and relationship building almost always benefit from increased Openness. In his research for the U.S. Navy, Will Schutz discovered that if it wasn't possible to create teams based upon compatibility factors, the next best thing was to create an environment where it was safe for people to be more open. Openness is not only a way to create depth in relationships; it is a key problem-solving tool. It is difficult, if not impossible, to deal effectively with relationship problems if you aren't willing to share your thoughts and feelings.

An important task for any team or organization that is generally low on openness, then, is to challenge themselves to flex up on openness to get all the information on the table about the specific issue, project, or problem. It is impossible to creatively solve problems if people aren't willing to say what is going on.

---

**BOX 7-7**

In his research for the Navy, Will Schutz discovered that if it wasn't possible to create teams based upon compatibility factors, the next best thing was to create an environment where it was safe for people to be more open.

---

This is why so much of our work is designed to create organizational environments where employees feel safe enough to increase their openness. If people aren't willing to tell the truth because it feels too dangerous, organizations perpetuate an environment where no one says the emperor has no clothes. This shows up in high turnover because employees aren't willing to openly discuss their dissatisfaction at work. It shows up in wasted effort and resources because no one is willing to say a project won't work. It shows up in failed relationships because people are unwilling to honestly express their needs and desires or their disappointments and disillusionment.

At an individual level, one potential consequence of a low-openness preference is that other people are likely to project their own feelings onto you or make up stories about what you are feeling. Since people don't get much information about what's going on inside of people with a preference for low openness, they will tend to fill in the blanks with their own stories. Low-openness people may also feel a little judged by high-openness people who always want "more" from them.

One consequence of having a preference for high openness is that you may not get others to share at the same depth you desire. Remember, if you are in the top of the high-openness scale, most of the rest of the world does not want to share at the same depth as you. If you can't be flexible for the circumstances you are in, you may always be a little disappointed by the unwillingness of others to self-disclose at a level you find satisfying.

A husband and wife attending a workshop were at opposite ends of the openness preference. She enjoyed high openness and wanted it from him. He preferred low openness. No area of discussion was off limits for her. She wanted to share all of her feelings, including her feelings about the sex lives of their adult children. He always felt flooded with information and would rather pull out his fingernails than discuss his feelings about their kids' sex lives. Both thought that they were normal and that their spouse was weird. They both judged the other as "wrong" on the issue of openness. An understanding of behavior preferences allowed them to appreciate that their spouse was simply different, not wrong. An understanding of their different preferences allowed them to talk in nonjudgmental terms and problem solve about their differences rather than engage in name-calling.

---

**BOX 7-8**

Problem solving and relationship building almost always benefit from increased openness.

---

Behavior preferences about openness are greatly influenced by our beliefs about the issue of likability (both ours and others'), and the underlying fear of feeling rejected.

## FIRO ELEMENT B ASSESSMENT AND SCALES

The FIRO Element B is a scientifically researched questionnaire that measures our preferences regarding Inclusion, Control, and Openness. To quantify preferences, the FIRO Element B uses a scale with 0 being the low end and 9 being the high end for each of the behaviors (Inclusion, Control, and Openness). Using this 0 to 9 scale, the FIRO Element B measures four aspects of each behavior: How we behave toward others; how we want to behave toward others; how others behave toward us; and how we want others to behave toward us.

The FIRO Element B also measures the difference between the way individuals behave and the way they want to behave, as well as the difference between the way others behave toward us and the way we want them to behave.

---

**BOX 7-9**

**FIRO Element B Structure**

| | What I See Happening Now | What I Want to Happen | Difference |
|---|---|---|---|
| **How I Behave Toward Others** | How I Behave Toward Others Now | How I Want to Behave Toward Others | The difference between how I behave and how I want to behave |
| **How Others Behave Toward Me** | How Others Behave Toward Me Now | How I Want Others to Behave Toward Me | The difference between how others behave toward me and how I want them to behave |

---

The differences are important because Schutz believed strongly that individual behavioral preferences are not hardwired into personality. Therefore, if individuals want to behave differently from how they are currently behaving, they can take action to behave differently. If individuals want others to behave differently toward them, they can make certain choices and change their own behavior in ways that will influence how others behave toward them.

For example, if Gary realizes he wants others to include him more, he can take a number of steps. He can be more open about his desire and tell people he would like to do more activities with others. Maybe he could join more social activities. If he is looking for more openness in his life, he can be more deliberate about whom he spends time with so that he has more time with friends who are open to greater depth and self-disclosure.

## LET'S LOOK AT AN EXAMPLE

Monica and Hank are colleagues on a project team. We can get a sense of where they may run into compatibility issues by looking at their scores. Keep in mind that if Monica and Hank can be flexible in their behavior when dealing with each other, they may be able to work together successfully. If they become rigid in their behavior, however, they will probably run into some compatibility issues.

The FIRO Element B scores can offer a wealth of information about the complexities of team effectiveness. For purposes of this discussion, however, we're taking a few examples and simply looking at how one person behaves toward another compared to how that other person wants to be treated. For example, we compare Monica's score on "I include others" with Hank's score on "I want others to include me." If there are large differences between what one person does and what the other wants, that is an area of *potential* conflict that can get in the way of a collaborative effort. We describe it as an area of potential conflict because the numbers themselves don't tell us whether a conflict will occur. If either of them gets rigid about their preference, it will likely result in conflict or at least a strained relationship. The keys to their compatibility are their abilities to know themselves, understand that they have some different preferences, be willing to talk openly about those differences, and be flexible in their behavior.

Take a look at the scores for Monica and Hank in box 7-10, and then we'll discuss them.

BOX 7-10

| MONICA'S SCORES | | HANK'S SCORES |
|---|---|---|
| | **Inclusion** | |
| 2 | I include others | 7 |
| 3 | I want to include others | 7 |
| 1 | *Difference* | 0 |
| | | |
| 6 | Others include me | 5 |
| 2 | I want others to include me | 7 |
| 4 | Difference | 2 |
| | | |
| | **Control** | |
| 4 | I control others | 6 |
| 4 | I want to control others | 5 |
| 0 | *Difference* | 1 |
| | | |
| 5 | Others control me | 3 |
| 6 | I want others to control me | 3 |
| 1 | *Difference* | 0 |
| | | |
| | **Openness** | |
| 3 | I am open with others | 9 |
| 5 | I want to be open with others | 9 |
| 2 | *Difference* | 0 |
| | | |
| 7 | Others are open with me | 4 |
| 5 | I want others to be open with me | 9 |
| 2 | *Difference* | 5 |

Regarding Inclusion, Monica prefers to include others at a level 2. Hank wants others to include him at a level 7. This presents an area of potential conflict or uneasiness in their working relationship if they become rigid. Because Monica prefers less inclusion, if she gets rigid, she may avoid activities necessary to the team's success if they require a lot of involvement with Hank. Monica may interpret (may even misinterpret) Hank's desire for greater involvement to be inappropriate or needy. Hank, on the other hand, may feel excluded by Monica. He may demand more contact than is really necessary to get the job done. He may misinterpret Monica's desire to work alone as avoidance or abandonment of him, which may lead to an inappropriate reaction on his part.

Regarding Control, Hank controls others at level 6 and Monica wants others to control her at level 6. Monica controls others at level 4 and Hank wants others to control him at level 3. Without knowing any more about their relationship, our hypothesis would be that they are probably quite compatible around issues of control.

Regarding Openness, Monica prefers to be open to others at level 3 and Hank wants others to be open with him at level 9. Monica has a different comfort zone about self-disclosure from Hank. Monica will probably feel pressure from Hank to disclose more, and Hank may end up being constantly disappointed about the level of personal sharing coming from Monica.

Whether the differences between Monica's and Hank's behaviors and desires create a problem for team effectiveness depends on the nature of the task assigned to the team, and the abilities of Monica and Hank to be flexible in their behaviors and expectations. Perhaps Monica can flex up on inclusion and openness in her relationship with Hank. Perhaps Hank can flex down in his expectations about Monica, knowing that her behavior has a lot to do with her own preferences and little to do with him personally.

If Monica and Hank were experiencing stress in their relationship, we would coach them in the following way:

## We Would Coach Monica as Follows

### Regarding Inclusion

Notice that Hank prefers to be included much more than you prefer to include people. So, you might take special care to acknowledge him and include him more than you usually do. He could misinterpret your preference for including others less as feeling he is not important, or he could feel that you are avoiding him or leaving him out of key involvements. While it is not your job to take care of him, it is your job to use your own self-insight to make sure you both work well together. Also, be aware that Hank will want to include you more than you generally prefer. So, talk with him about your desire for more individual space. It is also important that you resist the temptation to make up stories about him "invading" your space or intruding on you or not trusting you to work alone.

### Regarding Control

Notice that you and Hank have compatible scores on Control. The amount of control you express closely matches what he likes. The opposite is also true; the amount of control Hank expresses is just what you like. We would not expect much conflict in this area. However, one warning for both of you would be to make sure you both can flex up to take higher control and assert yourselves at critical moments in the project if the situation requires.

### Regarding Openness

Notice that Hank is going to want quite a bit more openness than you. He may be tempted to see your lower openness as being too businesslike or a little cold. He may think at times you don't like him. With his high inclusion and high openness, Hank is likely to want to visit a lot and just hang out. Make a special effort to be absolutely direct about your intentions, motives, and feelings about the project you are working on. It is fine to set boundaries about how much personal stuff you wish to share with him, but if being successful working together requires a high amount of self-disclosure, you may have to flex up and let him know where you stand on things. You should make a point of letting him know that you really do value and care about his contribution, and that if you don't talk all the time, it does not mean something is wrong.

## We Would Coach Hank as Follows

### Regarding Inclusion

Notice that you like a lot more inclusion than Monica does. So, let her have some space. She renews and refreshes by being alone; it does not mean anything about you. She might prefer most of your contact to be focused on work, so don't take it personally if she does not want to hang out or tell stories or visit after hours. Let her know it is fine for her to signal you when she's feeling it's too much. Also let her know that while you enjoy a lot of contact, it does not mean you're trying to invade her space. Keep inviting her, but don't be surprised if she doesn't show up very often. Give her credit when she does include you. Often it won't occur to her that it is important or pleasurable for others to be included.

### Regarding Control

Notice that you and Monica have compatible scores on Control. The amount of control you express is just what she likes. The opposite is also true; the amount of control Monica expresses closely matches what you like. We would not expect much conflict in this area. However, one warning for both of you would be to make sure you both can flex up to take higher control and assert yourselves at critical moments in the project if the situation requires. Also notice that because of your higher Inclusion and Openness scores, it is likely to be much easier for you to approach and assert toward others. You already like a lot of contact and self-disclosure, so your preferences are likely to make it easier for you to assert in conflict situations. This may also be true between the two of you. So, we encourage you to go first, and don't wait too long for her to initiate contact when you need to talk or work out difficulties.

### Regarding Openness

Notice you prefer a lot more openness. So be aware that Monica might experience you as a little overwhelming and feel flooded with too much information. Be aware that her more private preference does not mean she does not like you or care. She may not wish to share too much about her private life, so don't make up negative stories about that. You do need her to be straight about what she really thinks and feels about the work you are doing together, so gently ask her for her views. Monica's profile suggests she may not volunteer this information. Pay special attention when she does share. You need to recalibrate your expectations. While you might find it easy just to get it all out there, it may be a real act of courage for Monica to disclose more, so don't undervalue it.

**BOX 7-11**

### FIRO Element B and the FIRO B

We've not devoted any discussion to differences between the older FIRO B and the newer FIRO Element B. However, trainers, consultants, coaches, and other current users of the FIRO B may wish to investigate the benefits of the newer instrument. The FIRO B provides six scores; the FIRO Element B provides eighteen scores in a format that Will Schutz (creator of the FIRO B) believed was more user-friendly. The additional scores provide a richness of information that makes the FIRO Element B an excellent tool for self-development, personal growth, and coaching, as well as for relationship compatibility issues. It is also less expensive.

For example, looking at Monica's Inclusion scores without reference to anyone else's, notice that others include her at level 6 and she wants others to include her at level 2. This indicates some potential dissatisfaction in her life. She may be feeling some strain of being included too much by others and might benefit from coaching around setting clearer boundaries. Hank's Openness scores indicate that others are open with him at 4 and he wants others to be open with him at 9. Hank might benefit from coaching about how to create an environment where others feel safer being more open with him. These areas for increased self-analysis would not be available with the scores of the older FIRO B.

## FIRO ELEMENT B SCORES

In a few pages you will have the opportunity to explore your own behavior preference scores. Before you determine your scores, here are a few points to keep in mind when reflecting on your scores:

- The scores are merely a snapshot in time. They reflect what your preferences are here and now and are not a "terminal" classification. If you want to change your behavior, increasing your self-awareness is always the best starting point.
- No score is better or worse than another. There is no right or wrong or best score to have. If you have strong feelings that one of your scores is bad or good, you may want to take some time to explore the story you are telling yourself about why it is good or bad. That exploration may give you more information about your behavior than the actual score. Say, for example, you take the FIRO Element B online and score high on wanting to control

others. If you feel bad about that, it is not because there is anything wrong with a preference for high control. If you feel bad about your score, it is because you are making up a story about high control being bad. For example, we sometimes see this in women who have grown up under the myth that succeeding in the business world requires the attitude of a "controlling bitch." Rather than embrace their preference for high control and assertiveness, they may deny that they have such a preference because of the negative connotations they have learned about high control. So if you notice that you have strong negative feelings about your score, that can be helpful information about your self-judgment.

- If you choose to take the FIRO Element B online and get your actual scores rather than your own estimates, notice any reactions you may have to any of the scores. If you believe any of the scores produced by the instrument are inaccurate, it may be worth your while to explore the implication of the score as if it were true, even if you think it is wrong.

- Although Will Schutz was an extraordinary statistician and loved numbers, he always believed that the numbers were just a starting point for self-discovery and should be the beginning of the dialogue between people in a relationship, and not the end.

- The key is in knowing your preferences and having the ability to flex up or down the scale to be effective in whatever circumstances you face.

- Your score, by itself, will not indicate whether it is a preference from which you can flex, or a rigidity that may lead to relationship problems. You'll have the chance to explore your possible rigidities in chapter 8.

The *differences* between how you are behaving and how you want to behave, or how others are behaving toward you and how you want them to behave toward you, are also a rich source of data. Once again, however, the numbers (either high differences or low differences) are just a starting point for self-exploration. They are neither good nor bad; they are just information. The richness comes not from the numbers by themselves, but rather from the story you tell yourself about them, i.e., the interpretation you make of the numbers.

For example, on a scale of 0 (low) to 9 (high), if you include people at 3 and you want to include people at 8, that is a difference of 5. That could reflect that you recognize that you want to include others more than you have been, and that you are excited about changing your lifestyle to become more inclusive. You may have a clear plan to include others more by reaching out to others and taking more initiative or by joining more activities. You may see this difference of 5 as a positive reflection of the changes you are initiating in your life.

Or you may see this difference of 5 as a reflection of your deep unhappiness with the amount of contact you have with others, and maybe you have no idea what to do to change the situation. The number 5, by itself, tells you only that you are not currently behaving in the way that you want to behave. The story you are telling yourself about the difference can give you more information than the number itself.

The same is true if the difference is small. A difference of 0, 1, or 2 can reflect that you are happy with the way you are living your life. Or, it may reflect that you are unaware of areas of dissatisfaction in your life. If your differences are low, but you don't seem to have a lot of aliveness in your life or control over your destiny or a depth of intimacy, a low difference may reflect your lack of awareness about your dissatisfaction rather than a high level of satisfaction. Once again, the story you are telling yourself about the difference can give you as much or more information as the number itself.

Ron used the FIRO Element B in some work with a group of midlevel supervisors and managers in a manufacturing plant. Their scores reflected low differences between the ways they behaved and the ways they wanted to behave. The scores also reflected low differences between the ways others behaved toward them and the ways they wanted others to behave toward them. On the surface, this could indicate the group was pretty satisfied with the direction of their lives. The group, however, was lethargic and lacked the aliveness that you might expect to see in a group that was happy and satisfied with their lives.

After three days of what Ron terms "emotional dentistry" (where uncovering an emotion is like pulling teeth), the employees began discovering and revealing the dissatisfaction and unhappiness that they were experiencing. They were all midlevel employees feeling trapped in an unsatisfying system. They all had invested fifteen to twenty years of their lives in jobs that now seemed like a dead end. They felt that they couldn't leave because they would lose so much they had invested in their pension, yet they also had no room for advancement or fresh challenges. Instead of being aware of their dissatisfaction, they hunkered down and numbed themselves out, refusing to let themselves feel how stifled and miserable they were. This is another reminder of how the FIRO Element B scores should be seen as the starting point of the discussion about any relationship and not as a definitive description. Some of the individuals used this new information to deal more directly with the dissatisfaction they were feeling in their lives.[5] For example, one individual left his job and moved out of the area.

---

**BOX 7-12**

**FIRO Element B Scores**

1. The scores are a snapshot in time, not a permanent classification.

2. There is no right or wrong, good or bad, or best score to have.

3. Notice any strong reactions you have to your scores; they can give you helpful information about possible self-judgment.

4. If you feel the scores are incorrect, explore the implications of your scores as if they were accurate.

5. The scores should be the beginning of the exploration, not the end.

6. The key is to know your preference and be able to flex up or down the scale to be effective in whatever circumstance you face.

7. The score, by itself, will not tell you if it is a preference from which you can flex, or a rigidity that may lead to relationship problems.

8. The *Differences* scores are also a rich source of data, telling you if you are behaving in the way you want to behave and if others are behaving toward you the way you want them to.

---

## EXPLORING PREFERENCES USING FIRO ELEMENT B SCORES

Remember we are talking about scores in relationship to others. If your inclusion preference is 5 and a coworker has a preference of 9, you may look low on inclusion to that coworker. If another colleague has an inclusion preference of 0, you may look high on inclusion to that person. While you may feel your preference is stable and satisfying, you might receive conflicting feedback from your colleagues. FIRO theory helps us understand this dynamic, so an individual dialogue with each person you relate to is the key to building understanding and trust. Each relationship has an ongoing dynamic that requires mutual understanding and flexibility to work well.

---

**BOX 7-13**

In work with university students, research confirmed that the best predictor of success in selection for the shortest relationships, e.g., dorm president, was inclusion compatibility; the best predictor of success for selection of moderately long relationships, e.g., hitchhiking partner, was control compatibility; the best predictor of success for selection for long-term relationships, e.g., roommate, was openness compatibility.[6]

---

The primary usefulness of these scores is that they give a focused springboard to discuss similarities and differences regarding three major ways of relating to others. This understanding serves as a foundation for better working relationships and collaboration. It is helpful to realize that other people honestly perceive the world differently and that they are not simply being mean, hardheaded, stupid, or stubborn. FIRO theory is not an evaluative theory; i.e., it does not suggest where anyone "should be." It simply points out that people really do differ in the ways they prefer to interact. It is the open dialogue, the willingness to listen and self-disclose, that is essential in building understanding and mutual respect while exploring the scores.

- - - - - - - - - - - - - - - - - - - - - - - - - - - - - - - - - - - - - - - - - - - - - - - - - - -

Exercise 7-1

Now that you have an understanding of the three behaviors so important in interpersonal relationships, we invite you to explore your own preferences. You can do this in two ways. One is to reflect for a few minutes on your behavior and any feedback you may have received about your behavior and then to estimate what your scores might be. Then put those estimated scores into the worksheet on page 130.

The second method is to go online to www.radicalcollaboration.com, then click on "Fill Out a Relationship Profile," where you can fill out the FIRO Element B and have it scored. You can then put your actual scores into the worksheet on page 130. Taking the FIRO Element B online will take about twenty minutes, and the results will have been psychometrically validated.

- - - - - - - - - - - - - - - - - - - - - - - - - - - - - - - - - - - - - - - - - - - - - - - - - - -

We suggest that you explore your scores by inviting a colleague, coworker, supervisor, employee, or family member to join you in this exercise. On the next page there is a place to fill in scores for all the FIRO Element B dimensions for both yourself and a work colleague, friend, or spouse. If both of you take the FIRO Element B online, your discussion will be that much richer. After you either estimate the scores or get them online, fill them in below. Then proceed with the dialogue instructions following the scores below.

------------------------------------------------------------

| My Scores | | Scores of Your Colleague, Friend, or Spouse | |
| --- | --- | --- | --- |
| I include others | _____ | I include others | _____ |
| I want to include others | _____ | I want to include others | _____ |
| *Difference* | _____ | *Difference* | _____ |
| Others include me | _____ | Others include me | _____ |
| I want others to include me | _____ | I want others to include me | _____ |
| *Difference* | _____ | *Difference* | _____ |
| I control others | _____ | I control others | _____ |
| I want to control others | _____ | I want to control others | _____ |
| *Difference* | _____ | *Difference* | _____ |
| Others control me | _____ | Others control me | _____ |
| I want others to control me | _____ | I want others to control me | _____ |
| *Difference* | _____ | *Difference* | _____ |
| I am open with others | _____ | I am open with others | _____ |
| I want to be open with others | _____ | I want to be open with others | _____ |
| *Difference* | _____ | *Difference* | _____ |
| Others are open with me | _____ | Others are open with me | _____ |
| I want others to be open with me | _____ | I want others to be open with me | _____ |
| *Difference* | _____ | *Difference* | _____ |

------------------------------------------------------------

## Dialogue Instructions

Start by talking about your Inclusion scores and the implications of those scores. When you finish discussing Inclusion, then move on to Control. When you finish with Control, then move on to discuss Openness scores. Follow steps 1, 2, and 3 listed below for the groups of scores for each behavior (Inclusion, Control, and Openness). Then in step 4 you both take a few minutes for self-reflection.

### Step #1. I share and you listen regarding the following questions:

1. How do I see my behavior toward you (about Inclusion or Control or Openness)?

2. How satisfied am I with the way I am being (refer to Differences Scores)?

3. How do I see your behavior toward me (about Inclusion or Control or Openness)?

4. How satisfied am I with your behavior (are you too inclusive, too controlling, or too open, or not enough)?

5. What is my own sense of my capacity to flex?

### Step #2. You share and I listen regarding the following questions:

1. How do you see your behavior toward me (about Inclusion or Control or Openness)?

2. How satisfied are you with the way you are being (refer to Differences Scores)?

3. How do you see my behavior toward you (about Inclusion or Control or Openness)?

4. How satisfied are you with my behavior (am I too inclusive, too controlling, or too open, or not enough)?

5. What is your own sense of your capacity to flex?

**Step #3. We talk together about our scores, exploring the implications and potential conflicts because of our different preferences, using the following questions:**

1. Fill in your scores below (repeat for Control and Openness):

   I include others _____ and you want to be included _____.

   You include others_____ and I want to be included _____.

2. How does this play out in our relationship? What are some examples?

3. Does the nature of our relationship or work situation require a certain level of (Inclusion, Control, or Openness) to be effective?

4. Are we in agreement about that?

5. Are there any stories that either of us makes up about this?

6. Are there any deeper feelings or concerns that might be triggered by this dynamic?

**Step #4. After we have completed steps 1, 2, and 3 for each of the three behaviors, we take a few minutes for self-reflection around the following questions:**

1. Given the discussion we have just had, is there anything I want to start doing or stop doing to improve the relationship?

2. Since I am aware that Inclusion behavior is connected to deeper concerns about significance, what are two things I could do to help my partner feel even more significant and reduce their possible fear of being ignored, overlooked, forgotten, taken for granted, or not heard?

3. Since I am aware that Control behavior is connected to deeper concerns about competence, what are two things I could do to help my partner feel even more competent and reduce their possible fear of being humiliated, shamed, blamed, or embarrassed?

4. Since I am aware that Openness behavior is connected to deeper concerns about likability, what are two things I could do to help my partner feel even more likable and reduce their possible fear of being rejected, unlikable, despised, or unwanted?

## CHAPTER SUMMARY

Whether you want to improve a single relationship or change the culture of an entire organization, increasing the self-awareness of the people in the relationship is a great place to start. The research of Will Schutz in developing FIRO theory finds that the three primary behaviors regarding compatibility in relationships are Inclusion, Control, and Openness. Inclusion is defined as how much contact we want with others. Control is about how much influence we want. Openness describes the amount and depth of disclosure we want. Each person can be ranked somewhere along a scale of 0 (low) up to 9 (high) for each of these behaviors. No matter where your preference falls on the scale, about 90 percent of the rest of the world has a different preference from you.

People's behavioral preferences regarding Inclusion, Control, and Openness are greatly influenced by their beliefs of the significance, competence, and likability of themselves and others. They are also influenced by the fear of being ignored, humiliated, or rejected. While there is no best preference to have, preferences carry consequences. Preferences, however, don't cause problems for people; it is their inability to be flexible in circumstances that call for an approach different from their preference that creates a problem.

Unlike our beliefs about Inclusion and Control, we do have a strong bias about the advantages of becoming more open. *If your goal is to build more effective collaborative relationships, becoming more open is one of the most helpful things you can do.* In his research for the Navy, Will Schutz discovered that problem solving and relationship building almost always benefit from increased Openness.

The primary usefulness of the FIRO Element B scores (from 0 to 9) is that they create a focused springboard to discuss our similarities and differences regarding three major ways of relating to the rest of the world. It is helpful to realize that other people honestly perceive the world differently from us, and that they are not simply being mean, hardheaded, stupid, or stubborn. Readers are invited to take the FIRO Element B online, then, following a structured set of questions, discuss their scores with other people with whom they are in a relationship. It is the dialogue, the willingness to listen and be open, that is essential in building understanding, mutual respect, and collaboration.

# CHAPTER 8
# RIGIDITY IS THE ENEMY

**The key to** compatibility is flexibility. Rigid behavior in your relationships is the enemy. What causes problems is the inability to operate effectively outside your preferences for Inclusion, Control, and Openness when circumstances call for a different range of behavior.

---

**BOX 8-1**

Your preferred levels of Inclusion, Control, and Openness are not the key to compatibility. Flexibility in your behaviors is the key. Rigidity in your relationship behavior is the enemy!

---

## THE ROLE OF SELF-ESTEEM

People's feelings drive their behavior. More precisely, their feelings and beliefs about their own significance, competence, and likability will foster either flexibility or rigidity in their Inclusion, Control, and Openness behavior. The stronger their self-esteem, i.e., the more comfortable they are with their own significance, competence, and likability, the less defensive they tend to become. Strong self-esteem allows people to respond more authentically to the diversity of others without becoming defensive or overly offended by the differences of others. A positive self-concept also allows people to respond accountably, rather than defensively, to the consequences of their preferred behavior. For example, people with strong self-esteem wouldn't demand that everyone adjust to their desire for high inclusion or wouldn't get offended when other people tend to project their feelings onto them or invent stories about them because of their low openness.

With strong self-esteem people don't have undue anxiety about their own significance or the need to be included. They are comfortable being with other people and also comfortable being alone. They allow themselves a wide range of behavior around the issue of inclusion, depending upon the circumstances they face. If individuals are comfortable about their own competence, they tend not to have problems regarding control issues. They can feel comfortable either taking control or not taking control depending on the circumstances. They have flexibility to adjust their behavior to whatever circumstances arise. If people have a strong sense of their likability, they feel free to be open to whatever extent is appropriate. They can be very open, self-disclosing, and comfortable in close relationships, and also comfortable with less disclosure in relationships with some distance and less intimacy. Their amount of self-disclosure depends on the circumstances of the relationship.

There is no single profile for people with strong self-esteem. They won't all have similar preferences regarding Inclusion, Control, and Openness because they get to be any way they want to be. What they all have in common is a lack of defensiveness and a lack of rigidity.

Feelings and beliefs about people's significance, competence, and likability stem from many sources, such as parents, friends, and childhood experiences. Those feelings and beliefs become problematic when they are overly influenced by fear. Individuals may unconsciously not want to experience underlying fears associated with feeling insignificant, incompetent, and unlikable and may bury their awareness of their fears. They then project the turmoil outward in some way and become "rigid" in their behavior. This can happen so quickly and automatically that they do not notice the behavior as rigid.

---

**BOX 8-2**

People with strong self-esteem come in all shapes, sizes, and colors. They all have different preferences for Inclusion, Control, and Openness because they get to be any way they want to be. What they do have in common is a lack of defensiveness and a lack of rigidity.

---

## FEELINGS AND FEARS

FIRO theory associates certain fears with the three feelings of *significance*, *competence*, and *likability* and the related behaviors of *inclusion*, *control*, and *openness*. The three related fears are of being *ignored*, *humiliated*, or *rejected* (see chart on page 110).

## Feelings of Significance and Fears of Being Ignored

An individual's feelings of significance or insignificance and fears of feeling ignored greatly affect his or her behavior regarding inclusion. If people experience fears of feeling ignored (abandoned, neglected, worthless, or insignificant), that can cause great discomfort. When they arise, people choose to either let themselves feel these uncomfortable feelings or behave in a way that helps to avoid feeling that pain. For example, if people fear being ignored, they may always surround themselves with people. They may become the life of the party, the one with the lamp shade on their head, the one that nobody ignores because they are always in other's faces, making it impossible to be ignored. People make themselves the center of attention so they never have to feel pain associated with feeling ignored.

---

**BOX 8-3**

People's feelings of *significance* (or insignificance) and their fears of feeling *ignored* affect how much they include others and how much they want to be included.

---

People may also, however, choose a very different strategy to deal with the same issue. Instead of making themselves the center of attention, they may try to avoid contact with other people. They may never go to parties or socialize and never join groups. This is a different type of preemptive strike. Metaphorically, they go live in a cave as a hermit and choose a solitary existence. Nobody can ignore them because they have already separated themselves from everyone who could ignore them. They have no one left in their life to ignore them and therefore to remind them of the pain they feel about being ignored.

This goes to the heart of rigid behavior. Instead of exploring any uncomfortable feelings that might arise, people limit their range of behavior to that which lets them avoid feeling the pain. Notice that the same underlying fear of being ignored or insignificant can trigger defensive behavior in completely opposite directions. Some individuals might surround themselves with people to avoid feeling ignored or insignificant, while others might abandon contact with people. They avoid the risk of being ignored by abandoning other people before those people can abandon them. These strategies look very different, but they are driven by the same underlying fear.

While rigidity at the extreme ends of the scale is easier to notice, it is possible to get rigid at any place along the continuum of the scale of inclusion. Living like a hermit at the low inclusion end of the scale (0), or surrounding yourself with others all the time at the high end of the inclusion scale (9), are very noticeable behaviors. Being stuck in the middle of the inclusion scale (4–5) can, however, cause just as much stress in a relationship. It can appear as a halfhearted commitment to the relationship, or confusing in-and-out behavior.

## Feelings of Competence and Fears of Being Humiliated

Feelings of competence or incompetence and fears of being humiliated (shamed, embarrassed, or seen as incompetent) greatly influence people's desire for control. If people choose not to address their feelings and fears directly, but instead put their efforts into avoiding them, an unconscious strategy might be to rigidly always try to take control. The unconscious motivation behind such a strategy is that taking control or responsibility over the situation will reduce the chance of humiliation. Thus the workaholic takes control and puts in countless extra hours, not out of joy for the work, but rather unconsciously to avoid the possibility of failure and humiliation.

---

**BOX 8-4**

People's feelings of *competence* (or incompetence) and their fears of feeling *humiliated* affect the amount of control they seek.

---

The same fear may drive a completely opposite strategy. Instead of becoming a workaholic or a control freak to avoid humiliation, an individual may totally and rigidly abdicate any responsibility whatsoever, not even taking responsibility for the school bake sale, much less striving to become the sales manager at work. By avoiding any situation with a possibility of failure and humiliation, the individual cannot be held accountable and cannot be blamed for failure. These individuals will never have to face looking incompetent or being humiliated because they will never accept any obligation where they have to demonstrate any competence.

Once again, the same underlying fear of humiliation can cause very different behavior around how much control a person desires. At the low end of the control scale (0), someone rigidly refuses all responsibility. Being a control freak at the high end of the control scale (9) may unconsciously be motivated by the same fear of being humiliated. The fear can be so great that individuals limit their range of responses in various circumstances to what feels familiar and safe, rather than what is appropriate. Thus rigidity around the behavior of control is created.

Just as with inclusion behavior, individuals can get rigid at any place along the control continuum. Rigidity at midrange on the control scale might show up as having poor boundaries or as erratic control behavior, first wanting control then wanting to get rid of it.

## Feelings of Likability and Fears of Being Rejected

Feelings of likability or unlikability and fears of being rejected (despised or unlikable) greatly affect how open someone is in relationships. If people choose not to deal with their feelings and fears directly but instead put their efforts into avoiding them, an unconscious strategy might be to never disclose anything about themselves that may lead to being rejected. If people fear that they are not likable and worry that if other people find out what they are really like, they will undoubtedly be rejected, it is unlikely that they will want to disclose much about themselves. For example, "If people know me, they will reject me. Therefore I will never let anyone really know me. I won't ever share any real depth about myself because openness will just lead to rejection."

---

**BOX 8-5**

People's feelings of *likability* (or unlikability) and their fears of feeling *rejected* affect how much openness they want in their relationships.

---

The fear of rejection can also create rigidity in the opposite direction. An individual may flood others with details long before it is appropriate under the circumstances of the relationship. The underlying and unconscious strategy is to disclose everything about oneself that might lead to rejection before the relationship matters. For example, a workshop participant might introduce himself as follows:

"Hi, I'm Larry. I'm attending this workshop because my wife is getting ready to divorce me. I've never been able to maintain a long-term relationship. It probably has to do with my drinking problem, or maybe my drug abuse. Naturally I don't get along so great with my kids either. I think they probably resent all the time I spent in prison."

There actually is a strategy underlying this flooding with premature openness. Larry is going to disclose everything that might lead to his rejection before he has invested in potential relationships in the room. That way, rejection by others won't hurt so much because he is not yet invested in the relationship.

So once again, the fear of being rejected can cause radically different rigid behaviors. Rigidly disclosing nothing at the low end of the openness scale (0) or prematurely disclosing too much or too early at the high end of the openness scale (9) may unconsciously be motivated by the same fear of being rejected. An individual will lose the flexibility to be open at an appropriate level because he or she never wants to face the possibility of rejection.

Just as with the behaviors of inclusion and control, individuals can become rigid at any place along the openness continuum. Rigidity at midrange on the openness scale might show up as being very neutral or middle-of-the-road with unpredictable periodic sharing. If an individual's preference on any of the three scales is a 5, and they become rigid, their comfort zone may range from 4 to 6. But if you are in a situation that calls for you to behave at a 2 or a 7, you may be sweating bullets. Becoming rigid in the middle of the scale can cause people just as many difficulties as getting rigid at either end of the scale.

Now explore your own possible rigidities by looking at your preferences (your FIRO Element B scores) in relation to the rigidity charts on the following pages.

---------------------------------------------------------------------------

Exercise 8-1

## Looking for Rigidity

The FIRO Element B does not tell you if your score is a preference from which you can flex or if it reflects a rigidity. The best way to figure that out is to look at your behavior in relation to your scores. The charts on the next pages focus you on only three of your scores: *I include others, I control others,* and *I am open with others.*

First note what those three scores are for you, then go to the appropriate chart (page 141 for *I include others;* page 142 for *I control others;* and page 143 for *I am open with others.* On the charts there is a scale continuum from 0 to 9. Put an X on the scale in the spot that relates to your score. For example, if your score on *I include others* is a 1, it would look like this:

## INCLUSION RIGIDITY

0    **X**    2    3    4    5    6    7    8    9

| Low | Middle | High |
|-----|--------|------|
| If you have a preference for low inclusion and you get rigid, you may appear: | If you have a preference for midrange inclusion and you get rigid, you may appear: | If you have a preference for high inclusion and you get rigid, you may appear: |
| leaving | in/out behavior | acting out |
| withholding | lukewarm commitment | overinvolvement |
| not being available | overneutrality | taking credit |
| avoiding | halfheartedness | busybody |
| quitting | | notice-me behavior |

The next step is to look at the descriptions below your X to see if any of them fit you. In the above example, the person is a 1 on *I include others*, so that person would look at the descriptions *leaving*, *withholding*, *not being available*, *avoiding*, and *quitting*. If those descriptions seem familiar, or if you have received feedback from your colleagues, friends, or family that you behave in any of these ways, it is a strong possibility that your behavior reflects a rigidity. If your score regarding *I include others* is a 4 or 5, you would be looking at the descriptions *in/out behavior*, *lukewarm commitment*, *overneutrality*, and *halfheartedness* to see if they fit your behavior. If so, it would be an indication of some rigidity in your behavior.

When you finish with the Inclusion chart, go on to the charts for your scores on *I control others* and *I am open with others*, looking for possible rigidities in those areas. Remember, rigidities are caused by underlying fears. If your rigidity is around Inclusion, that may indicate possible concerns about your significance or fears of being ignored. If the rigidity is around Control, that may indicate possible concerns about your competence or fears of being humiliated. If the rigidity is around Openness, that may indicate possible concerns about your likability or fears of being rejected.

If none of the descriptions on the charts seem to fit your behavior, it is likely that you are flexible. In that case your behavior is not overly influenced by underlying concerns about your significance, competence, or likability, or fears around feeling ignored, humiliated or rejected. If you have any doubts about possible rigid behaviors or underlying fears, the best source for exploring the issue is getting feedback from a trusted colleague, friend, or family member.

In the following chapter, there are additional tools for gaining more insight about possible rigidities and for overcoming them.

## INCLUSION RIGIDITY

Ideal state: Flexibility (acting appropriately to a situation)

Ineffective state: Rigidity (acting inappropriately and rigidly to a situation)

| 0 | 1 | 2 | 3 | 4 | 5 | 6 | 7 | 8 | 9 |
|---|---|---|---|---|---|---|---|---|---|

| Low | Middle | High |
|---|---|---|
| If you have a preference for low inclusion and you get rigid, you may appear: | If you have a preference for midrange inclusion and you get rigid, you may appear: | If you have a preference for high inclusion and you get rigid, you may appear: |
| leaving<br>withholding<br>not being available<br>avoiding<br>quitting | in/out behavior<br>lukewarm commitment<br>overneutrality<br>halfheartedness | acting out<br>overinvolvement<br>taking credit<br>busybody<br>notice-me behavior |

**Key dynamic:**
Individuals unconsciously do not want to experience the feelings associated with being ignored and bury the uncomfortable/unaccepted/unfelt feelings. They then project the turmoil outward in some way and become "rigid" in their inclusion behavior. They hope to change the situation so that they can avoid the deeper conflict. This process is so quick, unconscious, and automatic they do not notice it happening.

## CONTROL RIGIDITY

Ideal state: Flexibility (acting appropriately to a situation)

Ineffective state: Rigidity (acting inappropriately and rigidly to a situation)

| 0 | 1 | 2 | 3 | 4 | 5 | 6 | 7 | 8 | 9 |
|---|---|---|---|---|---|---|---|---|---|
| Low | | | | | Middle | | | | High |

| If you have a preference for low control and you get rigid, you may appear: | If you have a preference for midrange control and you get rigid, you may appear: | If you have a preference for high control and you get rigid, you may appear: |
|---|---|---|
| passive | inconsistent behavior | threatening |
| complacent | few boundaries | only my way |
| nonassertive | plays martyr | shaming |
| not trying | blaming | hostile |
| avoiding responsibility | hostile teasing | domineering |

**Key dynamic:**
Individuals unconsciously do not want to experience the feelings associated with being humiliated and bury the uncomfortable/unaccepted/unfelt feelings. They then project the turmoil outward in some way and become "rigid" in their control behavior. They hope to change the situation so that they can avoid the deeper conflict. This process is so quick, unconscious, and automatic they do not notice it happening.

## OPENNESS RIGIDITY

Ideal state: Flexibility (acting appropriately to a situation)

Ineffective state: Rigidity (acting inappropriately and rigidly to a situation)

| 0 | 1 | 2 | 3 | 4 | 5 | 6 | 7 | 8 | 9 |
|---|---|---|---|---|---|---|---|---|---|

| Low | Middle | High |
|---|---|---|
| If you have a preference for low openness and you get rigid, you may appear: | If you have a preference for midrange openness and you get rigid, you may appear: | If you have a preference for high openness and you get rigid, you may appear: |
| withholding<br>overly silent<br>has nothing to say<br>none of your business<br>secretive<br>stonewalling | lacking passion<br>pleasantly neutral<br>unpredictable periodic sharing<br>middle-of-the-road<br>difficult to know if cares<br>overly influenced by context<br>runs hot then cold | superficially friendly<br>premature disclosure<br>overprocessing<br>inappropriate details<br>emotional flooding<br>shares "everything" |

**Key dynamic:**
Individuals unconsciously do not want to experience the feelings associated with being rejected and bury the uncomfortable/unaccepted/unfelt feelings. They then project the turmoil outward in some way and become "rigid" in their openness behavior. They hope to change the situation so that they can avoid the deeper conflict. This process is so quick, unconscious, and automatic they do not notice it happening.

------------------------------------------------------------------------

## CHAPTER SUMMARY

The key to compatibility is flexibility in your behaviors, not your preferences regarding the three relationship behaviors of Inclusion, Control, and Openness. Rigidity in your behavior is the enemy. The work of Will Schutz and FIRO theory conclude that rigidity regarding Inclusion stems from fears of being ignored or insignificant. Rigidity regarding Control stems from fears of being humiliated or incompetent. Rigidity regarding Openness stems from fears of being rejected or unlikable.

The same underlying fear may drive very different behaviors. If people are afraid of being ignored, some may rigidly avoid contact with people, while others may rigidly surround themselves with people. If people are afraid of being humiliated, some may rigidly avoid situations giving them any responsibility, while others may rigidly try to take control in all situations. If people are afraid of rejection, some may disclose little about themselves, while others may inappropriately disclose too much, too soon. Rigidities at the extreme ends of the behavioral scales, 0 (low) or 9 (high), are easier to spot; however, it is possible to get rigid at any place along the continuum. Rigidity at any place along the continuum will stress a collaborative relationship.

# CHAPTER 9
# BREAKING FREE OF THE PAST ONE THOUGHT AT A TIME

**People's reality consists** of their thoughts passing through their mind. A series of ideas, invented conversations, blessings, accusations, and monologues are racing though their mind at warp speed. A good portion of the time they are not even aware the stories exist. They play a huge role in how people see life and how they relate to others. The stories create both a person's joy and their desperation in life in general and in relationships in particular.

It is those internal thoughts, those stories, and the interpretations of those stories that people attach to the external events in their lives that give meaning to those events and relationships. Two individuals in the same circumstances can get laid off by their employer at the same time. One sees it as an opportunity, the other sees it as a disaster. An event may happen, but it is the story about the event that makes it positive or negative, safe or scary, joyful or sad. Those stories are more often than not unconscious and unexamined.

People too often come to believe these stories are true, as though they were cast in concrete. They appear in their lives like movie scripts that they are powerless to influence. The scripts seem independent of what people want to do now. They forget that the stories are of their own creation.

People learn their stories from their experiences. Individuals are all a bit like clay, molded by their past. If you grew up in a violent household, your current stories may tend to portray the world as unsafe, scary, unpredictable, and violent, even if your current existence is safe, predictable, and pleasant. If your father was weak and easily manipulated, your stories may support a belief that men are weak and must be controlled and manipulated for their own good. If your mother acted helpless and needed protecting, you may carry that with you in relationships with women. We invite you to explore your early histories with the intention of understanding and taking responsibility for yourselves, not to lay blame, make excuses, or get stuck in the past.

---

**BOX 9-1**

Our reality consists of stories we make up about the events in our lives. It is helpful to explore these stories to increase our understanding and take responsibility for ourselves. It is not for the purpose of laying blame, making excuses, or getting stuck in the past.

---

People's greatest teachers of who they are, both positive and negative, are those individuals who raised them, their parents or other adults who played a significant role in their childhood. People learn who they are and what the world is like early in life. The lessons they learn stay with them and are difficult to unlearn. It is easy and natural to make the incorrect assumption that people are their past. This is particularly true when they become fearful and can easily lose perspective because of their rigid thinking.

The past is impossible to change. It is what it is, good, bad, or indifferent, and everyone is stuck with his or her past. While people are greatly influenced by their past, however, they are not inseparable from it. Their past does not have to determine their present self-identity. More importantly, it certainly doesn't have to determine their future.

---

**BOX 9-2**

We are greatly influenced by our past, but not inseparable from it. The past is impossible to change, but it doesn't have to determine our future.

---

Some people find comfort and security by believing they are powerless to overcome the past. It saves them from even having to try. It saves them from having to face the possibility of failure, and from the unknown. Giving up the known can be frightening. The unknown is scary, but it can also be freedom. It is the freedom to sculpt one's own future; the freedom to become authentic and whole; the freedom to become the kind of person one wants to be.

Identifying and separating from your negative childhood influences can bring huge rewards, particularly in relationships with others. It is not an easy task, however. No new system, process, exercise, or simple tool can do it for you. They can help, but it is ultimately your job to create change in your life. You are the CEO of your own redevelopment project, which will consist of relearning the implications that your past has on your present and future. This has to be done one thought at a time, one feeling at a time, and one gut reaction at a time.

---

**BOX 9-3**

You are the CEO of your own redevelopment project.

---

## CREATING NEW WAYS OF THINKING

This chapter describes eight tools that our workshop participants use to let go of their past and reclaim their future. Their common denominators are attempts to increase awareness and encourage fresh thinking patterns. These tools encourage readers to break away from old, learned ineffective patterns of behavior by focusing attention on more effective ways of being. In some exercises readers will spend a fair amount of time reflecting on the past. The purpose is not to change the past, but to consciously identify and acknowledge the impact that the past has on the present.

This also frees up unconscious energy about the past that people don't even know they carry around with them. Most people think that their past is behind them. Yet many people carry their past like a shield in front of them, not behind them, to protect themselves from their stories. Then they are perplexed in relationships when they feel that something is between them and others. But something is actually between them, the old baggage of both people.

Many people spend a lifetime dragging around their baggage from the past. A lifetime of feeling like a hopeless victim, or aggressively charging into arguments with sword and shield, pouring energy into fighting, hiding, running, avoiding, holding back, fearful of taking risks, fearful of letting anyone see what's really going on inside. Thinking it isn't safe, people don't take the plunge into the here and now, and it has cost them everything. It mutes day-to-day lives and relationships.

People will find, however, that the more they invest in really working these issues, the more they will be able to live in the here and now, not in the past. Working these issues can free the energy that has kept them tethered to the past and instead shift that energy into aliveness and authenticity. This requires compassionate self-honesty and more than a little detective work.

---

**BOX 9-4**
We think our past is behind us, yet most of us carry our past out in front like a shield, wondering why we can't seem to get as close to others as we want.

---

## DON'T FORGET TO BREATHE!

In several exercises, we have you start by taking a few deep breaths. The body needs oxygen for life. Paradoxically, when people become fearful or agitated, they often don't get the oxygen they need. When they get charged up or fearful, their breathing usually gets shallow as they tense up their musculature. When they get defensive or angry, they breathe inefficiently, depriving the brain of needed oxygen. It's helpful to develop the capacity to breathe deeply, taking the time to center yourself. As simple as it seems, one of the most important things to remember when you get into a stressful situation is *keep breathing*.

## EIGHT TOOLS FOR LETTING GO OF THE PAST

It is always more effective putting energy into becoming whom you want to be, rather than putting energy into avoiding whom you don't want to be. Yet, if we are riddled by unconscious and unexamined thoughts and feelings from our past, it will be difficult to be intentional about our future. The eight tools offer different perspectives for gaining self-awareness, wholeness, and authenticity. So try them out to see which ones are helpful. Try them all, then continue to use the ones that are helpful and discard what is not helpful. Stay as open as possible and take note of any strong feelings or thoughts that arise during any of the exercises. Pay particular attention to the things that you resist, because resistance can sometimes tell you where you need to go, rather than where you want to go.

**Parental traits exercise** looks at how negative traits of your parents may still be playing an important role in your current relationships.

**Mental rehearsal** can help discharge the impact of early negative childhood programming, replacing the negative thoughts and feelings with a sense of being significant, competent, and likable.

**Body-mind imagery** creates grounding within the body, building alignment and harmony between three centers of the body: head, heart, and belly.

**Developing an objective observer** is a practice of self-observation allowing a different perspective from outside the experience to become a part of the inner experience.

**Distortion log** is a tool for tracking and consciously disputing distorted negative self-talk.

**Light visualization** is a shortcut to a sense of calmness and grounding prior to an anxiety-provoking event.

**Accountable friends** is taking the opportunity to gain insight through honest feedback of friends.

**Individual daily reflective practice** is setting aside a time every day for some method of deliberate self-awareness and self-reflection.

------------------------------------------------------------

Tool 9-1

# Exploring Parental Traits

We start with an exercise to help you gain awareness of just how your past may be influencing you and preventing you from addressing your problems. The following tool will help you understand how the negative traits of your parents may be influencing your current relationships. Start by thinking of a current business problem that seems to involve some interpersonal relationship difficulties. You may want to write out a sentence or two below, describing the situation:

_____

_____

_____

For most people, their parents played the most significant role, both positive and negative, in their development into adulthood. Those whose parents were not the ones raising them can just substitute the two most significant adults in their childhood. Don't be put off because the tool concentrates only on negative traits. Most people also received positive messages from the positive, supportive traits of parents. Those positive traits, however, are not the ones that are causing relationship problems. So, for this exercise, concentrate on negative traits.

**List two negative traits for your mother and two negative traits for your father that showed up in relationships.**

**MOTHER** _____    _____

**FATHER** _____    _____

Some people find this exercise easy because of the many negative traits they could list. Others find it more difficult, perhaps because they are not observant or because they are in denial about the negative traits of their parents or because they had positive supportive parents. But everyone has a few negative traits. Even absolutely wonderful parents have at least two negative traits. So, for those of you having difficulty identifying any negative traits of your parents, the following page contains a list of negative traits that commonly affect relationships. It's not necessary to pick traits from this list, which is only to jog your thinking.

**BOX 9-5**

**Negative Trait List**

| | | |
|---|---|---|
| Violent/abusive | Accusing | Cowardly |
| Arbitrary | Faultfinder/nitpicker | Paranoid |
| Antagonistic | Cynical | Dependent/clingy |
| Pushy | Self-righteous | Self-effacing/compliant |
| Greedy/selfish | Rigid | Self-conscious |
| Resentful | Impatient | Easily hurt |
| Jealous | Condescending | Nervous laugh |
| Sarcastic | Puritanical/moralistic | Disappointed |
| Argumentative | Negative | Lack of concentration |
| Nagging | Blaming/shaming | Martyr |
| Teasing | Never satisfied | Addictive |
| Prying | Prideful | Unemotional |
| Silent treatment | Superficial | Overly emotional |
| Dominating/controlling | Status seeker | Joyless/humorless |
| Demanding | Exhibitionist | Pouting |
| Energy sucking | Compulsive | Unimaginative |
| Favoritism | Can't say no | Indifferent |
| Manipulative | Elitist/snob | Stingy |
| Guilt flinging | Conceited | Tactless |
| Has to have last word | Name-dropper | Disrespectful |
| Interrupts | Hypocritical | Oblivious |
| Always right | Narcissistic | Unreliable |
| Untruthful | Suspicious/distrustful | Procrastinator |
| Competitive | Worrier | Perfectionist |
| | Pessimistic | Deceitful |

After selecting four negative traits, take a look at how they may have affected your ability to form trusting collaborative relationships. It can work in many ways, so sometimes it's easy to miss the connection.

---

**BOX 9-6**

The strong negative traits of your parents are most likely still affecting your own ability to form relationships in one of the following ways:

1. You *adopt* the trait and become just like your parent.

2. You *rebel* from the trait, doing exactly the opposite, but are still controlled by it.

3. You *project* the trait out onto the world, expecting the world to treat you as your parent did.

4. You *collude* with significant others, teaching them to act as your parent did.

5. You *self-inflict* the trait, treating yourself just as your parent did.

---

The negative traits of people's parents almost always show up in their own relationships in one of the following five ways:

**Adoption.** This is the easiest connection to make. Your mom was manipulative in relationships. She was never straightforward, but rather scheming in a deceitful way to get others to do what she wanted. You learned from a master and have adopted her manipulative way in relationships. You may not even recognize that you are being manipulative. This behavior may seem normal because it is the only way you learned to get things done in a relationship. You have adopted her negative trait, and to this extent you have become your mother.

**Rebellion.** This is also pretty easy to spot. Say your father was a tyrant. He ranted and raved, bullying everyone he had contact with. You hated that about him and the effect it had on you and everyone else with whom he had a relationship. You swore you would never ever be like that. You'll show him how much you hated that trait by becoming exactly the opposite of him. You'll never raise your voice or take a strong stand, even when it might be appropriate. You are so afraid that you may be seen as a tyrant that you won't even stand up for yourself. You are proving to your father that you are not like him. Of course, you are still controlled by his behavior. You are acting the way you do not out of free will and authenticity, but rather to prove to the world that you are not like your father. In feeling compelled to be the opposite of him, you are still a prisoner of his behavior.

**Projection.** Now it gets a little trickier to spot. You project your parent's negative trait out into the world and expect the world to treat you the same way. Perhaps a parent was unpredictable in relationships, running hot and cold, and couldn't be depended upon. As a result of your projection, you've come to believe that the world is unpredictable, erratic, and undependable. Your belief is not based on any evidence of unpredictability out in the world, but rather entirely upon your projection. Possibly all your relationships are in fact reliable and predictable. In spite of all the evidence that your current relationships are stable, however, you still mistrust the relationships, maintaining your belief about the unpredictability of relationships because of your projection of the trait of your parent onto the rest of the world.

**Collusion.** Here you teach others to treat you the way you learned and expected to be treated as a child. Perhaps your mother was a real bitch. She nagged and picked on you in the most caustic ways. She was always on your case, never giving you a moment's rest. When you married, you looked for a wife who was not a bitch. She seemed caring and kind when you got married. Two years later, however, she has become similar to your mother. She nags you all the time to get things done. She is impatient with you and talks to you using the most caustic language. She wasn't like that when you married her, but you have trained her to respond to you the way your mother did. You learned growing up that was the appropriate way to be treated, so you have re-created that same environment by training your wife to treat you like the bitch that your mother was.

**Self-infliction.** Here you've taken over the role of your parent, and now you treat yourself using your parent's trait. Perhaps your father was tight with money, a real miser. You never received the nice present you wanted on your birthday. You wore hand-me-downs not because your family didn't have enough money, but rather because your father prided himself in not wasting money on his children's clothes. You, however, have grown into a generous adult. You freely give to others out of a caring spirit, not to get anything and also not out of rebellion. You have both a sincerely generous heart and the money to help others. While you may be generous with others, however, you treat yourself miserly. You wouldn't hesitate buying your child a new sweater at the start of winter; however, you can make do with the same sweater you've used for the past six winters. You convince yourself that you are not like your father because you are so generous with your children. In one respect, however, you've taken it upon yourself to become your father, at least to the extent that you lack generosity to yourself. This may well be the most devastating, creating an unconscious sense of self-betrayal in your self-concept.

## Instructions

You now have an understanding of five ways your parents' negative traits may show up in your own relationships (adoption, rebellion, projection, collusion, and self-infliction). Take some time to reflect on the four traits of your parents that you have selected. Think back on the current business problem that you identified at the beginning of this exercise. See if you can identify how the negative traits may be affecting this business problem.

My current business relationships are
**Mother's Trait #1**          affected by this trait in the following way:

_____          _____

_____

_____

_____

_____

**Mother's Trait #2**

_____          _____

_____

_____

_____

_____

**Father's Trait #1**

_____    _____

    _____

    _____

    _____

    _____

**Father's Trait #2**

_____    _____

    _____

    _____

    _____

    _____

------------------------------------------------------------

Tool 9-2

## Mental Rehearsal

People learned most of their fears and rigidity during their childhood. They often bring those childhood fears with them to every meeting or encounter and every relationship via their unconscious. By consciously recognizing that they are no longer living in their childhood and that those childhood beliefs may no longer be true and helpful, people can change their perception of their current circumstances. Changing people's unconscious beliefs into more conscious attitudes about their own significance, competence, and likability can play a powerful neutralizing role. Over time this can free them from phantom childhood fears that are no longer applicable to their present life.

    We suggest you read through the example below, then go back and do it yourself.

## MENTAL REHEARSAL EXAMPLE

Remember back in chapter 2 when Karen was talking to her boss John about an idea for a company project? As Karen was talking, John turned and reached for his coffee cup. Karen's immediate reaction in her mind was "Oh damn; he must not want to hear this. He probably thinks it's really stupid." Karen experienced a high charge of energy throughout her body and started talking faster, flooding John with information. She became confused and less articulate, creating the very situation that she feared, i.e. that her boss did not want to hear what she had to say.

After the meeting, Karen tries the Mental Rehearsal:

1. **Recall a recent experience where you became fearful and rigid in your thinking or behavior.**

    Karen thinks of her experience with her boss.

2. **Identify the negative traits, attitudes, or behaviors that you exhibited. Also identify any fears of being ignored, humiliated, or rejected.**

    Karen noted that she became rattled and inarticulate, and lost her train of thought. She started talking very fast as though John was disinterested and was going to cut her off at any moment. She noticed strong fears of being ignored and humiliated.

3. **Think about where you first learned these traits, attitudes, or behaviors. If possible, try to remember a specific scene early in your life where you first learned this fearful behavior.**

    Karen recalled being at her family's dinner table trying to get a word in edgewise and being ridiculed by her father and siblings. She remembers trying to talk really fast to get her ideas understood before the family ridicule started.

4. **Notice how the circumstances of your recent experience are different from those when you first learned these negative traits, attitudes, or behaviors.**

    Her boss does not have a history of ridiculing Karen. In fact, all the evidence Karen has indicates that John would be interested in her ideas about the project. He seemed pleased when she first offered to share her ideas.

5. **Imagine yourself in the present as significant, competent, and likable and let these feelings flow throughout your calm, centered being.**

Karen relaxes, closes her eyes, takes a couple of deep breaths, and then imagines herself as a very significant, competent, and likable person. She lets this feeling flow through her body and mind for several minutes, basking in the warmth of the feeling.

6. **Now, in your mind, reenvision your recent experience with this new conscious awareness of your own significance, competence and likability. Continue to breathe deeply as you let yourself integrate your new feelings into this recent experience. Imagine yourself reexperiencing that recent experience, creating an outcome you would have liked to have experienced. Notice what is different in your behavior, in your internal interpretation of the event, and in your capacity to respond authentically.**

Karen reenvisions her meeting with her boss. She feels confident in her ideas and her ability to communicate them to John. When she imagines John turning away from her to get his coffee, Karen doesn't see this as a rejection of her, but rather John simply wanting a drink of coffee. Feeling grounded and present, Karen imagines herself continuing to share her ideas with John in a calm, relaxed, and articulate manner.

7. **Notice how you are feeling about the experience now.**

Karen is feeling calm, and a little less attached to her old childhood patterns that she will be ignored or humiliated. She is looking forward to the next opportunity she has to talk to her boss, and feels confident she will feel more grounded and relaxed during their next meeting.

Now that you've read the example, try doing it. Close your eyes and relax your body, taking several deep breaths. Notice if there is any tension in your body that you can get rid of by shifting your position. Pay attention to your breathing. Settle into a rhythm of breathing deep, slow breaths. To the extent possible, breathe down into your belly. Once you are feeling relaxed, follow the steps listed in the example.

------------------------------------------------------------

Tool 9-3

## Body-Mind Imagery

Imagine three centers in the body: head, heart, and belly, i.e., your gut. It takes all three centers to support a strong relationship. If one center overpowers another, you have a lopsided contributor to the relationship. You may lack the balance necessary for a strong relationship and can easily overwhelm others or be overwhelmed yourself. Without enough heart you may lack the depth necessary for empathy, compassion, or love. Without a connection to your belly you may lack strength, grounding, intuition, and passion. Without a connection to your head you can do some really stupid and thoughtless things that can ruin even the best of relationships.

When the three centers are in balance, energy flows through the body creating a sense of harmony within the individual and a sense of connection with other people. When the centers are not in alignment, the energy bounces around in your body like a herky-jerky roller coaster, creating chaos and instability not only within you but within all your relationships.

When your energy is chaotic and your centers are out of balance or alignment with each other, fear and rigidity can be the result. The following exercise is a way to create balance among the body centers.[1] It also can create better alignment among the head, heart, and belly in a course of action to improve a relationship. You may wish to read this through several times before you try it so that you don't have to break your visualization to take the next step. Or, you may have someone else read it to you slowly, giving you plenty of time to take each step. Another possibility is to read it into a tape recorder to play back to yourself at your own pace.

## Exercise

Create a comfortable, quiet environment for yourself where you won't be disturbed. Think of a relationship that you would like to improve. Notice how you feel in your body when you reflect on that relationship.

Now close your eyes and relax your body, taking several deep breaths. Notice if there is any tension in your body that you can get rid of by shifting your position. Pay attention to your breathing. Settle into a rhythm of deep, slow breaths. To the extent possible, breathe slowly down into your belly.

Start relaxing your entire body starting with your toes. Moving slowly up your body, focus your attention on each body part as you consciously let the tension release from that part. Take your time, moving on to the next body part only when the previous part lets go of any tension. When you have finally relaxed the top of your head, imagine you are standing at the top of a flight of stairs. As you slowly descend the stairs, notice that you are becoming more relaxed with each step you take.

When you reach the bottom of the stairs, suspend all of your thinking. Transform all of that thinking energy that you are no longer using into a river of cascading energy. Let it flow down into your chest and through your heart, feeling your heart open as the energy flows through. Imagine the river continuing through your chest and flowing all the way down into your belly, warming your belly, keeping it soft and relaxed, and then flowing down into your legs and through the soles of your feet. The energy leaves your feet and flows deep into the ground, so that you can feel what it is to be connected to the earth by a giant web of roots.

Imagine the energy creating a stable base that grounds you solidly to the earth, then let that energy flow back up through your feet and legs, back into the belly, which supports your strength, passion, and intuition. Then it flows up through the heart, the place of compassion, forgiveness, empathy, and love, and up to the head to achieve mindfulness.

The river of energy continues to flow up and out the crown of your head into the universe like the branches of a mighty oak tree. Notice your solid connection with the earth below and the universe above.

From this place of connection and harmony ask yourself three questions:

1. Ask your head, "What thoughts can I express to strengthen this relationship?" Then take your time and wait to see what answer you receive.

2. Ask your heart, "What feelings do I need to express to strengthen this relationship?" Then take your time and wait to see what answer you receive.

3. Ask your belly, "What action should I take to strengthen this relationship?" Then take your time and wait to see what answer you receive.

After you receive your answers, and when you are ready, open your eyes and spend a few moments reflecting on the experience and any insight you may have gained. Notice how you are feeling in your body and remember that feeling. If it feels helpful, you may wish to write for a few minutes about the experience.

- - - - - - - - - - - - - - - - - - - - - - - - - - - - - - - - - - - - - - - - - - - - - - - - - - - - - - - - - - - -
Tool 9-4

## Developing an Objective Observer

In any relationship, people can often get caught up in the moment and lose track of what is happening within themselves. If people had just a little more awareness of what they were doing and feeling in the moment, they might be able to make a slight correction in their demeanor or direction that could have a big impact on the outcome of that particular interchange. A slight increase in awareness, in the moment, might be enough to keep them operating in the Green Zone, rather than sliding unconsciously into the Red Zone.

Developing an Objective Observer is not so much an exercise as it is a practice to develop and use regularly. It encourages you to be present in any experience, but also to have a small part of you outside the experience, observing the experience from a slight distance. It is a practice of self-observation. It is as though you are stepping outside of the circle of what is happening in the moment, while it is happening, and noticing the experience as if you were an objective observer. Your Objective Observer should not be concerned so much with the content of any interchange, but rather with the process and feelings that are having an impact on the experience.[2]

Ask your Objective Observer to be on the lookout for the following:

- Am I participating from the Green Zone or the Red Zone?
- Am I listening effectively by summarizing and feeding back what I am hearing?
- Am I being open and truthful?
- Am I calm, present, and relaxed in my body?

- Is my body language congruent with what I am saying?
- Do I notice any defensiveness? If so, can I become more centered?
- Do I seem open to new ideas or am I rigid in my thinking?
- Am I being inclusive?
- Am I helping my partner feel significant, competent, and likable?

---------------------------------------------------------------

Tool 9-5

## Distortion Log

Self-talk is the ongoing conversation people have with themselves, but only in their own mind. They almost never share it with others. It is usually the most truthful and accurate picture of what people are thinking. Since people never share it with others, they never have to worry about censoring it. When this self-talk comes from a grounded, intelligent, and reflective voice, it can be motivating, encouraging, self-enhancing, and energizing, and create a positive life force.

Some people, however, are filled with self-critical self-talk from an ungrounded, demeaning little voice. It can sound like stream-of-consciousness self-bashing: *Nobody at work likes me. Of course, why would they like me? I'm really not as smart as they are. I wish I were better looking. I don't contribute much to this relationship. I'll bet they're avoiding me. They probably go to lunch all the time and never ask me. I've never been popular. Not much chance I'll ever find a good relationship. I'll probably never make friends here at work.* People's heads are filled with noise from their own worst critic.

Who you become as a person is to a great extent a reflection of your internal self-talk. It can become a self-fulfilling prophecy. Positive self-talk can build your confidence and help you be more open and available to positive relationships. Negative self-talk can be one of the worst things you can do and the best way to sabotage yourself. If you keep telling yourself that you will never find good relationships, you certainly decrease the chances of being open to relationships when the opportunity arises.

People can be unaware that these self-critical thought processes are conditioned from childhood and can be fraught with distortions. Too often people mindlessly accept the thoughts as true, without subjecting them to the same content analysis that they make regarding the comments of others. The next exercise encourages you to examine some of your critical self-talk, searching for possible distortions. It requires you to subject your negative thoughts to the same scrutiny that you would subject the assertions of your relationship partners.

| **BOX 9-7** Identify Negative Thoughts | Identify Distorted Thinking | Implications of the Distortion | Replace with More Positive Thought |
|---|---|---|---|
|  |  |  |  |

In the first column, identify the self-critical thought.

In the second column, test that self-critical thought against all the objective evidence that you have about the substance of your negative thought. Scrutinize the thought to see if it has any basis in fact or if it is merely distorted thinking based on old childhood conditioning and fears.

In the third column, identify the possible consequences of your distorted thinking. It is important for you to realize that your distorted thinking has significant implications for your behavior, attitude, and your ability to be in collaborative relationships.

In the fourth column replace your distorted thought with a more realistic positive thought. Whenever you catch yourself engaging in your original negative distorted thinking, immediately substitute, in your mind, this more realistic positive thought. Review the example in Box 9-8, and then try it yourself with one of your possible distortions.

| **BOX 9-8** | | | |
|---|---|---|---|
| Identify Negative Thoughts | Identify Distorted Thinking | Implications of the Distortion | Replace with More Positive Thought |
| *This deal will fall through. No one will sign this agreement. No one will trust me with this job. They don't want to do business with me. I'm such a screwup.* | *What am I saying? They actually approached us about this alliance! This could be a productive and profitable business relationship for all of us. All the evidence indicates they do want to do business with me. I really jump to negative conclusions whenever I get anxious.* | *If I keep engaging in my distorted thinking, I'll probably lose faith in this deal and will waver out of fear of rejection. I may not pursue the contract as vigorously as I should. I'll be sending them a negative message and sound pessimistic. They may begin to question my commitment to this deal, which is exactly the opposite of what I want to happen.* | *Since all the indications are that they want to do business with me, I will continue with an optimistic, confident attitude. This will be a profitable deal for all of us and can lead to additional business opportunities. I will project positive thoughts in my communications with them, letting them know I am a solid, enthusiastic partner.* |

--------------------------------------------------------------

Tool 9-6

## Light Visualization

Indulge us for a moment with this next quick little visualization. It may seem a little too "California" for you. But, if you are open to it (i.e., you don't get rigid in your thinking about visualizations being stupid), it can be an excellent way to feel more grounded and centered right before you have to deal with any anxiety-provoking event. Try it at least once. You may find it "enlightening."

## Exercise

Close your eyes and take a couple of deep breaths. Imagine a shaft of soothing golden light entering the top of your head and slowly filling every space in your body. Imagine the golden light displacing all your negative thoughts and energy, cleansing your whole body with a warm glow. Fully experience yourself as calm, grounded, present, and authentic. When you are ready, open your eyes and notice how you are feeling.

Repeat this exercise right before you go into a stressful event.

--------------------------------------------------------------

Tool 9-7

## Accountable Friends

Nothing improves a person's self-awareness like a good friend telling him or her the truth. Time for self-reflection with friends is a powerful tool for growth. If people are open to it and can stay nondefensive, they can gain a great deal of wisdom from feedback about their mistakes as well as their successes. The times they have failed themselves and others, being inauthentic and not living up to the values they profess, can offer rich insight into who they are, as well as who they are not. People can also learn a lot about themselves from their successes, the times they did live out their truest values, when they had clarity of thought and purpose and a powerful combination of passion and focus.

Knowledgeable and courageous friends willing to give you honest feedback, hold you accountable, and celebrate even your smallest victories can support individual growth by creating a cultural norm within the relationship. Members of the relationship not only commit to "I want to be authentic in this relationship," they also commit to "this is the way we expect to be treated."

Think of a good friend or two whom you could approach about creating an opportunity for genuine feedback. Perhaps you and a colleague can spend an hour a month at work reflecting upon one area where you want to grow and develop. Start small and let it develop as you find it useful.[3]

-----------------------------------------------------------------
Tool 9-8

## Individual Daily Reflective Practice

One of the most valuable things you can do to support yourself is to cultivate daily reflective practice. This means setting aside a time every day for some method of deliberate self-awareness and self-reflection. Many meditation practices recommend setting aside at least twenty minutes a day. Research is clear that if you want something to become a regular habit, you must practice conscientiously. It is strange that most people know that if they want to become good at something, like putting a golf ball, the centerpiece of improving performance would be regular practice. Even after they had achieved high performance, they would still set aside time for continued practice.

It is much the same for developing the quality of mind of the Green Zone. So, each morning, you might find a calm place to just sit and practice breathing or some other meditative technique. You may wish to read something inspirational or restate a personal vision statement. You may wish to use this calm, centered time simply to reflect on the path you have chosen for your personal growth.
-----------------------------------------------------------------

## OTHER METHODS

There is no correct or best way to gain self-awareness and reduce fear. Life is a series of trial and error, and so is growth. We've said before that any method that fits you is a good way to proceed. From meditation to the martial arts, or therapy to theology or spirituality, perseverance is the key, building the future one thought, one feeling, or one gut reaction at a time.

## CHAPTER SUMMARY

It is people's internal thoughts, their stories, that they attach to the external events in their lives that give meaning to those events and relationships. People learn their stories from their experience. The past is impossible to change. It is what it is, good, bad, or indifferent, and everyone is stuck with his or her past. While people are greatly influenced by their past, however, they are not inseparable from it, and it doesn't have to determine their future. Most people think that their past is behind them. Yet most people carry their past like a shield in front of them, not behind them, to protect them from their stories.

The common denominator of the tools in this chapter is an attempt to increase awareness and create new patterns in the brain, which can encourage fresh thinking. The tools encourage readers to break away from old, learned, ineffective patterns of behaviors by focusing attention on more effective ways of being. Working these issues can free the energy that keeps people tethered to the past and instead shift that energy into aliveness and authenticity. This requires compassionate self-honesty and detective work.

## PART 5
## 5TH ESSENTIAL SKILL

# PROBLEM SOLVING AND NEGOTIATING

Congratulations! You've worked your way through the first four skills and are now ready to learn the fifth skill that is essential to building collaborative relationships. This fifth skill differs from the earlier skills that you have already learned. The first four skills required some soul-searching, since they have to do with you and your interior landscape. You learned the importance of collaborative intention, truthfulness, self-accountability, self-awareness, and your awareness of others. However, even the most self-aware, accountable, truth-telling, nondefensive people will have a difficult time maintaining successful relationships if they aren't skilled at negotiating their way through conflict.

A big part of success at collaborative relationships is knowing how to resolve conflicts. If people aren't skilled at managing conflicts, it can tear relationships apart. This fifth skill is the ability to solve problems and negotiate your way through conflict in a way that supports collaboration. The next part of the book, chapters 10 to 17, moves from the interpersonal readiness covered earlier to what we call Skillful Problem-Solving Methods.

Chapter 10 offers specific strategies to encourage collaboration. Chapters 11 to 17 teach readers Interest-Based Problem Solving. It is a specific step-by-step approach to negotiating your way through conflict.

# CHAPTER 10
# STRATEGIES FOR COLLABORATIVE SUCCESS

**Everyone claims to** be collaborative and lists collaboration high in most organizational values. In practice, however, behaviors are often dominated by hidden or unconscious, adversarial attitudes. These adversarial attitudes and behaviors typically show up when the relationship is under stress. People often don't even realize they are acting adversarially because their attitudes are so automatic and unconscious. That's why it is so important to increase self-awareness about attitudes, fears, and defensiveness. Neil Bodine, one of the premier labor lawyers in the country, describes the approach as analogous to certain martial arts, in both philosophy and goals: "Like a martial art, it requires external and internal practice—an external technique and an inner attitude."[1]

Unconscious attitudes are like the bulk of an iceberg, which is hidden below the surface. Most of what people do is based on attitudes and beliefs that are below the surface of their own consciousness. This "below the surface" material gets people into trouble. As Professor Vance Kennedy says, "The hardest part of conflict resolution is the internal work that must be done before collaboration can occur."[2]

---

**BOX 10-1**

This book does not simply advocate a nicer, less aggressive strategy. What it advocates requires a great deal of awareness and deliberate action.

---

Successful collaborative relationships require conscious and deliberate action. When we're working to build collaboration among team members, or between departments, divisions, organizations, or even individual employees, we have often used simulations, case studies, and game theory to dramatize the difference between adversarial and collaborative attitudes.

In these exercises, participants play various roles and get to experiment with different strategies to achieve success, however they may define it. They must think strategically and anticipate the reactions of other participants, who may or may not be inclined to collaborate. The exercises reflect the classic dilemma of most people entering into new relationships. The unknowns of the situation are a breeding ground for the unconscious hopes and fears of all the participants. One of our favorite simulations is called the Radiant Transit Exercise, where a board of directors of a transit company is given the opportunity to choose either an adversarial or a collaborative strategy to increase profits.[3]

There has been a great deal of research on similar game theory and business decision-making strategies.[4] Based upon this research, as well as our own experience debriefing participants in this exercise hundreds of times and experience with our client companies, the following ten strategies are recommended to build effective long-term collaborative relationships. They require a great deal of awareness and deliberate action.

---

**BOX 10-2**

**Ten Strategies for Building Collaboration**

1. Go first.

2. Be open and direct about your intent to collaborate.

3. Pay attention to responses.

4. Keep talking.

5. Forgive quickly (respond positively when others cooperate).

6. Agree ahead of time on systems for conflict resolution.

7. Conduct regular reviews and actively monitor relationships.

8. Use graduated sanctions.

9. Make a commitment to a higher ethical standard.

10. Use Interest-Based Problem Solving to negotiate disputes.

---

# TEN HELPFUL STRATEGIES

## 1. Go First

This is not about who makes the first offer, but who makes the first effort to be collaborative and build a long-term relationship.[5] Those seeking long-term relationships will tend to be more willing to take risks earlier in the relationship. They know that it is generally more effective to be proactive in building relationships. They also know that over the long haul there is a greater opportunity to recoup any early losses. Clearly communicating your intentions at the beginning, rather than sitting back and waiting for the other person to make the first move, creates a much greater chance of influencing the direction of the relationship. One of the more common, and least effective, strategies for building a relationship that we see regularly is for one person to sit by the phone and wait for the other person to call first. Don't squander precious time; be willing to go first.

## 2. Be Open and Direct about Your Intent to Collaborate

If you want to build a collaborative relationship, you have a much better chance of success if you clearly communicate your desire to the other party. People are not mind readers. Often they are simply waiting until it seems safe before they try to build a relationship. Being open and direct about your intentions can create that safety net for the other parties.

If you are clear about your intent to collaborate, you have a much better chance of salvaging the situation if unexpected circumstances occur. If people know your intentions, they are less likely to make up negative stories to fill in for any missing facts. If other people know that building a collaborative relationship is a high priority for you and something surprising happens, instead of immediately jumping to the assumption that you can't be trusted, they may be thinking, "I wonder what happened," or, "That's curious, we'd better look into that."

It's also important to remember that actions also speak. Are your actions consistent with the message you are trying to send? It is helpful to ask yourself, "How might my message or my actions be misconstrued?" If there is a good possibility that the message could be misconstrued, your work isn't finished. You need to keep crafting the message to make your intention clear.

---

**BOX 10-3**

Everything you say and do, as well as everything you don't say and don't do, sends a message. Pay attention to the message you are sending.

---

Individuals sometimes fear that telling the other side what they really want gives the other side additional power over them. That may be true in rare instances; however, our experience is that you dramatically increase the chances of getting what you want if you are open and direct about what you want. We're always a bit dismayed by some people who put effort into tricking the other side into giving them what they want, when the other side would probably be open to giving it to them in the first place. Remember, we're talking about strategies for building better relationships. Holding your cards close to your vest may be an effective strategy in a poker game. It will not serve you well in a collaborative relationship.

### 3. Pay Attention to Responses

Most negotiations include efforts to both create value and claim value. Creating value means expanding the size of the pie before it gets divided. It is inventing lots of options to meet the mutual interests of the parties. Claiming value means dividing the pie. It is making sure that your particular interests are met to the fullest extent possible. Don't get lulled into a sense of security that the other side is taking responsibility for getting your interests met, i.e., you getting your fair share of the pie. That is often not the case, and if you do not remain vigilant to the circumstances you face, you can easily be taken advantage of.

In the old comic strip *Peanuts*, Charlie Brown was consistently suckered into trying to kick a football that was held by Lucy. Just as Charlie Brown would kick at the ball, Lucy would pull the ball away and Charlie would land on his rear end. He was always naively hopeful that Lucy's promise not to move the football was true this time. Charlie Brown would continually ignore that Lucy would always pull the football away just as he was starting to kick it. If you fail to pay attention to the responses you are receiving from others, you may repeatedly end up on your butt.

> **BOX 10-4**
>
> When trying to collaborate, it's easy to get lulled into an unrealistic belief that the other side is taking responsibility for your getting your interests met. Without vigilance, you can be taken advantage of.

People who pay close attention to their circumstances can respond with a wider range of actions/reactions and typically fare better than individuals whose response is limited by a fixed mind-set. For example, when faced with unpredictable behavior by a counterpart, some people may always interpret that as an aggressive competitive move, because of their own rigid mind-set. Other people, however, might wonder why their counterpart is acting unpredictably. They may not be limited by preconceived notions of what the behavior means, so they can ask themselves "What might this mean? Is their move defensive or aggressive? Are they trying to tell us something? How could we have contributed to this? Given this move, how might they react in the future? How can we protect ourselves without sending the wrong message?" These are all questions reflecting flexibility and an openness to a range of responses not available to those with rigid thinking.

A good strategy is to be completely trustworthy but not so wholly trusting that you become blind to your circumstances. Acting appropriately to your circumstances requires you to pay attention to those circumstances.

## 4. Keep Talking

Never pass up the opportunity to talk, ask questions, and listen. It is always in your interest to communicate effectively and always better to err in favor of too much communication rather than too little. If people don't understand what you are thinking or feeling, they will make up their own stories about you to fill in the information they lack. When they make up these stories, they are rarely as generous to you as you might wish. People are always making assumptions based upon incomplete information. It is impossible to escape the necessity of making assumptions; however, if you pass up the opportunity to talk, you are forgoing the opportunity to test those assumptions.

The more complex the issues, or the higher the stakes, the more important it is to communicate at every opportunity. It doesn't need to be a formal meeting. It can be as simple as picking up the phone and letting people know about some action you are considering that might affect them. Remember that you are always sending a message, even if you don't do or say anything. Be aware of the messages you may be sending. Making the effort required for clear communication will not guarantee success; however, not doing so will almost always guarantee failure.

---

**BOX 10-5**

Clear, consistent communication will not guarantee success; however, poor communication will almost always guarantee failure. A notable example of how refusing to talk will guarantee failure is the relationship between the United States and Cuba.

---

Great examples of the importance of efforts to communicate are Begin and Sadat with President Carter at Camp David; de Klerk and Mandela in South Africa; Arafat and Rabin in Palestine; and Nixon and Chou En-lai in China. They each made inroads in the peace process because they were willing to keep talking. A notable example of how refusing to talk will guarantee failure is the strained relationship between the United States and Cuba. The United States has been refusing to talk to Castro for decades, and it is pretty clear that nothing will happen in that relationship until Castro dies.

Sometimes people shy away from talking to their relationship partners because they are ashamed of their earlier tactics or betrayals. Sometimes it is because their feelings are hurt or they are angry or disappointed with something the other person has done. Sometimes they are simply trying to be "nice" by not bringing up an uncomfortable issue. Whatever the reason for not talking, the issue is still there, getting bigger and bigger.

We call these unspoken issues "elephants in the room." They are huge and can be sitting right in the middle of the relationship. They can reflect a betrayal or unexplained or puzzling behavior such as changes in previous strategies. Maybe one team member undermined another, maybe the boss is an alcoholic, or perhaps an important member of the team is all of a sudden doing poor-quality work. If there are elephants in the room in your relationships, it is even more important that you be willing to talk about them. Talking about them is the only way to jointly create methods of avoiding reoccurrences or of repairing the damage. Ignoring them will cause them to grow out of proportion, harming the relationship, and will insure that your relationship stays at a superficial level.

The training staff of the California labor-management project that we've talked about in the preface and appendix 1 learned a little ritual from one of its clients that we have continued whenever we work with separate teams, departments, or organizations that must interact with other teams, departments, and organizations. The client reported that when they had an "elephant in the room" that needed to be talked about, they brought a little stuffed elephant to their meeting and placed it on the table, saying "there's an elephant in the room that we need to discuss." They found it an effective way to raise a sensitive issue and minimize hostility. Now, at the end of many of our training programs, we give toy elephants to the leaders of each group or organization. We explain that whenever either side feels there is an elephant in the room, they are to bring their toy elephant to the meeting, set it in the middle of the table, and announce, "We believe there is an elephant in the room that we should talk about." Having the toy elephant sitting in front of everyone on the table is always a great reminder not only that it is essential to deal with the elephants in the room, but also that it can be done from the Green Zone.

## 5. Forgive Quickly (Respond Positively When Others Cooperate)

Holding a grudge does not serve you well. Getting locked into a long series of mutual recriminations will often doom a relationship. By "forgive quickly" we are not urging you to forget about any past betrayals or unreliability, or to be blindly positive. Rather, we are urging you to be open and receptive to opportunities to resume cooperation. It may be that before you begin cooperating again you will need to build insurance policies into the relationships. For example, if your counterpart, like Lucy, has pulled the ball away several times in the past, you may want her to post a bond insuring she complete her responsibilities. You can start by openly discussing your fears of untrustworthiness and then jointly invent ways to reduce future risk and insure future compliance.

## 6. Agree Ahead of Time on Systems for Conflict Resolution

The worst possible time to invent systems for resolving your conflict is when you are right in the middle of that conflict. Conflict exacerbates defensiveness and rigidity, which in turn reduces creativity. You are far better off planning ahead for conflicts you may face in the future. People are often hesitant to raise this at the start of a new relationship out of fear that it sends the wrong message. But it is precisely your willingness to deal with realistic fears that can strengthen the relationship.

We were once negotiating a partnership agreement where we had great enthusiasm about the future. No one wanted to raise the possibility that the relationship might not work out over the long haul. We were all concerned that we might jinx the new relationship by focusing on negative possibilities. The dissolution section of the contract was the most difficult section to negotiate because nobody wanted to face that the partnership might not survive. Years later, however, when circumstances changed for all of the partners, we were able to dissolve the partnership, resolving all sorts of thorny issues. We were able to remain close friends, willing to support each other's individual paths in a way we would not have been able to if we hadn't had a system of conflict resolution in place ahead of time.

A conflict-resolution and grievance policy is usually one of the first and most important sections negotiated in labor-management contracts. An established process for dealing with conflict when it arises almost always creates a sense of certainty and stability that can significantly reduce tension when a dispute arises.

## 7. Conduct Regular Reviews and Actively Monitor Relationships

"Trust but verify" is one of the wisest ways for not overloading trust. Parents who have tried to get their kids to brush their teeth know that explaining the benefits of brushing may work one or two times, but won't ensure clean teeth over the long run. It takes regular monitoring until the habit is solidly in place. The same is true for collaborative relationships. Regular reviews should be conducted to insure that the parties are meeting their obligations in the relationship. This keeps little problems from growing into big, relationship-busting problems. Several employers we've worked with conduct regular budget overviews with all the employees. Inviting the employees or alliance partners to regularly conduct financial reviews, for example, insures that money is being spent according to plans previously agreed upon, eliminating surprises and building credibility.

## 8. Use Graduated Sanctions

If you simply look the other way when a violation of trust occurs, you send the wrong message and encourage future breaches of trust. It is important to deal directly with violations to insure that unacceptable behavior is stopped. If, however, you overreact with a punitive melt-down when something minor occurs the first time, you may unnecessarily stress the relationship and also encourage future breaches of trust. It is helpful if you can negotiate an understanding of graduated sanctions into any system for conflict resolution that you may agree upon.

## 9. Make a Commitment to a Higher Ethical Standard

The Enrons of the world eat away at the very soul of our corporate culture. Fortunately, most of us are not faced with the seduction of wealth and power at such a high level. In ongoing relationships, however, it's typically not the big betrayals that erode the relationship over the long term. It's usually the little things that never get cleared up that do long-term damage. A cut corner that hurts a partner or takes advantage of something because "they'll never know" can create a permanent disillusionment when it does eventually come to light. We're not advocating a rigid moral code here, simply suggesting that we are all faced with many more opportunities to be ethical than we are usually aware of. How often have you photocopied a few pages from a book without even thinking about the copyright violation, or downloaded music from the Internet without paying a royalty, or used pirated software, or bad-mouthed and bitched about someone to a third party but not had the integrity to raise your complaint directly with that person?

It's just this simple: making an effort to be more conscious of your ethical standards will result in greater authenticity. Greater authenticity will result in stronger, more collaborative relationships. It's not easy, but it is simple!

## *10. Use Interest-Based Problem Solving to Negotiate Disputes*

Conflict is a regular and natural part of any ongoing relationship. When disputes arise in a successful collaborative relationship, parties try to use the opportunity not only to resolve that dispute, but also to help avoid other disputes in the future. They look for compliance-prone agreements, i.e., agreements where obligations are likely to be fulfilled.

The organizers of the California labor-management project looked at many different methodologies for negotiating the way through the inevitable conflicts that arise in any relationship. The one they found to be the most effective was the Interest-Based approach to problem solving: "Interest-Based" because it is based upon a thorough understanding of the underlying interests of the stakeholders rather than the all-too-traditional method of sticking to your favorite position without concern for the other side's interests. The use of the Interest-Based methodology was one of the most significant factors leading to an 85 percent reduction in the rate of disputes filed with the State of California over a three-year period.[6] Research has also shown that participants over a six-year period who were trained in the Interest-Based method felt they were almost 45 percent more effective at getting their interests met in conflicted situations.[7]

No process or methodology will guarantee success in all cases, but the use of the Interest-Based approach to negotiate your way through conflict will substantially increase your chances of a successful relationship. We devote the last third of this book to this methodology because it produces measurable positive results.

Take a moment to reflect how your behaviors around these issues may affect your relationships. Using the scale on the next page, you can reflect upon a specific relationship or just generally in your life.

Exercise 10-1

# Collaboration Reflection

Take a few minutes to reflect on your life. On a scale of 0 (low) to 9 (high), to what degree do you participate in these behaviors?

Going first _____

Being open and direct about your intent to collaborate _____

Paying attention to responses _____

Always taking opportunities to communicate _____

Forgiving quickly _____

Agreeing ahead of time on systems for conflict resolution _____

Conducting regular reviews and actively monitoring the relationship _____

Using graduated sanctions _____

Maintaining a high ethical standard _____

Using Interest-Based Problem Solving _____

Thinking of one or two specific relationships, what could you do to be more proactive regarding these behaviors?

_____

_____

_____

_____

## CHAPTER SUMMARY

Behaviors are often dominated by hidden or unconscious competitive attitudes. Successful collaborative relationships require conscious and deliberate action. People often don't even realize they are acting adversarially because their attitudes are unconscious. Unconscious attitudes are like the bulk of an iceberg below the surface of the water. Most of what people do is based on attitudes and beliefs that are below the surface of their own consciousness. This below-the-surface material gets them into trouble. That's why it is so important to increase self-awareness about attitudes, fears, and defensiveness and to engage in deliberate strategies and action to further collaboration.

We have suggested ten deliberate strategies to increase your effectiveness in building collaborative relationships. They are:

1. Go first.

2. Be open and direct about your intent to collaborate.

3. Pay attention to responses.

4. Keep talking.

5. Forgive quickly (respond positively when others cooperate).

6. Agree ahead of time on systems for conflict resolution.

7. Conduct regular reviews and actively monitor relationships.

8. Use graduated sanctions.

9. Make a commitment to a higher ethical standard.

10. Use Interest-Based Problem Solving to negotiate disputes.

# CHAPTER 11
# WE'VE GOT A PROBLEM; NOW WHAT DO WE DO ABOUT IT?
## (An Overview of the Interest-Based Approach to Negotiating)

**If your relationship** doesn't bump up against some conflict every once in a while, you're either in complete denial or overly medicated. Anytime you get two or more people together over the long haul, they are going to have some interests that clash. Author Ellen Wachtel notes that "a dysfunctional family is any family with more than one member."[1] People and organizations aren't fully alive if they don't occasionally have conflict. However, resolving conflict requires courage and skill.

Conflict presents a good opportunity to stretch, grow, and gain perspective and wisdom. Without something to grind up against, both people and organizations can become stale and stagnant. Conflict reflects some passion in the relationship. Something exciting and interesting is happening in the relationship. Conflict is with us for life, and what we have conflict about can define us just as clearly as what or whom we love, and whom or what we surround ourselves with.

Yet most people avoid conflict as much as they avoid physical pain or public speaking. The problem usually isn't the conflict. It's the way we handle conflict that creates the stress around it. And it's what we do with conflict that makes a difference. When we choose to see it as an enemy, we're using all our energy and creative power to resist it. Then we're back to spending our energy on self-preservation rather than problem solving. If we view conflict as threatening our survival, it is bound to push us into a negative, adversarial Red Zone attitude. If we see it as a natural part of life, knowing that we have tools and skills to deal with it, that helps us keep a more positive, nondefensive, Green Zone attitude.

Conflict is just a situation. It's not good; it's not bad. If we see conflict as bad or scary or exciting, that's just the story that we're telling ourselves about it. The story is not the conflict; it's our interpretation that comes from our history, our attitudes, and our choices.

The fifth essential skill for successful collaborative relationships is a method of negotiating your way through conflict as it arises, Interest-Based Problem Solving: "Interest-Based" because it is based on a better understanding of the underlying interests of the parties to the dispute. We have found that the methodology we are suggesting in the next few sections has dramatically improved people's relationship skills by helping them resolve conflict in more direct, creative, and collaborative ways.

## THE INTEREST-BASED APPROACH PRODUCES MEASURABLE RESULTS

The method is not a generalized pep talk or motivational process simply urging you to be more collaborative. Rather it is a specific step-by-step approach to negotiating your way through conflict. Following it will make you more effective dealing with the inevitable conflict in every relationship. At first it may seem a bit like a paint-by-the-numbers approach, but that's all right. We urge you to follow the steps and paint by the numbers for a while. In a short time you will begin to internalize the process and discover that your thinking is changing. You'll begin to face conflicts by thinking first about the underlying interests of all the people involved, rather than by clinging rigidly to your favorite solution.

---

**BOX 11-1**

Interest-Based Problem Solving is a specific step-by-step approach to negotiating your way through conflict. Following it will make you more effective dealing with the inevitable conflict that arises in every relationship.

---

The approach can also have a profound impact on the attitudes of people within an organization, about how they approach conflict. This is the conflict culture of an organization, which in large part determines the collaborative potential of any organization or relationship. In some organizations conflict is rampant and openly expressed, reflecting a culture of hostility. In others it is hidden below the surface like the bulk of an iceberg, reflecting a more passive-aggressive culture. Interest-based methods can help people deal with conflict more directly and in a less toxic way.

In California school systems, some of the most dysfunctional, adversarial Red Zone labor-management relationships reduced their conflict by an average rate of 85 percent over three years by adopting this as their primary-problem solving methodology.[2] This wasn't just a handful of lucky relationships that happened to pull off something special. The research involved almost one hundred troubled bargaining relationships over three years. Conflict among all organizations involved in the research was reduced by an average rate of 67 percent. These weren't just perceptions or estimates of participants. The State of California had accurate data about the conflict among these parties both before and after the adoption of an Interest-Based approach to problem solving. This methodology fueled a substantial improvement that was sustainable over the long term. It resulted in a measurable improvement to the bottom line, significantly reducing the cost of conflict.

---

**BOX 11-2**

Some of the most dysfunctional, adversarial Red Zone or polarized relationships turned things around by adopting this as their primary problem-solving methodology. The research surveyed almost one hundred troubled organizations over three years. After adoption of an Interest-Based approach, the reduction in conflict averaged 67 percent. Some of the most dysfunctional organizations reduced their conflict by an average rate of 85 percent over three years.

What would an 85 percent reduction in conflict do to your company's bottom line?

---

Imagine the impact to the bottom line of your team, business, or organization if you reduced conflict by 65, 75, or 85 percent over the next three years. If you're a skeptic and believe those numbers are too ambitious, cut it in half and think about a 30 to 35 percent improvement. Don't think only in terms of dollar savings in the "direct" cost of conflict. Think about the potential profits from the creativity that will be freed up. Think about the extra time that supervisors and managers will have to spend on their real work if they don't have to spend it refereeing disputes. It's great for a company to be able to produce measurable dollar savings; however, indirect benefits to the bottom line may be even more impressive. Imagine the savings in lower turnover and higher employee motivation when people can work and create in an atmosphere that is free of mistrust and intrigue and the fear of betrayal. Imagine the potential improvement in customer service and problem solving if when something goes wrong, instead of finger-pointing you hear comments like "Let me tell you about my contribution to the problem" or "What can I do to make it right?" or "Here's what I could improve on next time." It's life in the Green Zone.

We've worked with groups of NASA employees for many years and were fortunate to be able to observe one of their debriefing sessions after the *Columbia* shuttle disaster. In the group we observed, they were remarkably accountable. They sincerely worked to understand what had happened and focused their attention, intellectually and emotionally, on problem solving rather than searching for scapegoats and trying to blame someone else.

You should notice that we will use the terms *problem solving, conflict resolution,* and *negotiations* interchangeably. The terms overlap so much that we believe any distinction is blurred to the point of being useless. Unless your problem or conflict is one of those rare instances that involves only you, it will take some negotiation to work through it. It is not an overstatement or exaggeration to say that "life is a negotiation." If you are negotiating anything, it is because you have a problem or a conflict. You either want more or less of something in your life, or someone to start or stop doing something. You may not consider it a conflict because no hostility may be involved, but it is still a negotiation.

## WHAT IS THE INTEREST-BASED APPROACH?

The Interest-Based approach is both a tool for gaining understanding and preparing to resolve a dispute, as well as a process to follow when you are meeting with your counterparts.

Mark Twain once said, "The person who grabs the cat by the tail learns about forty-four percent faster than the one just watching." The best way to learn the Interest-Based method is to use it on something real and immediate in your life. We urge you to do this. Don't try to learn the process using the biggest, most irresolvable recurring nightmare of the past thirty years of your life. Start with something a bit more manageable and move on to the nightmare after you've had a little practice under your belt.

First use the Interest-Based approach as a planning tool to prepare to resolve your dispute. Then follow the methodology as a step-by-step process, working with your counterparts to resolve the dispute. The method involves the following steps:

1. Set the tone and discuss the process. Be open and direct about your intentions regarding problem solving as well as your intentions about the relationship. Try to reach agreement about what process you will use to resolve the issues.

2. Define the problem and develop a statement of issues that need to be resolved together.

3. Gain understanding of the underlying interests of the parties involved in the dispute. Interests are the wants, needs, or desires that underlie the issues that need to be resolved.

4. Develop a contingency plan. What will you be able to do on your own without the help or permission of the other side if you can't agree on a resolution?

5. Invent creative solutions. Work jointly to create a large number of potential solutions to meet as many interests of all the parties as possible.

6. Evaluate possible solutions against interests and contingency plans. Narrow the possible solutions and reach clear commitments and agreements where it is possible to verify compliance. Communicate to any constituencies in a manner that builds the relationship.

--------------------------------------------------------------------------------

Exercise 11-1

## Identifying a Current Conflict

Take a few minutes to think of a real dispute or conflict that is current in your life. Jot down a few notes about that problem, and keep the problem in mind as you read through chapters 12 through 17.

_____

_____

_____

_____

_____

--------------------------------------------------------------------------------

## CHAPTER SUMMARY

The fifth essential skill for successful relationships is a method for resolving conflicts. The Interest-Based approach is the most effective problem-solving methodology for building collaborative relationships. It is a specific step-by-step approach for planning and negotiating your way through conflict. It has produced measurable and sustainable culture shifts in organizations that have adopted this approach. In California, almost one hundred Red Zone organizations reduced their conflict by an average rate of 67 percent by adopting the Interest-Based approach as their primary problem-solving methodology. Ten of the most severely polarized Red Zone organizations reduced their conflict by an average rate of 85 percent over three years. Interest-Based Problem Solving can foster an atmosphere where people have the ability to spend their energy on their work, free of mistrust, intrigue, and the fear of betrayal. The Interest-Based approach is a powerful tool for maintaining a more constructive attitude and staying in the Green Zone.

**BOX 11-3**

**Steps of the Interest-Based Approach**

1. Set a positive tone and discuss the process.

2. Create a statement of issues to be resolved.

3. Understand the underlying interests of all the parties.

4. Develop a contingency plan.

5. Jointly invent creative solutions.

6. Evaluate possible solutions, reaching clear commitments and compliance-prone agreements.

# CHAPTER 12
# HOW DO WE GET STARTED?
## (Deciding What Process to Use, and Helping People Feel Included)

**Good starts make** for good endings. In his research about group compatibility, Will Schutz found that groups first face inclusion issues.[1] This means people want to know whether they belong. Will they be included, are they significant, will others pay attention to them, or will they be ignored? People's belief about their significance in the group can play a large part in determining whether they have a positive or negative attitude, and operate from the Green Zone or the Red Zone.

It is to everyone's advantage to help each other stay in the Green Zone, with a positive approach, particularly when dealing with conflict. So, the first things you should resolve with your colleagues or counterparts are inclusion issues. How will you be clear with your intentions about both the conflict and the relationship? How will you help your counterparts feel included and significant in the process, to the extent they feel comfortable?

Have you ever given any thought to how important being included is to your relationship partners? Think for a few minutes about their FIRO Element B scores for inclusion. If they have high-inclusion preferences, it may be helpful to have a lot of face-to-face meetings to address the matters at hand. If they have low-inclusion scores, you may want to consider doing some of your preliminary work through memos, e-mails, or phone calls rather than face-to-face meetings. Give some thought to your own Element B inclusion scores. How do your preferences match the preferences of the others? Can you be flexible to make it more comfortable for the others, or might some of your own rigidity be getting in the way of a more compatible process?

## CHEAP TRICKS DON'T WORK

Older books on negotiation strategy often suggested little tricks to put the other party at a disadvantage. Make them come to your office. Put them in shorter chairs so you can look down on them. Have your own coffee, but don't offer any to them. Arrange the room so the light will shine in their faces, creating glare. Make their chairs uncomfortable. Make sure you're sitting at the head of the table. Take telephone calls during the meeting to signal that other issues and people are much more important than they are. Make sure you have more information than they do, and make sure they know you do. Keep them waiting in your office or show up late to the meeting location. Announce that you need to leave early because you have important things to take care of. Deliberately have your staff interrupt you during the meeting with other issues. The list is long.

Our experience is that the older books were right to some extent. These tactics can have a profound impact on the process and eventually on the outcome. If your goal is to build collaboration, however, these techniques do not work. They only give you an advantage if your goal is to destroy trust, intimidate, or manipulate. Tricks like these are guaranteed to push individuals into the Red Zone and become more antagonistic. They are designed to make people feel insignificant, incompetent, and unlikable, which are the three issues that can trigger fears and foster rigid behavior. If you are trying to resolve conflict rather than create it, and to keep people in a positive Green Zone rather than a negative Red Zone, avoid petty tactics.

---

**BOX 12-1**

Petty negotiating tactics only give you an advantage if your goal is to destroy trust, intimidate, or manipulate. They don't build relationships.

---

Instead, anticipate the amount of inclusion your counterparts are comfortable with and create that environment. Remember that everything we do and say, as well as what we don't do and don't say, will send a message. So be conscious of the message you may be sending. Give thought to how your actions will be interpreted or possibly misinterpreted. Using whatever words and actions are comfortable and congruent for you, make clear that you have both short-term and long-term interests in the relationship as well as in solving the immediate problem.

## BE CLEAR ABOUT YOUR INTENTIONS

If you want to build a collaborative relationship, tell them that. On many occasions during a mediation one side would tell us, "I don't know why they're being so distant. We want to build a relationship, why don't they?" We would ask, "Have you told them that?" and they would often reply, "Well, no, but they ought to be able to figure that out. Why else would we be here?" If they don't have any information from you about your interest in finding a solution and building a relationship, they will typically fill in the blanks with their own story, which usually is not as favorable as you might wish.

Communicating that you want to reach a solution that is in the interests of all concerned, and that you are open to persuasion about how to resolve the issue, invites others to join you as an ally with a common purpose, rather than becoming an adversary. This is an excellent time to propose that both parties use the Interest-Based method to work the issue. We've had some clients who have sent their counterparts an outline of the process along with an invitation that they try the process during the upcoming meeting. They tell the other party that it is a nonadversarial method they've learned that may help resolve the issue while building their relationship.

Another client scheduled some Interest-Based training for their own employees and invited several of their suppliers to join the training at no cost. They explained that the training was about a collaborative method for resolving disputes, and since they wanted stronger, more collaborative relationships with their suppliers, they were inviting them to train together. This is a nice, clear way to tell the other party that you value the relationship, that they are significant to you, and that you desire stronger collaboration. It is also an excellent way to build a common culture between two organizations, whether they are separate companies or departments or teams within a company.

## TALK ABOUT PROCESS ISSUES TO AVOID SURPRISES

It is important to try to reach agreement on the process you will use so that you can avoid as many surprises as possible. You can discuss procedural issues before your meeting or wait until you actually meet. Examples of process issues that have come up in groups we've worked with are meeting protocols such as whether to use a facilitator or flip charts or how agendas would be set. Timing issues are usually important. How often will the parties meet? Will they meet for an hour at a time or for a full day, once a week or once a month, or around the clock until the matter is resolved?

Information sharing is often an important issue. Some groups agree to exchange key information such as their perspective of the problem, or financial data. Some groups use this as an opportunity to discuss what information will be helpful. Other groups plan out a joint effort to search for information that will be helpful, so that the search for relevant information also reinforces collaboration in the relationship. Labor-management groups using Interest-Based negotiations will sometimes form joint labor-management committees to gather information about health-care costs or budget issues prior to beginning their negotiations.

This is also a good time to clarify decision-making authority. It's stressful to a relationship if, right at the end of the process when one side is ready to sign an agreement, they learn they have different levels of authority and the other side announces that they have to take it to a higher level to get approval.

For most of these process issues there is no right or wrong or best practice to use. The point is to make those decisions jointly, not unilaterally. When we work with groups, we often rearrange the room so that they are not sitting across the table from each other. We may arrange the chairs in a semicircle facing a flip chart so that parties are focused on the flip chart rather than each other. These are small things that can sometimes foster a more positive Green Zone environment; however, they shouldn't be done unilaterally.

We once had a client who had seen the room rearranged like that during a different project and liked it. They wanted to create the same positive Green Zone atmosphere with a different partner with whom they had a more traditional and slightly adversarial relationship. So, prior to an important meeting they removed the table from the room and rearranged all the chairs so they were facing a single flip chart. They even went so far as to have their team members sit in every other chair before the other party arrived for the meeting. They believed that interspersed seating around a flip chart instead of across a table would create a less "we vs. them" mind-set, and would instead foster a feeling of a single team. They believed these were all helpful little inclusion steps.

When the second group arrived and saw how the room was set up, their comment was "Who appointed you God? We like having a table to write on. We'll come back after you fix the room." Later, when they debriefed that issue, it became clear that the room setup was not the real issue. In fact the table didn't really matter much at all; the second group eventually came to enjoy not having a table between the parties. What they were really upset about was that they hadn't been included in making the decision. The first group's good intentions were interpreted by the second group as just another example of insensitive, noninclusive thinking.

---

Exercise 12-1

## Identifying Process and Inclusion Issues

Think of the problem, dispute, or conflict that you identified in chapter 11 to follow along in this process. Please reflect on what you can do to clarify the conflict-resolution process and help your counterpart feel included. Review the example below and then complete the worksheet that follows.

### PROCESS AND INCLUSION WORKSHEET

1. How much inclusion do I believe my counterparts want? How do I know this? (When in doubt, ask.) What specific action can I take to make my intentions clear and include them and their opinions?

   *Victor has mentioned in the past that he hates traveling and long meetings and would rather work by himself, so he probably has a preference for low inclusion. I can do a lot of the negotiations and preparation over the phone and with e-mail. I'll tell him, both over the phone and in e-mails, that my intention is to work to build a long-term relationship with his company. I will invite him to share his ideas at all stages of the negotiations.*

2. What can I do to help my counterparts feel significant, competent, and likable?

   *I can acknowledge his preference to avoid meetings and make sure he knows I will respect his preference. I will schedule enough time so that our phone calls don't have to be rushed. I will tell him I'm willing to travel to see him if that would help. I will restate his interests out loud, rather than just assume they are clear. I will ask for his input and will listen carefully, checking for understanding and feeding back to him my understanding. I will keep him updated on any changes in my thinking or planning. I will make sure he knows how happy I am to have the opportunity to work with him.*

3. On what process issues would it be helpful for us to reach agreement?

*We need to set a schedule of meetings well in advance, to accommodate travel schedules. Whom else should we bring to our meetings? When will we involve lawyers in the negotiation? How will we share financial information ahead of time? How can we protect confidentiality? Joint press releases vs. we're on our own. Do we each have final authority, or does any decision need to be approved?*

## PROCESS AND INCLUSION WORKSHEET

1. How much inclusion do I believe my counterparts want? How do I know this? (When in doubt, ask.) What specific action can I take to make my intentions clear and include them and their opinions?

_____

_____

_____

_____

_____

2. What can I do to help my counterparts feel significant, competent, and likable?

_____

_____

_____

_____

_____

3. What process issues would it be helpful for us to reach agreement on?

_____

_____

_____

_____

_____

--------------------------------------------------------------------

## CHAPTER SUMMARY

A natural starting place for groups dealing with conflict is to talk about what process to use to resolve that conflict. Do what you can to help your counterparts feel included. It is important to clearly communicate your intentions about both the relationship and the problem-solving process. If you want to build a more collaborative relationship, tell that to the other side. When deciding upon process issues, be sure to do that jointly. That you are making the process decisions together is usually as important as the substance of the decision.

# CHAPTER 13
# WHAT REALLY IS OUR PROBLEM?
## (Defining the Issues That Need to Be Resolved *Together*)

**It was a $90 million** dispute; big stakes, with a lot of publicity. The parties had been negotiating the dispute off and on for almost eighteen months without success. Jim was asked to try mediation with the parties because it had finally reached the litigation stage. In his first meeting with the parties Jim asked each side to educate him about the dispute. He needed to know the details of the dispute. What problem were they trying to resolve?

The first spokesperson started by giving a little history. She spoke for about forty-five minutes, explaining in great detail the substance of the problem. At the end of the lengthy explanation the second spokesperson turned to her and said, "What in the hell are you talking about? That's not the problem at all!"

They had never had a good discussion of how each organization saw the problem. Both sides were using language that was similar enough to lull the other side into believing they were trying to solve the same problem. But they weren't. Each time they made proposals, they sounded close enough to be working on the same problem, but in fact they were like passengers on two trains on parallel tracks heading in similar directions. They weren't ever going to meet until they both started working on the same problem.

---

**BOX 13-1**

If you can't agree on the problem, you're unlikely to agree on the solution.

---

If the head of manufacturing believes the goal is to reduce absenteeism, and the head of human resources believes they are trying to raise low morale, these may overlap enough that it sounds as if they are working on the same issue. When it comes time to reach closure, however, each side may be a little mystified and frustrated by the other's lack of enthusiasm for their proposed solutions.

It's a little like drawing a curved line in the sand and asking people if it is convex or concave. It depends entirely on where you're standing. What is your perspective? People standing on either side of the line could argue for a long time and never reach an agreement. Compromise certainly won't help. Nobody would be willing to compromise by splitting the difference and agreeing that the line was straight. If people on the left defined the problem as "How can I get these other people to see that the line is concave?" and the people on the right defined the problem as "How can I get these other people to see that the line is convex?" they will merely have increased their own rigid thinking about the problem.

If they can agree on a common problem statement like "What is the nature of this line?" then they can work together to find a solution. The people on one side might then be willing to go to the other side to see a different perspective. After doing that, they might invite the people on the other side to come across to see it from their perspective.

Without a common definition of the problem they won't be able to successfully work as a team to solve the right problem. A thorough discussion and explicit agreement about the issues to be resolved is a prerequisite to a good solution for the same problem.

## DON'T INCLUDE SOLUTIONS

Rick and Harry are business partners we've worked with. Rick is on the road a lot, incurring travel expenses on the company credit card. He admittedly is not meticulous about saving receipts, but doesn't think it's that big a deal if he loses an occasional receipt because the company gets a monthly bill from the credit card company. Harry has responsibility for financial issues and is enormously frustrated by Rick's failure to turn in all his receipts.

Rick defines the problem as "How can I get Harry off my back about lost receipts?" Harry defines the problem as "How can I get Rick to be more responsible and turn in all his receipts?" Neither of these, however, is effective as a problem statement. Each is more about a favorite solution rather than the underlying problem. Harry's favorite solution is to get Rick to change his behavior. Rick's favorite solution is to get Harry to change his behavior. Including a solution in the problem statement will just entrench everyone's position about the issue rather than open up a helpful dialogue. One solution may in fact be for Rick to do a better job of turning in receipts. But imagine how open Rick will be to trying to solve the problem of "How do I get Rick to be more responsible and turn in all his receipts?" It will just seem like more nagging on Harry's part. Another potential solution may be for Harry to lighten up about the receipts and accept the credit card bill as enough documentation. But Harry is less likely to move in that direction if the subject of their meeting is "How do I get Harry off my back?"

If these two partners define the problem as "How can we design a system to account for travel expenses and credit card receipts?" they are both more likely to embrace the problem-solving process. Neither will feel the need to defend himself going into the process.

If you include solutions in the problem statement, you may also inadvertently eliminate other potentially good solutions. For example, in a joint venture between a U.S. manufacturer and a Chinese distributor of the product, assume the problem was stated as:

1. Which partner will determine the sales profit margin on imported goods?

   Or

2. How will the export sales manager set profit margins?

Both of these statements of the problem include preconceived solutions and exclude other possible solutions. Number one assumes that the profit margin has to be set by either one partner or the other. The second problem statement assumes the margin will be set by the export sales manager. Both tend to reduce the number of creative options the two sides might invent if they weren't starting with those preconceptions. They might never consider the possibility of a joint U.S.-Chinese price/profit committee, or the possible option of setting a floor price and letting distributors set their own profit margins above the sales price.

## DON'T SHAME OR BLAME

In the Rick and Harry example, both will probably be more open to a solution if they are not blamed or shamed about the current situation. Attacking an issue rather than demonizing a person will reduce your counterpart's defensiveness as well as send a message that you want to work with the other side to find a solution. A nonjudgmental problem statement will also invite people to solve the problem from the constructive Green Zone.

A common question we get when we urge this strategy is "What if the person is the problem?" We see this in teams quite often where a single member of the team is rude or disruptive or has ineffective communication skills. There we urge parties to define the behaviors as the problem rather than the person. You are much more likely to solve the issue of "How can I get my phone calls to Bob returned in a timely manner?" or "How can I improve communications with Bob?" rather than "What can we do about Bob? He's such an insensitive jerk."

## KEEP IT SIMPLE

We also urge parties to keep their problem statement simple. If it takes more than a sentence or two to describe, you're probably getting into too much detail too early in the process. A simple statement allows parties to easily refer back to their original focus if they are getting off track.

---

**BOX 13-2**

Keep the problem statement simple. If it takes more than a sentence or two, you're probably getting into too much detail too early in the process.

---

In planning, you may have to speculate about how your counterparts might define the problem. It is important to give this some careful thought. Do a little role reversal and put yourself in their place. Ask yourself how they might describe the situation, including its impact on the relationship. Then see if you can draft a problem statement that would be acceptable to all of you.

Once you actually start meeting with the other side, it is important that you verify that your understanding of the problem from their perspective was correct. You'll need all your of active listening and feedback skills. It is also an opportunity to check out any assumptions that you may have been making.

Don't just announce what the problem is that must be resolved. Use this as an opportunity to demonstrate that you've been giving the matter some thought from their perspective. You might introduce a proposed problem statement with something like "I've been trying to think about this problem from both our perspectives and define it in a way that we could both agree so that we are both trying to find solutions to the same problem. Please let me know if I've misunderstood anything from your point of view or left anything out." Then introduce your proposed problem statement and discuss it to see if it works for both of you.

By introducing it that way you are signaling that you've made an effort to understand the other's point of view and that you want to work together with them to find a solution. It is an invitation to search for solutions from the constructive set of Green Zone attitudes and behaviors.

------------------------------------------------------------

Exercise 13-1

## Writing a Problem Statement

Now take a few minutes to reflect on the problem you've chosen. Then in the space below write a problem statement of the issues that need to be resolved. Use the following guidelines:

1. It should be a statement of issues that need to be resolved.

2. The problem statement must be acceptable to both parties.

3. Do not include potential solutions in the problem statement.

4. Avoid shaming and blaming . . . don't demonize people.

5. Keep it simple.

The issues that we need to resolve together are . . .

_____

_____

_____

_____

------------------------------------------------------------

## CHAPTER SUMMARY

If you can't agree on the problem, you'll never agree on the solution. Without a common definition of the problem you won't be able to operate as a collaborative team trying to solve the right problem. When it comes time to reach closure, each side will be frustrated by the other's lack of enthusiasm for their proposed solutions. The definition of the problem must also be acceptable to both sides to get full buy-in for any solutions. Do not include potential solutions in the problem statement. Including them will usually trigger defensiveness and rigid thinking on the other side, and you may also inadvertently eliminate other good potential solutions. To keep everyone in the Green Zone, focus on the issue without shaming or blaming each other. Finally, remember the adage "keep it simple." A short, concise statement allows parties to refocus easily if they are getting off track.

# CHAPTER 14
# WHAT DOES EVERYBODY REALLY NEED?
## (Understanding the Underlying Interests)

**I ask for** the moon to give myself plenty of "bargaining room." You, of course, offer only a fraction of what you think is fair, to give yourself plenty of "bargaining room." Then typically we spend a tremendous amount of energy trying to convince each other of the "rightness" of our position and the fallacies of the other's position.

Eventually, positioning gives way to some movement, usually through compromise or serial concessions. Sometimes it is simply the superior strength of one side or the other, or possibly the intervention of some outside political or market pressures. Sometimes people just run out of time or energy and give in. If there is enough movement to get to an acceptable solution, the parties may reach agreement.

This is the negotiation process that most people were taught when they were young. A lot of people, including some pretty high-powered business, political, and international negotiators, still use this process. It can still be seen in boardrooms, sales meetings, labor negotiations, Congress, the White House, geopolitical settings, and flea markets, among many other venues all over the world.

Eventually agreements are usually reached and parties carry on with other matters. This occurs, however, not because they've done a good job of meeting the interests of the parties, but rather because they ended up at a common denominator that was acceptable. Agreements are something everyone can live with. They are reasonably tolerable. If one of your goals is to build long-term collaboration among the parties, however, it is a particularly ineffective and destructive method of negotiating conflict because it pits parties against each other rather than joining them as a problem-solving team.

The Interest-Based method of problem solving takes a different approach, and this part of the process may seem the most different from what a lot of us learned growing up. By focusing on the underlying interests of the parties rather than starting off arguing about the rightness of your favorite solution, i.e., your rigid position, you will dramatically increase the chances of finding a better solution, and doing it in a way that is less toxic to the relationship. In the research about the California project we've previously referred to, almost all participants surveyed said that the methods had a highly positive impact on both their process by making it less adversarial and thus less toxic interpersonally, and on their products by their reaching agreements that did a better job of meeting the underlying interests of all the parties involved.

## WHAT'S AN INTEREST?

Let's start by defining interests. Interests are the wants, needs, and desires that underlie the problem-solving efforts in the first place. Contrast that to a position, which is simply one way of fulfilling that desire or meeting that need. An interest reflects an underlying need while a position reflects a favorite solution.

The following dialogue between two friends illustrates how much more helpful an understanding of interests can be for resolving a dispute or finding solutions to a problem:

Ryan:    I've been thinking about buying a used truck. I know that you had talked about selling yours a while back, and I wondered if you would sell it to me now. I'll give you $7,000 for it and I could come get it this Friday.

Doug:    Sure, I would be willing to sell it to you. I wouldn't sell it for less than $7,500, however, and I wouldn't want you to pick it up until next month.

Ryan:    OK, I'll agree to pay you $7,500, but I still want to get the truck this Friday.

Doug:    I'm sorry. That won't work for me.

What we learn from this brief conversation is the *positions* both men have taken. Ryan's opening position was an offer of $7,000 and he wanted to pick up the truck on Friday. He then changed his position and raised his offer to $7,500. He maintained his position about when he would pick up the truck. He wanted it on Friday. Doug started out asking $7,500 for the truck and maintained his position on price. He also maintained his position about when Ryan could pick up the truck. Doug wanted to wait until next month and he offered no movement on that issue.

Knowing their positions does not help the two parties reach an acceptable agreement. What would help them reach an agreement is an understanding about why each took his position. If Ryan and Doug had spent some time asking questions, or explaining why they took these positions, they would have discovered their underlying *interests*. Ryan wanted a truck because he was starting up a package delivery service next month and he was trying to build up a fleet of trucks. He needed to pick up the truck this Friday because he had leased new office space for his new business and he had to move out of his old office by this Sunday. He was hoping to have the truck over the weekend to help with the move.

Doug, on the other hand, has a son going off to college next month and he needs $7,500 to pay for college expenses. He also wants to have the truck to be able to move all of his son's possessions to his new college residence next month.

Charting interests, to keep track of them and to keep them as a reference during negotiations, is helpful. For this simple example, the Interests Chart might look like this:

**BOX 14-1**

| Interests | |
|---|---|
| **Ryan** | **Doug** |
| A truck to build his fleet | Money for his son's college expenses |
| A way to move his office next weekend | A way to move his son off to college next month |

## WHY FOCUS ON INTERESTS?

We'll come back to Ryan and Doug in a few minutes to see how much easier it is for them to reach agreement when they focus on their interests. First let's look at three main reasons why it is more effective to focus on interests as opposed to positions. The first reason is that in any given conflict or problem there typically exist many interests, not just those that are apparent on the surface. A good example from the United States is the dispute between groups favoring or opposing gun ownership. The group favoring gun ownership is the National Rifle Association. Its members are typically hunters and sportsmen. Other groups, known as the gun control lobby, support legislation prohibiting the ownership of certain types of guns. These two groups take different stands on pending legislation so often that most people assume that they are opposed on every issue.

If, however, you were to review the literature each group publishes, you would learn that both groups have a strong interest in anticrime legislation; both groups have a strong interest in a system for quick and easy background checks on people legitimately wishing to buy guns for hunting or protection; and both groups have a strong interest in keeping guns away from criminals. Both groups have an interest in fighting terrorism.

It would be easy to assume that these two groups had no common interests by just focusing on their most publicized adversarial positions. Once you focus on their underlying interests, however, you learn that they have significant common interests. If these two opposing groups were to join forces on those common interests, they would be a powerful political force and could no doubt get Congress to pass legislation to those ends. This shows how focusing on interests rather than positions can help discover areas of mutual interest, which dramatically increases the chances of successfully negotiating your way through conflict.

In many cases, even in situations where the positions conflict, the underlying interests may not. Linda and Shelly are two sisters arguing over who should get to use the family car that afternoon. Each takes the position that she should get the car because the other sister drove it last. Their father can't remember who got it last, so he flips a coin to see who gets the car. One sister wins; the other loses.

The outcome would have been different had they talked about their underlying interests. Linda wanted the car so that she could go to the movies. Shelly wanted the car so that she could go study at the library. The theater and the library are less than a mile apart. Had they discussed their interests, one sister could have had the car and dropped off the other sister on the way, then picked her up on the way home. Their positions conflicted, their interests did not.

A real-life example of this occurred during a labor strike in

Southern California. Management and the union had reached agreement on just about everything except salary. The union was rigid in its position that it had to get a 5 percent raise for its members and nothing else would do. The district was growing rapidly and management knew it would be in better shape financially next year, but was adamant that it couldn't afford anything more than 2.5 percent for the current year. The parties were at loggerheads; neither side would budge. They simply kept repeating their demands while thousands of kids were out on the streets instead of in classrooms.

When the discussion finally shifted away from their intractable positions and to their underlying interests, it became clear that the union had painted themselves into a corner. They had realized much too late that the available funds would not support a 5 percent raise, but they had promised their members they would improve the salary schedule by 5 percent. The union realized their underlying interest wasn't so much the money as it was in keeping a promise to their members. Once this was clear, the negotiators started work on a different problem: How do we increase the salary schedule by 5 percent with only 2.5 percent money? Since management believed their financial position would improve the following year, the parties agreed to give a 5 percent raise, but had it start more than halfway through the school year.

The union met its interest in keeping its promise to their members by getting a 5 percent increase in the salary schedule. Management met its interests of staying within the budget and avoiding deficit spending. The positions of each side, 5 percent for the union and 2.5 percent for management, were directly conflicting. The underlying interests of both sides, staying within the budget for management and keeping their promise to their members for the union, did not conflict.

The third and most important reason for focusing on interests instead of positions is that for every interest there are usually many ways of satisfying the interest. Any position taken is merely one way of satisfying the underlying interest. If parties focus on positions, they often exclude many other possible solutions that may work just as well as, or even better than, their favorite position.

Now look back once again on the negotiation between Ryan and Doug over the sale of the truck. Knowing what their interests are, as opposed to their positions, many more options are apparent. For example, they could make the sale on Friday and Ryan could lend the truck back to Doug for the weekend he moves his son off to college.

Perhaps they could make the sale next month and Doug could lend the truck to Ryan this weekend to move his offices. Perhaps Ryan could pay Doug an extra $500 so that Doug could have all of his son's stuff shipped off to college. Maybe Ryan could even offer to move the son's stuff with his new delivery business at a discount. These are all options that might not have been apparent had the parties only looked at positions rather than their interests.

---

**BOX 14-2**

Three Reasons It Is Easier to Reconcile Interests Than Positions

1. Often, multiple interests are involved.
2. Interests may not conflict even though positions conflict.
3. There are usually several methods of satisfying any interest.

---

## DISCOVERING INTERESTS

Many parties in conflict will only have a vague sense of the interests of the other party. A surprisingly large number of parties don't even have a good understanding of their own interests, much less the interests of the other side. Failing to understand interests is a huge roadblock to successful problem solving. If you are trying to establish a long-term, mutually beneficial business relationship, it is crucial that you develop a good understanding of the interests of all the stakeholders in the conflict.

-------------------------------------------------------------

Tool 14-1

## Role Reversal

In preparing for a negotiation, one of the best ways to understand the interests of the other party is to do a "role reversal." Put yourself into the place of the other side. Try to articulate what they are seeking from the negotiation and, more importantly, why they are seeking it.

We have used this common technique with great success in legal settlement conferences, executive coaching, counseling with married couples, and business groups in conflict. We start by asking the parties to educate us about the dispute. In a legal dispute we might start with the plaintiffs; however, we wouldn't ask them to explain their side of the dispute. Rather, we would ask them to explain the respondents' side of the dispute. When they finish, we turn to the respondents and ask if the plaintiffs' description was accurate and complete. Usually it isn't. We then ask the respondents to talk about what is missing or why the plaintiffs' description is not accurate. Then the plaintiffs are asked again to state the respondents' argument to the satisfaction of the respondents. This may take several rounds of clarifying and explaining, but when done, the plaintiffs typically have a different, and more thorough, understanding of the dispute.

The same process is repeated with the other side until both sides not only have a thorough understanding of the other side's case and underlying interests, but also can articulate them to the satisfaction of the other side. Not until then is it worthwhile trying to invent options leading to an agreement.

Obviously, in your preparation for a meeting you won't usually have the opportunity for a role reversal with the other side present. You will, however, be able to switch places with them in your imagination. Perhaps you can assign part of your team or a friend to play the role of the other party. The object is simply to try to get a better understanding of the other party's interests.

---

**BOX 14-3**

Put yourself into the place of the other side. Try to articulate what they are seeking from the negotiation and, more importantly, why they are seeking it.

---

Tool 14-2

## Worst Critic Analysis

Another tool is the "worst critic analysis." With this tool you focus on the worst internal critic the other party will have to deal with before they agree to any settlement. Ask yourself, "What will the critic's strongest points be? How will the critic argue against any solutions?" This can give a better perspective of the difficulties faced by the other side. It can also help you invent solutions and communications strategies to assist the other side in "selling" any proposed settlement to its constituencies.

If you're trying to form a relationship with the plant manager of a manufacturing company and you believe that the manager of their design engineering department is opposed to the deal, you'd better understand the interests of the engineering manager. Anticipating the arguments and underlying interests of the engineering manager will help you support the plant manager and build the relationship.

------------------------------------------------------------

## HISTORY PLAYS A ROLE

History can also have a powerful influence on the interests of the parties. When Iraq invaded Kuwait, the United Nations assembled an enormous multinational fighting force to combat Iraq. At the same time the United Nations was building up its forces, it was asking Israel, which was clearly the most heavily armed country in the region, to avoid involvement. Israel was urged not to react when Scud missiles were landing on its cities. The interests underlying this strategy would make no sense to anyone without a good understanding of the Arab-Israeli conflict. Having that historical understanding made it easier to see that it was not in Israel's interest to join the UN forces. Other Arab countries would not have been so unified against Iraq if Israel had joined their ranks.

When the San Jose Unified School District became the first school district in the history of California to go bankrupt, it had a profound impact on the interest analysis of the parties for a long time. For years after the bankruptcy, the school board wanted to maintain a larger than average ending balance in their budget so that they wouldn't have to fear budget shortfalls. Employees had interests about security issues that we didn't see in other school districts in the state during that time. Without some knowledge of the history of the bankruptcy in that district, it would have been impossible to do an accurate interest analysis.

## IS IT SYMBOLIC?

Sometimes what may appear to be an interest is really only a symbol for a much deeper interest. For example, a person may try to justify a new purchase of an automobile because of an interest in better transportation, or a new cell phone because of an interest in better telecommunications. By digging deeper, however, it's possible to discover that better transportation or telecommunications may not be the real interest. What may in fact be the real underlying interest is the individual's need to impress his in-laws, who claimed he would never be successful.

If this person's employer tried to solve a transportation problem by giving him a used bicycle or arranging a car pool or investigating possible bus routes, it would not satisfy the employee's true interest. If the employer tried to solve his telecommunications problem by giving him money to use in a pay phone, it would also fail to satisfy the real interest. The new car and the new cell phone are only symbolic of the real underlying interest of building esteem in the eyes of his in-laws.

If the employer wanted to satisfy the real interest, it wouldn't waste time or money trying to solve transportation or telecommunications problems. Rather, it would recognize the interest of impressing the in-laws and, if it chooses to, assist in that area by possibly giving the worker a new, more impressive job title or other recognition of success.

## INTANGIBLES ARE IMPORTANT

Don't forget about the intangible interests of all humans to be treated fairly. All people want to have their views fully heard and understood (even if they are ultimately rejected), and not to feel taken advantage of. Over the years a huge number of disputes could easily have been settled with an honest and sincere apology, in recognition of those intangible interests. If they are delivered in a believable way, words like the following can often satisfy the most basic interest of being treated with respect:

> We are truly sorry for the hurt and stress we have caused you. We did not realize it would affect you the way it did and have taken steps so that it will never happen again.

These intangible interests come into focus most often when they are not being met. If things are going well, we tend not to worry about them. If, however, meetings are canceled arbitrarily, phone calls are not returned, or negotiators are personally rejected or humiliated in other ways, intangible interests take on great significance.

## BE AWARE OF CULTURAL ISSUES

Cultural issues can also play a role in understanding interests. We were in China with Dean Judy Teng of City College of San Francisco negotiating a new training program. The negotiations seemed to go well. We didn't get a contract; however, we did get invited back for another round of negotiations. The next time we didn't get a contract either; but we did get a letter of intent that said, in a vague way, that at some point in the future the Chinese company intended to do business with us. It took several more trips to agree on a contract.

This could have been more frustrating than it was, had Dean Teng not been aware of the cultural issues involved. The contract was really not the issue, because even if we did get a contract, it would be difficult if not impossible to enforce; certainly not practical considering the costs and difficulties of trying to litigate in China. The business arrangement we were negotiating would not be governed by a contract. It would be governed by the strength of our relationship. The underlying interest, which was driven by cultural issues, was in having a strong relationship, not in having a strong contract.[1] Negotiating a contract was simply a tool for building a relationship.

---

**BOX 14-4**

**Cultural Issues Affect Our Interests**

The early bird gets the worm.
*American proverb*

The lead bird in the flock is the first to be shot.
*Chinese proverb*

Don't just sit there; do something.
*Protestant value*

Don't just do something; sit there.
*Zen value*

---

## ARTICULATING INTERESTS

The easiest way to gain understanding about interests is to ask probing questions such as "Why is that in your interest?" or "Why would our solution not be in your interest?" Remember to ask your questions from the Green Zone. You should be asking for education, not justification. It should be more like "Help me understand why this is important to you" rather than "What makes you think you deserve that?" Your questions should communicate a sincere desire to better understand the interests of the other side.

Be hesitant to move on to the next step until you can articulate what you believe are their interests. You should understand the interests to the point where they seem to be a rational basis for any action or positions the other side has taken, or you expect them to take. Most people act rationally considering their beliefs about their own interests. If their actions seem irrational based upon your understanding of their interests, it is a safe assumption that you don't really understand their interests.

---

**BOX 14-5**

If the other person's actions seem irrational, it's probably because you don't understand their underlying interests.

---

Keep in mind that when you are doing your preparation and trying to understand the interests of the other party, you are often making assumptions about their interests. People rarely have enough information to make a completely accurate interest analysis of someone else's interests without a dialogue. It is crucial, therefore, that when you do have the opportunity to meet with the other party, you take time to verify the accuracy of your assumptions. A positive way to do that might sound like this:

Hi, Janelle. I've been giving thought to what our interests are regarding that contract we need to renegotiate. I'd like to take some time to tell you my understanding of your interests. I don't want to forget any or misinterpret them, so I was hoping you could give me some feedback about my understanding. If I've left anything out or misunderstood anything, maybe you can let me know. At some point I'd also like to explain all my interests to you as well, so we both have a better understanding of what we're dealing with.

Notice if you have any resistance in trying to understand and to articulate the interests of the other side. If your resistance is preventing you from seeking that understanding, you will be well served by taking time to look at that resistance. What is keeping your mind closed? What are you worried about learning? Your resistance is a telltale sign of your own defensiveness.

---

**BOX 14-6**

Your resistance to understanding the interests of the other side is a major sign of your own defensiveness. If you feel resistance, go directly back to chapter 2. Do not pass Go. Do not collect $200.

---

Let's practice with a case study:

--------------------------------------------------------------------------------

Exercise 14-1

## Monica and Andre Interest Analysis

Read the conversation between Monica and Andre in the box below and list a few of the interests they are identifying.

---

**BOX 14-7 MONICA AND ANDRE DIALOGUE**

**Andre:**    I think we should buy that last three-bedroom house we looked at.

**Monica:**  It sure is close to where we both work. I hate that commute of ours; all that stop-and-go traffic is killing me.

**Andre:**    Me too. I'd rather look for another job than spend much more time in traffic like this.

**Monica:**  I'd rather buy that first house we looked at. Although one thing is clear; we need to have three bedrooms.

**Andre:**    It was nice that it had three bedrooms so Junior could have a room of his own and we could also have our office. I don't think we could get by without space for an office.

**Monica:**  The last house was so expensive. I don't think we could still afford to put money away for Junior's college fund.

**Andre:**    Yeah, I agree. If we don't put money away for college now, we'll never be able to save enough by the time he's ready to go.

---

List a few of the interests you noticed here:

_____

_____

_____

_____

_____

If you listed a three-bedroom house, a shorter commute, and money for Junior's college, you're close, but not quite there yet. The three-bedroom house is a possible solution, not an interest. The real underlying interest is a bedroom for Andre and Monica, a bedroom for Junior, and space for an office. A three-bedroom house would satisfy those interests; however, there might also be other ways to satisfy them. For example, there might be a two-bedroom house with a place in the garage or an attic that would work well for an office but not as a bedroom.

If you said a shorter commute, once again you've focused on a solution, not necessarily on the underlying interest, which is to not spend time in traffic. Another possible solution might be to move farther away from work but live close to a commuter train line. Their commute might actually be longer, but they would be able to spend that time more productively on the train and they would still be spending less time in traffic.

It is easy to miss the real underlying need unless you form a habit of asking yourself, "Why do they need that and what underlying need does that really satisfy?"

## GET THE INTERESTS OF ALL THE PARTIES

Often several parties are involved in a dispute or problem. It is important to do an interest analysis for each party. In a typical teachers' strike, we would do an interest analysis for the teachers' union and the management team headed by the superintendent. The school board, however, also has interests, which may or may not overlap with the interests of the management team. Don't forget that management is appointed, but the school board is elected, so their constituencies are not identical. Usually there is a parent-teacher group that has its own separate interests, as well as a taxpayer group. Although the bus drivers, aides, maintenance workers, and clerical and food service employees may not be at the bargaining table, any settlement may have a potential impact on their pay or working conditions, so they need to be considered also.

You can see that in multiparty situations an interest analysis can get complex. If you expect to create an agreement that has a high chance of compliance, it's important to take the time to understand the interests of all the stakeholders.

------------------------------------------------------------------

Exercise 14-2

## Understanding Interests

This is a chart for you to do an interest analysis for your own problem that you have selected. If you have more than two parties to the dispute, just get an additional piece of paper to do an interest analysis for each party.

| BOX 14-8 | |
| --- | --- |
| | **Interests** |
| **Our Interests** | **Their Interests** |
| | |

------------------------------------------------------------------

## CHAPTER SUMMARY

People typically learn to negotiate their way through conflict by asking for the moon or offering little. Then through compromise, trade-offs, or the superior strength of one side over the other, they reach a solution that is usually acceptable. However, agreements reached that way may not be optimal. The Interest-Based approach is a process where instead of leading with your favorite solutions, you spend your energy understanding all of the underlying interests of the parties involved, both yours and those of the other people. Not until you have a good understanding of everyone's interests can you move on to creating solutions.

Focusing on interests is more productive than arguing over positions because often there are multiple interests. An interest reflects an underlying need as opposed to a position, which reflects a favorite solution. Some interests may overlap and form the beginning of an agreement. Also, interests may not conflict even when positions do. Finally, there are usually several ways to satisfy any interest.

A good tool for gaining an understanding of interests is to put yourself in the role of the other party. Imagine the problem from their point of view. Until you can articulate their interests to their satisfaction, you don't really understand them. A "worst critic" analysis is a tool that also helps you anticipate the internal opposition the other side will need to deal with. It is an additional way of understanding the interests as perceived by critics on the other side. Also don't forget to look at the history of the parties when trying to understand interests, as well as cultural issues and the intangibles of being fairly treated and fully heard.

In your planning, you are speculating and making assumptions about the other side's interests. Once you get together, it is crucial that you have a thorough dialogue to check those assumptions and become fully educated about all the interests involved.

# CHAPTER 15

# WHAT SHOULD WE DO IF WE CAN'T REACH A SOLUTION?
## (Developing a Contingency Plan)

**What are you** going to do if you can't find a solution? If you don't know that, you're not prepared. You will be at a tremendous disadvantage in your negotiations if you do not have a well-thought-out contingency plan in case negotiations fail. Someone without such a strategy will have no measure of success. Their only reference point to measure the value of possible solutions is their hopes and dreams or fears. People trying hard to build collaborative relationships are vulnerable to the seduction of agreeing with the other side just to build the relationship if they have no well-thought-out contingency plan.[1]

Without a well-thought-out contingency plan it may be too easy to enter into an unfavorable agreement out of a sense of desperation. The opposite is also true. Negotiators may get rigid on a given issue and may be willing to sacrifice an entire agreement even though it is better than any other available opportunities. In either of these situations, a thorough understanding of a contingency plan could have saved the negotiators from a mistake.

In the first example, they would have realized that the negotiated deal would not be as advantageous as the contingency plan. They would have rejected the agreement and moved on to their contingency plan. In the second example, they would have realized that the negotiated agreement, although not including all that they had hoped for, was nevertheless better than any other course of action available.

---

**BOX 15-1**

People who want collaborative relationships and have no contingency plan are vulnerable to the seduction of agreeing with the other side just to build the relationship.

---

## CAN YOU IMPROVE YOUR CONTINGENCY PLAN?

It is always time well spent doing whatever you can to improve your contingency plan. The stronger your plans that are separate and apart from any negotiated agreement, the stronger you will be in the negotiation.

Imagine that you own a small café with outdoor tables shaded by large trees. One day your neighbor has cut down some trees that you believe were on your side of the property line. You want the trees replaced or at least to be reimbursed for the cost of replacing them. You want to maintain a good relationship with your neighbors, so you are trying to resolve the dispute using a neighborhood mediation service. If you can't reach a settlement with your neighbors, you figure you have three possible contingency plans. You could replace the trees yourself at a cost of about $3,000 and considerable time and effort on your part; you could do nothing and live without any trees on that side of the café; or you could go to small claims court and if you win, you would get reimbursed for all your expenses.

After reviewing these three possibilities, you believe your contingency plan will be to go to small claims court. You've researched the issue and know you have a strong legal case. You don't feel completely comfortable with this plan, however, because you aren't quite sure how small claims court works and you're a little afraid you'll make a mistake when you are in front of the judge.

Some ways of improving your contingency plan might be for you to go to the library to check out some how-to books about small claims court. You could also spend an afternoon or two watching Judge Wapner on TV to see how people do it in his court. You could even go down to the local small claims court and sit in on a few cases to become more familiar with how it works and how to tell your story. You could rehearse telling your story to a friend. These are all ways of improving the strength of your contingency plan. Once you feel more comfortable that you can do a good job in small claims court, you are in a much stronger negotiating stance.

A manager and an employee are in a dispute that might result in the employee being terminated if they can't reach an agreement. The employee might improve his contingency plan by seeking legal representation or updating his résumé and looking for other work. The manager might improve her contingency plan by preparing for litigation or searching for other candidates to replace the employee if the employee is eventually terminated.

If you are having conflict with a parts supplier, it will strengthen your negotiating hand if you spend time finding other possible suppliers. If you have only one source for the parts, you have a weaker contingency plan than if you have three other possible suppliers lined up.

## AGREEMENTS MUST BE BETTER THAN ALL CONTINGENCY PLANS

It is helpful to understand, as best as you can, your counterpart's contingency plan. Any final agreement will have to be better than the contingency plans of both parties. Any party with a contingency plan better than the negotiated agreement will probably reject the agreement. If your counterpart has opportunities that are better than anything you can offer, it would save you a lot of wasted time and energy to find that out early.

Likewise, it would be a tremendous advantage knowing that your counterpart has no other opportunities available and may be quite desperate to reach an agreement with you. If that is the case, of course, they're unlikely to share that information with you. You will then have to make some assumptions about their contingency plan. Any chance to check those assumptions will be worth the effort. Doing research, asking questions, and looking at past actions or patterns all give you a more informed understanding of your counterpart's other opportunities.

It may be helpful or necessary to share your contingency plan with the other party. If you have a better contingency plan than what is being offered and your counterpart appears to be unyielding, it may be helpful to say something like "The proposal before us now is simply not in our interest to accept. We have other opportunities that will offer us a greater return (or more control or whatever the sticking point is)."

---

**BOX 15-2**

Your contingency plan is your measure of success. It will keep you from entering into a bad agreement or rejecting a good one.

---

## CAUTIONARY NOTES!

There are three cautionary points about sharing your contingency plan. First, it is crucial that if you share your contingency plan, you share it with the intent and effect of educating your counterparts rather than threatening them. If it is communicated as a threat, e.g., "You'd better yield on this point or we'll go someplace else," it will have a negative impact on relationship issues and drive others into a Red Zone reaction. People typically find education helpful, but react to threats in counterproductive ways, i.e., getting rigid themselves.

The second caution is, do not cry wolf. Don't use your contingency plan as a bluff, because your counterpart may call your bluff. If you are not prepared to implement your contingency plan, it is not effective. One of our past clients, a U.S. company, sells parts to a Chinese company. The sale was in the tens of millions of dollars. The Chinese company demanded that the U.S. company match what the Chinese company said was a price offer of a competitor. The U.S. company felt that it would have to take a loss if it lowered its price that low, so it broke off negotiations and prepared to return to the United States.

The negotiating relationship changed rather dramatically two hours later when the Chinese delegation came to the hotel and asked to reopen negotiations. It seemed that while the competitor's price had been lower, other factors made that deal unacceptable to the Chinese company. They had no other offer that they could actually accept. The bluff had been called, and their deception had been uncovered. This not only put the U.S negotiators in a significantly stronger bargaining position with the Chinese company, but also caused a great loss of face for the Chinese negotiators. When the deception became obvious, it also lowered the trust level for future negotiations.

The third and final caution is to be hesitant in revealing your contingency plans if your counterpart can block them or reduce their effectiveness. A contingency plan that can easily be influenced by your counterpart is ineffective and should ideally be revised and improved or at least not volunteered. If you're negotiating with Thomas to do all your local shipping and your contingency plan is to hire William, the only other trucker in town, and William and Thomas are brothers, you don't have much of a contingency plan unless the brothers are not getting along well.

Some negotiation books urge not only that you try to improve your contingency plan, but also that you try to worsen the other side's possible contingencies. This makes a lot of sense if you are talking about a one-shot negotiation, or if you plan on maintaining an arm's-length relationship with the other side. This book, however, is about building long-term collaborative relationships. We have seen it backfire time after time when a relationship partner does something to undermine the other side's possible contingencies. It's best to assume that such actions will always be discovered, and when they're found out, it will be destructive to the relationship. If you are in a relationship and the other side has a contingency plan available that is much better than anything you can offer, you are probably better off in the long term giving them your blessing to take the other deal.

---

**BOX 15-3**

**Cautionary Notes!**

1. If you decide to share your contingency plan, do it to educate others, not to threaten them.
2. Don't ever cry wolf, using your contingency plan as a bluff. Your bluff may get called to your great disadvantage.
3. Avoid sharing your contingency plan if your counterparts have the ability to block it.

---

Exercise 15-1

## Contingency Plans

Take some time to reflect on the contingency plans for both yourself and the other side in the problem you've chosen to work on using this process. Using the chart on the following page, list as many possibilities as you can for each side. Then go back and develop the most effective and coherent plan you can for what you would do if you are unable to reach an agreement. Also develop what you believe is the most likely plan that your counterparts can exercise.

---

BOX 15-4

## Contingency Plans

| Our Plans | Their Plans |
|---|---|
|  |  |

## CHAPTER SUMMARY

Your well-thought-out contingency plan is your best measure of success in negotiations. A good understanding of your plan will prevent you from entering into a bad agreement or rejecting a good agreement. It is always worth your while to try to improve your plan. The stronger your possibilities that are independent of a potential agreement, the greater leverage you will have in the negotiations. It is important that you try to understand the other side's available contingencies as well as your own. Any agreement will have to be better than the contingency plans of both sides. If either party has a contingency plan that is better than any proposed agreement, they shouldn't enter into the agreement.

If you decide to share your plan, make sure you do it from the Green Zone, trying to educate the other side rather than threaten them. Don't use your contingency plan as a bluff. If you can't carry it out, it isn't a contingency plan: it's just smoke and mirrors that will work to your disadvantage when the smoke clears. Finally, avoid sharing you contingency plan if your counterpart has the ability to block it or lessen its effectiveness.

## CHAPTER 16
# NOW WE GET TO THE FUN PART!
## (Inventing Creative Solutions)

**Now is the** time to switch from the investigative to the creative. You have set an inclusive tone, agreed upon the problems that need to be resolved and the process to resolve them, and understood each other's interests. You also know what you'll do if you can't reach an agreement. Now it's time to move to the creative part of the process. This is where you invent creative solutions to the conflict.

## TEN GUIDELINES FOR INVENTING CREATIVE SOLUTIONS

Here are some guidelines about inventing solutions.

### Guideline #1: Be firm about getting your interests met, but flexible about how you get them met.

Some people have a mistaken idea that being collaborative means being weak. That is not what we are urging. We urge you not to give up or compromise unless it is in your interest to do so. We want you to be absolutely tenacious about getting your interests met. However, we urge you to be flexible about how you get those interests met. There are usually many ways to meet any given interest.

Think back about the sale of Doug's truck to Ryan from chapter 14. When we looked at the interests involved and not just the positions, it was easy to invent several solutions that met all their interests well. They didn't have to compromise or give up anything. By being flexible about how they got their interests met, they were able to get them met 100 percent. The key is to invent lots of different ways to meet those interests.

## Guideline #2: Always look for mutual gains.

Try to exploit mutual interests. We sometimes come across parties who refuse to take an action in their own best interest because it will also benefit the other side. They want to get something for it, as though it were a concession. If one party refuses to do something in their own best interest simply to put pressure on the other side, it sends a negative, spiteful message that the relationship is of little value.

If one side takes action early that can result in a benefit not only to themselves, but also to the other side, it sends a positive message about the value of a long-term relationship. One school district we worked with applied for special federal funding that would result in increased salaries for some of its employees even though the district was under no obligation to renegotiate salaries for another two years. It sent a strong message to employees and the union that the district was seeking real solutions to salary issues and not simply positioning itself for the next round of negotiations.

## Guideline #3: Take advantage of complementary interests.

If, however, your interests aren't mutual, try to have your interests *dovetail*. Four partners in a construction company were experiencing great conflicts over their work assignments. During a mediation session they discussed all their interests and discovered that two partners loved building commercial office buildings. Another partner preferred the custom residential market because he felt he could be more creative and he enjoyed tailoring his work to the needs of individual clients. The fourth partner found it exciting to speculate in real estate rather than construct buildings. This led to a more effective distribution of their work that allowed their complementary interests to dovetail. One partner spent time acquiring land for the others to build on. Two partners concentrated on commercial buildings, and the other partner concentrated on residential custom homes.

If your interests don't dovetail, try to fulfill them in a way that doesn't do damage to the interests of the other side. The four construction partners mentioned above had a problem with a piece of property they all owned. The partner specializing in residential construction wanted to put two custom homes on the property. The two partners doing commercial building were worried about that because the company also owned a larger adjoining piece of property where they wanted to build a large office complex. The commercial builders believed that having two expensive custom homes next to their proposed office complex would make it more difficult for them to get the building permits they needed from the city planning department.

All four partners worked together to find a contractor specializing in apartments and condominiums, and they agreed to a real estate swap. Having apartments and condominiums next to their office complex would be beneficial rather than detrimental. The residential builder got an equally attractive location for his custom homes. Although the interests of the partners at first seemed conflicting, they were all able to get their interests met without doing damage to the interests of the other partners by working together to trade real estate with a third builder.

To recap, first exploit any mutual interests you have. If your interests aren't mutual, then try to have them dovetail or at least get them met without doing damage to the interests of the other party.

---

**BOX 16-1**

**Getting Your Interests Met**

1. Exploit mutual interests first.

2. If interests aren't mutual, then try to have your interests dovetail.

3. If you can't have your interests dovetail, then try to get your interests met without doing damage to the interests of the other party.

---

## Guideline #4: Separate the process of inventing options from judging or evaluating those possible solutions.

If people evaluate options as they are trying to invent them, it often stifles creativity. Everyone is under incredible pressure to solve problems instantly and move on to the next problem. People typically evaluate ideas as they invent them and will often adopt the first possible solution that seems to resolve the conflict. By doing that, they usually never get to the second, third, or fourth possible option, which might be much better than the first option. We're not saying that the first, most obvious solution isn't the best. If, however, you adopt the first option, it should be because it is your best option, not because it is your only option.

Evaluating ideas as they are being invented also discourages individuals within groups from sharing their creative thoughts. No one wants to be thought of poorly. If ideas are to be judged by the group as they are proposed, the natural tendency is to try to work out all the potential flaws in a proposal before offering it to the group.

To experience this, try a brainstorming session where participants are encouraged to put forth ideas no matter how improbable, incomplete, or silly they may appear. Then try a different issue with the ground rules changed. This time, give the same instructions except that after each participant makes a proposal, have the group have a thorough discussion of the value of that proposal.

In most cases, the output of the two groups will be dramatically different. In the first method, where the parties are free to make any proposal, people tend to offer ideas even though they are not well thought through. This, however, gives the group the chance to build on incomplete ideas, to piggyback ideas, or to use bits and pieces of the thought processes of various members of the group. The second method, where proposals are evaluated each time, tends to limit the number of proposals put forth. Participants tend not to offer incomplete or partial ideas, but rather hold those ideas and thoughts in their mind, working out the details until they are more complete. This robs the group of the possibility of packaging or piggybacking incomplete ideas.

---

**BOX 16-2**

To generate lots of ideas, separate inventing them from evaluating them. The goal is richness, not rightness.

---

Separating the two processes can also provide powerful protection in groups that have traditionally had an adversarial atmosphere, such as a labor-management negotiation. Parties will often not propose a solution for fear it may signal that they are willing to agree to such a proposal, when in fact they are only willing to think about it and evaluate it. If the ground rules are clear that proposing possible solutions is different from agreeing to solutions, both sides are much freer to propose ideas for consideration without the strings attached to authorship.

---

**BOX 16-3**

By suggesting an idea for future evaluation, neither party is sponsoring the proposal, neither party is claiming it as their own, and most important, neither party is agreeing to any proposal.

---

## Guideline #5: Invent as many options as possible.

We were both raised in Northern California close to where California's gold rush began in the 1800s. In the Sacramento area, one of the rites of passage, therefore, is that every youngster, at one time or another, tries panning for gold. For those of you who have never tried panning for gold, let us explain it. You take gravel, wash the gravel by swirling it around in a large pan, and eventually strain out larger pieces of gravel and hopefully reveal nuggets of gold left in the pan. The theory is that gold is heavier than the gravel and will therefore sink to the bottom of the pan as the gravel gets washed over its slanted sides.

Our experience was that panning for gold is an extremely exciting adventure for a young boy . . . for about three minutes, maximum. After that first pan of gravel, which never included a big golden nugget, we were always more interested in going swimming in the river or fishing. Jim's mother, however, would typically come by and remind everyone that you have to go through a lot of gravel to find a gold nugget. The same is true when looking for good solutions to a problem. The more possible solutions you invent, the greater your chances of providing a good solution.

---

**BOX 16-4**

You have to go through a lot of gravel to find a gold nugget. In our mediation work, we have found the same to be true. It's important to go through a lot of options (i.e., gravel) to find the gold nugget that is the elegant solution to the problem you are trying to solve.

---

## Guideline #6: Do not assume a fixed pie.

Many people believe that negotiations are a zero-sum game: the size of the pie is fixed, and the negotiation is simply the process by which the pie is divided. It is worth both parties' time trying to increase the size of the pie.

For example, California school districts had the option of taking money out of their general fund to put into a special maintenance fund, in order to get matching federal grants for maintenance. They weren't required to do this, but it could expand the size of the budget before they had to divide it up. Municipalities can often look to the federal government to get funds supporting economic development. These are ways of increasing the size of the pie for which parties are negotiating.

Two businesses dividing the profit from the sale of a product developed by a joint venture may have more flexibility if they negotiate the future profits on new products as well. Even two colleagues deciding where to have lunch can expand the size of the pie to create more solutions by agreeing where to go to lunch for the next two or three times rather than the single upcoming lunch. For example, we will go to your choice this time, but my choice next time. These are all simple examples of expanding the size of the pie, which increases flexibility, creativity, and the possibility of an acceptable solution.

The tendency is to assume that most negotiations center on big-ticket monetary items. Most day-to-day conflicts, however, arise from nonmonetary issues, where opportunities for increasing the size of the pie are abundant. For example, who gets which office is often a highly contested nonmonetary item. When and where to hold the company's annual conferences, who gets to go to which training programs, where to go on a family vacation, and what movie to rent need not end up as zero-sum negotiations.

---

**BOX 16-5**

Remember, even if you can't expand the pie, bad negotiating can shrink the size of any pie.

---

Just as important, keep in mind that it's possible to shrink the size of any pie through bad negotiating. All too often parties lose potential mutual gains because they get rigid in their thinking and overlook possible gains.

## Guideline #7: Put as much energy into solving the other side's problem as you do your own.

What you should be seeking is a productive and profitable long-term relationship. That cannot occur if either side is not getting their needs met over the long term. If one party has no faith that the other side is also concerned about their problems, trust in the relationship and optimism about its success will certainly be diminished. A one-sided relationship also tends to further rigid thinking. A party whose interests are not taken into consideration will be less likely to be flexible when the other side has problems. Just as in a personal relationship, a business marriage does not thrive if the problems on one side are neglected. One-sided agreements are not compliance-prone. They tend to promote passive-aggressive behavior.

## Guideline #8: Look to objective standards for potential solutions, if appropriate.

A great source of "fair solutions" can be standards that are outside the control of the immediate parties and that are readily accepted as legitimate by both parties.

For example, if parties to a joint venture were negotiating the starting salary levels of new engineers, it would be logical to look to industrywide comparability studies, i.e., what other companies are paying new engineers. This information can be obtained from local universities, human resources associations, or business surveys.

Industry practices are also good sources of objective criteria. If it is an industry custom for the local partner to pay the real estate taxes, that may be readily acceptable to both parties simply because it is a well-established procedure. Throughout the United States, the payment of certain escrow fees for the purchase or sale of real estate rarely provokes a heated negotiation simply because a standard industry practice has been accepted by both sides to a transaction as normal. For example, in Sacramento County, the county and city transfer taxes are typically split fifty-fifty between the buyer and seller. The recording costs, pest control costs, and title searches are paid by the seller. The buyer pays any loan appraisal fees and a home warranty fee if the buyer chooses to purchase a warranty. This doesn't mean it always has to be done this way. Either party can seek to negotiate allocation of any closing fees using a different formula or split, but absent a negotiated change, those local customs apply.

If parties were negotiating over the value of land for a new factory that was contributed by one party, a survey of selling prices of similar property would be relevant. Thus, the market value could be independently determined by sales prices of similar properties.

Statutory standards may form the basis of potential solutions. For example, if labor-management negotiators are negotiating new safety standards, they may look to the federal government's Occupational Safety and Health Administration (OSHA) guidelines to determine what is reasonable and fair, or at a minimum required by law.

Objective criteria such as these can offer the parties a way out of confrontational situations. Applicable objective criteria can provide a good starting point upon which parties can mold an acceptable solution. The acceptability of such standards is also increased if they are the result of a joint search for fair criteria. Parties can increase the likelihood of success by starting with a conversation about what would constitute good data and fair standards before they start their search.

### Guideline #9: When equally legitimate interests are at stake, look for fair procedures.

Certain procedures that are accepted by both parties as "fair" can also form the basis of creative solutions. Procedures are different from standards because they can help parties deal with equally legitimate, yet conflicting interests. If, for example, the costs of negotiations in terms of travel expenses and time are disproportionately borne by one side, the parties might agree to taking turns over who travels and where the negotiations occur.

If parties have conflicting interests, they may be willing to agree to a mediator or an arbitration process. Thus, they agree upon a fair procedure to be implemented when they cannot agree on certain substantive issues. This third-party process is often used to resolve disputes about contractual rights.

A slight variation of this theme is "final offer" arbitration. Here the parties do their best to reduce the gap between them. Then they each submit a final, last, best offer to an arbitrator. The arbitrator's authority is limited to picking which of the parties' last offers is to be implemented. The theory behind this procedure is that sometimes parties facing arbitration will maintain an extreme position in the belief that the arbitrator tends to split the difference. In final offer arbitration, the parties know the arbitrator cannot split the difference and is therefore more likely to pick the most reasonable final offer. Thus, the parties will work harder to make their final offer the most reasonable.[1]

To determine who goes first on a particular issue, the parties may agree to flip a coin. It is a quick, easy, and readily acceptable method of resolving equally legitimate interests.

If you have raised children, you will undoubtedly, at some time, have used the "one cuts and the other chooses" procedure for dividing a scarce resource such as the last piece of cake or a single container of modeling clay. If there is even the appearance of goods not being divided exactly equally, one child will be unhappy and the rivalry will be increased rather than reduced. By having one side divide the resource and the other side pick which division it receives, blame for an unequal division is eliminated. This procedure can also work well for two partners dissolving a business and deciding how to divide the assets.

Weighted voting is a variation of cut and choose. Here the disputing parties are each allotted a certain number of points that they can distribute among the items in dispute. The points are assigned as in an auction, with the item going to the highest bidder. If one party wants to spend most of their points on one item, then they run the risk that it will be the only item they end up with. For a thorough and sophisticated discussion of the merits of various methods of dividing assets, we suggest you look at *The Win-Win Solution: Guaranteeing Fair Shares to Everybody,* by Steven J. Brams and Alan D. Taylor. This book is a must read for anyone attempting high-stakes business mediation where assets must be divided.[2]

There is a difference between objective standards, which are sources of information you can refer to in order to determine the value of something, and fair procedures, which are processes you can use to make decisions. Objective standards such as comparability studies, market value, or industry practices are most helpful when seeking solutions to substantive issues such as how much should be paid, what the factory is worth, what discounts distributors should receive, what referral fees brokers or consultants should receive. Fair procedures, such as flipping a coin, taking turns, agreeing to use a third party, or one cuts and one chooses, are most effectively used to resolve legitimate conflicting interests. Standards have a substantive orientation, while fair procedures focus on process. That leads to the final guideline in inventing solutions.

---

**BOX 16-6**

**Fair Standards and Fair Procedures**

Fair *standards,* such as comparability studies, market value, or industry practices, are most helpful when seeking solutions to substantive issues such as how much should be paid, what the factory is worth, what discounts distributors should receive, what referral fees brokers or consultants should receive.

Fair *procedures,* such as flipping a coin, taking turns, agreeing to use a third party, or one cuts and one chooses, are most effectively used to resolve legitimate conflicting interests.

Fair *standards* have a substantive orientation, while fair *procedures* focus on process.

## Guideline #10: Be willing to negotiate over process-related criteria as well as substantive criteria.

We were advising an international airline on the repurchase of one of their early-model airplanes that had been sold to a collector decades earlier. The company had been negotiating for many months over the purchase price. Both sides wanted to complete the transaction, but each side had a very different perception of the value of the airplane. Neither side was willing to make the next move. What changed the dynamics of the negotiations was for the parties to stop negotiating over price and start negotiating over a process to find a fair price.

By shifting the focus from substantive issues to process issues, parties are often able to invent better options. This is particularly true if negotiators are not the actual decision makers and are just acting on orders from above. By negotiating a process to determine fair solutions, each side's negotiators are also given more tools for educating their own constituencies.

---

**BOX 16-7**

**Ten Guidelines for Inventing Solutions**

1. Be firm about getting your interests met, but flexible about how you get them met.

2. Always look for mutual gains.

3. If interests are not mutual, try to have them dovetail or get interests met without damaging the interests of the other side.

4. Separate the process of inventing options from judging or evaluating those possible solutions.

5. Invent as many options as possible.

6. Do not assume a fixed pie.

7. Put as much energy into solving the other side's problem as you do your own.

8. Look to objective standards for potential solutions.

9. With equally legitimate interests at stake, look for fair procedures.

10. Be willing to negotiate over process-related criteria as well as substantive criteria.

## TEN METHODS OF INVENTING CREATIVE SOLUTIONS

Keeping the above *guidelines* in mind, we've listed ten *methods* of generating creative solutions that have been helpful for our clients.

### Method #1: Brainstorming

Brainstorming is one of the most effective techniques for developing creative options. It works best in a group setting, when working on a specific problem. As a group, review the goals and ground rules. For example, generate lots of ideas, refrain from judging them, record all ideas, and encourage piggybacking of ideas.

When some members of the group tend to dominate meetings, try the nominative group technique. In this method of brainstorming, participants are asked to spend a few minutes quietly writing out their own ideas before recording ideas as a group. Each person is then asked for one idea. After several turns around the group, open the discussion, allowing anyone to offer ideas. This insures that the group benefits from everyone's input.

After generating a large number of ideas, allow discussion for clarification; then eliminate duplications. Then do a critical evaluation of the ideas, keeping in mind the interests you are trying to meet.

### Method #2: Approaching the Problem from a Different Perspective

We tend to get locked into certain mind-sets based upon the circumstances of our particular situations. Individuals with different backgrounds, however, will often resolve problems in radically different ways. The president of the chamber of commerce may approach a problem differently from the local priest; the small-business owner thinks differently from the corporate executive; the student looks at things differently from the high school principal; and the parent has a different approach from the child.

In one of our open-enrollment workshops, one participant drove a Jaguar and was meticulous about its upkeep and maintenance. At one point in the workshop he was complaining about his relationship with a colleague. He said he used to enjoy the relationship, but now the only time they spoke was when there was a problem, and it wasn't fun any longer. Another workshop participant who was a mechanic responded, "Too bad he's not your Jaguar. If you put as much energy into preventative maintenance of that relationship as you do your Jag, it probably wouldn't break down as often." The Jaguar owner hadn't thought about how little energy he put into maintaining the relationship until he compared it to his car by looking through the eyes of a mechanic.

If a problem or issue seems unsolvable, try putting yourself into the shoes of people in radically different circumstances from yourself. Analyze the problem as you think they might and develop solutions as you think they would. If it is difficult to imagine how they might approach the problem, seek them out and ask them. Our experience has been that if you explain what you are seeking, people are more than happy to offer advice.

## Method # 3: Alternating between General and Specific Views

Another way to change perspectives is by looking at the problem in either a more general or a more specific context. This helps prevent losing the forest for the trees. For example, if negotiators are trying to develop a better dispute-resolution system for their two companies forming an alliance, it can be helpful to define the issue in its most general terms, i.e., "we are trying to create a method of resolving alliance interface disputes." Then the negotiators might switch to a narrow perspective, examining the most minute details of the current system to see how well it fits the general goal. By switching back and forth between general and specific views, participants will often discover inconsistencies in past approaches and identify opportunities for improvement.

## Method #4: Dividing Single Issues into Their Various Parts

Often parties are able to resolve all of their differences except for one because there appears to be nothing left to trade off or compromise. This is frequently the case in labor strikes Jim has mediated, where the parties have been able to resolve all issues except for wages. By dividing the single issue of wages into several sub-issues, the negotiators create a greater opportunity for compromise, trade-offs, and linkages of issues.

For example, if parties are down to the final issue of wages and get stuck, they can divide that single issue into smaller issues such as timing of the pay or distribution of resources. A salary increase could be negotiated either for the full year or for only part of the year. It could be offered "across the board" equally to all employees or skewed to encourage new employees into the system or more senior employees to retire. The raise might permanently affect the salary schedule or could be a onetime bonus. Other items of value, such as time off or company-built products, could be substituted for dollars. Thus by viewing wages as numerous issues, rather than a single issue, negotiators increase their chances of finding a creative solution.

---

**BOX 16-8**

Dividing a single issue into several sub-issues creates a greater opportunity for compromise, trade-offs, and linkages of issues.

---

If the sale price is the last issue upon which negotiators are stuck, they might divide the issue into smaller issues such as whether the price is in current or future dollars or dollars at all. Maybe the price could be set in yen, tankers of vodka, or future services. A contractor we worked with who had severe cash-flow problems was able to cover the cost of insurance payments by wallboarding the inside of a building owned by the insurance company. He was able to separate the payment issue into two issues: the total amount, and how it would be paid. Then he was able to create a different way of paying the insurance bill. He paid with services rather than money. By creating more issues, you create more opportunity for flexibility.

## Method #5: Reframing

How many different ways can you describe the issue you are trying to resolve? One of our favorite true stories is an excellent example of reframing that we heard on National Public Radio. An employee loved all aspects of his job except for one: he disliked his boss. After agonizing over the problem for a long time, he finally decided he was going to have to escape from his boss and find another job in spite of what he would be giving up. He called an outplacement firm to help him look for a new job and was told to bring in his résumé the next day.

Fortunately, his wife was teaching a creativity course at a local community college. That night, when discussing the issue with his wife, she helped him to reframe his problem from "How do I get away from my boss?" into "How can I get my boss away from me?" Instead of taking his résumé to the outplacement firm, he took his boss's résumé and hired the firm to find a better job for his boss. When they found one, they made a cold call to the boss and offered him an interview. The boss was eventually hired and left the company. That not only solved the problem as originally defined by the employee, but created a promotional opportunity for him as well.

## Method #6: Reorganizing from the Start

Options are often created based upon the incorrect assumption that existing circumstances are cast in concrete. For example, if a salary plan is being negotiated, the negotiators often focus on how to add new money to the existing plan. It might be more effective for them to develop a completely new plan by looking at the total pot of money available for salaries.

Assuming that the existing structure, processes, or policies cannot be radically altered limits creativity.

## Method #7: Making Wish Lists

Companies or associations with large numbers of employees or members may generate a large number of creative ideas simply by asking for them. An announcement in the employee newsletter or over e-mail about the problem and a request for solutions can mobilize the creative forces of many different perspectives.

The keys are making it easy for people to share their ideas and making sure the employees know their ideas are being considered. The Eastern Region of the U.S. Forest Service increased the number of ideas submitted under the employee suggestion program from an average of sixty-three per year up to six thousand a year by taking the employee input more seriously. They didn't offer money incentives; they simply said that if management did not respond to any employee suggestion within thirty days, the employee was free to go ahead and implement the suggestion as long as it was legal. Employees were more than happy to share great ideas if they believed they were being taken seriously.[3]

## Method #8: Changing the Starting Point or Working Backward

When faced with a problem, most of us will analyze our current situation and then work toward a solution. We get partway to a solution, then hit a stumbling block. By working backward you don't work toward a solution, but instead from the solution.

First ask yourself what the situation would be like if the problem were solved. Maybe you would consider the problem solved if absenteeism was half what it is currently, or your cash flow was stronger, or your work teams were less conflicted and more creative. Once you visualize what the solution would look like, then ask yourself, "What was the last step we had to put in place before the problem was solved?" Then, "What was the next-to-the-last step before the problem was solved?" and so on, working from the solution toward your current circumstances, rather than from your current circumstances toward a solution.

A variation of this method is to simply start your problem solving at a different point in the process. If you know you will reach a stumbling block on your way toward a solution, just start your problem solving on the other side of that blocking point. By diverting your attention from the blocking point, you may find that what you thought was an impenetrable barrier was not even necessary to the process.

## Method #9: Playing "What If" Games

Creativity is tied directly to our ability to fantasize. This method urges participants to change current circumstances through fantasy, and to judge the impact of those changes upon their current goals. Participants might be asked to answer the questions "What if we had twice as much money to run this organization?" or "What if we had to restructure with only half as big a budget as we have now?" or "What if we merged with our competitor or spun off all marketing to another company?" or "What if we let employees work at home or set their own work hours?" A department facing a 10 percent budget cut might gain valuable insight about their true priorities by first discussing a 50 percent cut.

A training company we consulted with faced some belt-tightening because of the loss of a major client. The owners figured they could survive and balance the books if they reduced expenses by 10 percent. Instead of just trying to find a 10 percent savings, however, they discussed how they would organize the company if they were just starting up and had little capital. In doing so, they realized that two areas of their work required huge efforts to maintain, yet produced little income. So instead of cutting back by 10 percent, they decided to eliminate those two areas, cutting overhead by 25 percent, which increased profitability.

## Method #10: Looking for Differences

Many of us work hard to avoid dealing with differences out of fear that raising the issue will drive the parties apart. Negotiators with divergent positions, however, may find a richness of ideas by getting their differences to dovetail rather than ignoring them.

It is helpful to understand the type of differences you face. Certain types of differences lead to certain types of solutions. Individuals with *different skills* will probably be better off *combining their skills* rather than competing against each other, or both trying to do all tasks well.

In just about every teachers strike, negotiators dispute the size of the school district budget's projected ending balance. One side believes the ending balance will be large and the other side believes it will be small, and they base their negotiating strategies on those beliefs. They have a *difference in probability and risk assessment*. That type of difference suggests a *contingency agreement*. The parties agree that if the actual ending balance is larger than a certain amount, then plan A goes into effect. If the actual ending balance is less than that amount, then plan B goes into effect.

---

**BOX 16-9**

Negotiators with divergent positions may find a richness of ideas by focusing on blending their differences, rather than ignoring them.

If individuals have a *difference in time preference*, they might resolve their dispute by *altering their schedules*. Jim's son and daughter shared a bathroom when they were in high school, and getting ready for school in the morning was always a potential disaster. However, their differences in time preferences averted many problems. Ryan was a late-night person, often staying up late doing homework, then sleeping until the last five minutes before he needed to leave for classes. Janelle was a morning person, up at the crack of dawn to give her plenty of time to get ready for school. One obvious solution for sharing the bathroom was for Ryan to take showers at night and Janelle to take showers in the morning.

The classic difference that arises in most negotiations is a *difference in value*. The first person has something that is valued by the second person. The second person has something that is valued by the first person. The natural solution is to *trade* the objects.

---

**BOX 16-10**

**Ten Methods of Generating Creative Solutions**

1. Brainstorming

2. Approaching the problem from a different perspective

3. Alternating between general and specific views

4. Dividing single issues into their various parts

5. Reframing

6. Reorganizing from the start

7. Making wish lists

8. Changing the starting point or working backward

9. Playing "what if" games

10. Looking for differences

---

## CAUTIONARY NOTES!

1. Remember that in your planning, before you have a chance to have a dialogue with your relationship partners, your creative solutions are based to some extent on your speculation about your

partner's interests. Your ideas may contain many assumptions. So don't get wedded to any particular solution before you have a chance to see if it will indeed meet the interests of your partners.

2. Nobody likes to have solutions imposed upon them. The whole point of this process is to foster collaboration. That's why the search for creative solutions needs to be a joint effort. If you march into a meeting and announce that you've created several possible solutions, and you are not open to looking at any new ideas or suggestions from your partner, you will have shot yourself in the foot, completely undermining the whole collaborative process.

--------------------------------------------------------------------

Exercise 16-1

## Inventing Creative Solutions

Use the space that follows to generate as many potential solutions as you can for the real problem you are choosing to work on. You will notice that there is no line drawn down the center of the page as was the case for the "Interests" and "Contingency Plans" charts. That is because we don't distinguish "our solutions" and "their solutions." Since there is no sponsorship of, or agreement with, any option simply by suggesting that the parties evaluate it, it doesn't matter who suggests the possible solution. We just add all of them to the list for our evaluation later in the process.

--------------------------------------------------------------------

BOX 16-11

**Creative Potential Solutions**

## LET'S PRACTICE

Now let's go back and practice identifying Problem Statements, Interests, Contingency Plans, and Solutions.

---

Exercise 16-2

## The Clear Lake Cabin

Roy and Florence are considering remodeling their cabin at Clear Lake. They meet with Terry, their contractor, to discuss the project. In the negotiation between Roy and Florence on one side and Terry on the other, determine whether the statements below reflect Problem Statements, Interests, Contingency Plans, or Solutions.

For Problem Statements (the issue to be resolved) mark P.
For Interests (the reason why, need, or motivation) mark I.
For Contingency Plans (can be done without agreement) mark C.
For Solutions (possible solutions requiring agreement) mark S.

1. ___ Who should design the changes to the house?

2. ___ Roy and Florence hope the job can be finished before their children and grandchildren visit in two months.

3. ___ Roy and Florence could decide not to have the work done.

4. ___ What method of payment will be used?

5. ___ Roy could help Terry do the plumbing.

6. ___ Terry could do the job for $27,000.

7. ___ Roy and Florence could hire someone else to do the job.

8. ___ Roy and Florence could pay 50 percent down and make monthly payments for a year.

9. ___ The job would enable Terry to keep the crew busy during the winter.

10. ___ Terry could refuse to take the job and lay off the company's excess employees for the winter.

11. ___ Roy wants a shower area large enough that he doesn't keep hitting the shower walls each time he turns around.

12. ___ They could build an outdoor shower.

## Answers to Clear Lake Cabin Exercise

1. P  Who designs the changes is a Problem Statement because it is an issue that needs to be resolved in the negotiation between Roy, Florence, and Terry. One possible Solution would be for Terry to design the work. Another possible Solution is for Roy and Florence to do it themselves. They haven't yet resolved this issue.

2. I  Roy and Florence want to get the remodeling done before their family visits them in two months. They have an Interest in getting the job done soon.

3. C  Roy and Florence could decide not to do the job without any agreement from Terry. It is one of their Contingency Plans because they don't need Terry's agreement for this decision.

4. P  This is a Problem Statement because it is an issue that will have to be decided between Roy and Florence and Terry. Roy and Florence can't unilaterally decide to pay with a credit card (which is one possible Solution) if Terry doesn't accept credit cards. Terry can't unilaterally determine the payment method will be cash (another possible Solution) without the agreement of Roy and Florence. This is an issue that still needs to be resolved in their negotiation.

5. S  One possible Solution is that Roy and Terry could agree that Roy will help with the plumbing, thus lowering the cost. A different Solution would be for Terry to do all the work without help from Roy.

6. S  It is a possible Solution for Terry to do the work for $27,000. Other possible Solutions might be for Terry to charge $25,000 or $31,000. This will require the agreement of both Roy and Florence and Terry.

7. C  Roy and Florence can unilaterally decide not to use Terry to do the job. If they can't reach an acceptable agreement with Terry, possible Contingency Plans might be to look for someone else to do the work or perhaps decide not to do the work at all.

8. S  One possible Solution they could all agree on is for Roy and Florence to make a down payment of 50 percent and then pay the balance in monthly installments. Another possible Solution is for Roy and Florence to pay the remaining 50 percent at the completion of the job instead of in monthly payments.

9. I  This reflects Terry's possible underlying Interest in having work for the crew so that the company doesn't have to lay them off during the winter.

10. C  If Terry can't reach an agreement with Roy and Florence that is acceptable, one possible Contingency Plan is to decline the job and lay off some employees during the winter.

11.  I    Roy has an Interest in having a shower that is big enough for him to be comfort-
          able taking a shower.

12.  S    One possible Solution for meeting Roy's interests in a large shower is a fanciful
          idea he's always had, to build a shower outdoors where there is much more space.

----------------------------------------------------------------------------------

## CHAPTER SUMMARY

Parties are now engaged in the creative part of the process, trying to find solutions that will meet as many interests as possible. They should be tenacious about getting their interests met. However, since there are usually many ways to satisfy any interest, they should be flexible about how they get their interests met. Always look for mutual gains. If you find you have mutual interests, exploit them. If interests aren't mutual, then try to align them so they dovetail. If that isn't possible, at least try to get your interests met without doing damage to the other side's interests. The best way to end up with a good solution is to have a large number of options to work with. That is best accomplished by separating the creative inventing process from evaluating the ideas. Invent as many options as possible to find the gold nugget. Look to see if there are ways to expand the size of the pie before you try to divide it.

To create a compliance-prone solution you must address the needs of your partners, so give their problems just as much energy as your own. A rich source of ideas for solutions is objective standards such as industry practices, comparability studies, and wage surveys. If there are equally legitimate interests at stake, look for fair procedures such as taking turns, flipping a coin, using seniority, or one cuts and the other chooses. Finally, always be willing to negotiate over how you can find a fair solution.

# CHAPTER 17
# PUTTING THE PUZZLE TOGETHER
## (Reaching Closure)

**You're in the** final stretch. Now it's time to put the puzzle together.

In the beginning, the parties have concentrated their efforts on building the relationship. They have not rushed into substantive negotiations, but rather have taken ample time to help people feel included in the process. They are clear about their intentions and have come to agreement about the process they will use. The parties then agree on a statement of the problems they need to resolve. In contrast to typical business negotiations, people stay in the Green Zone and don't get rigid or positional about their favorite solutions. Instead the parties focus on understanding the interests of both sides.

The parties have each developed a contingency plan in case they can't reach a mutually acceptable solution. If they can't reach an agreement that's better than their contingency plans, they won't agree to a deal. They engaged in a joint effort to invent a large number of options that meet as many mutual interests as possible. Parties will be firm about getting their interests met, but stay flexible about how they are met.

The next step is to mold those possible solutions into a workable agreement. It will depend a lot on factors such as the size of the group, the type of dispute, time pressures, and the authority of the negotiators to reach final agreement. For example, if the conflict is limited to the two decision makers, it might be as simple as discussing all the potential solutions. Then one person might take the lead by saying something like this:

> Well, after evaluating all of our options against all of our interests, I think a solution that meets our interests and seems fair might be . . . (*spells out the proposal*). How would that work for you?

They then have a proposal on the table they can work from.

It may take more discussion to insure that they meet as many interests as possible. All the while, parties will be comparing any proposal to their contingency plans. When they find a solution they are happy with, they check for both clarity and commitment. That can be as simple as restating the agreement and a handshake, or a written agreement.

The opposite of that is a large group with many constituencies, and representatives who lack the authority to reach a final agreement. We've worked with disputes such as large multiparty bankruptcies and disputes involving international airlines, governments, and regulatory agencies where each step of the process took months, because both of the complexity of the issues and the number of relationships involved.

Steve Barber,[1] one of the leading consultants on the use of Interest-Based methods, was an early proponent on the West Coast of Interest-Based negotiation. He routinely works with large multiparty disputes. A number of his cases have involved from fifteen to forty parties and have taken years to reach agreement.

## USING A STRAW DESIGN TO REACH CLOSURE

A method that's effective in a group situation is to first review and discuss all the options to clarify any questions, eliminate duplication, and eventually eliminate those possible solutions lacking any obvious merit or support. The next step is a thorough discussion of how various options meet the interests of each side and fall within objective criteria. Each party should independently be reviewing all possible solutions against their contingency plans.

Typically, during the discussion about how the options meet interests, a pattern starts to develop and a vague outline of a possible agreement begins to emerge. When that happens, we usually suggest that one party or a subcommittee of both parties fashion a package called a straw design. It's called a straw design because it's not cast in concrete. Criticism cannot hurt a straw design. It's only made of straw and can easily be changed.

Once a straw design is complete, it is presented to the group. But the group isn't asked to approve or reject a proposal at that time, but rather is asked for feedback about how the straw design can be improved to better meet the interests of the parties. That feedback is incorporated into the proposal and a new design is created. That new straw design goes through the same review process, not for approval, but for suggestions for improvement until people are happy with it or it's apparent that it's as good as it is going to get. Only then will negotiators seek a commitment.

For large groups working with complex issues and strong constituencies, this may be a lengthy and time-consuming process of meeting, then taking time to report the straw design back to constituencies, getting feedback from constituencies, then meeting with the negotiations group to revise the straw design based upon the feedback.

---

**BOX 17-1**

**A Straw Design as a Closure Tool[2]**

**When to use a straw design:**

- After a large number of possible solutions have been invented, clarified, and evaluated against the interests of all the stakeholders.

- After the list of possible solutions has been reduced by eliminating clearly unworkable or undesirable solutions.

- When there appears to be a predominance of support for a particular solution or combination of solutions.

**How to make a straw design:**
An individual or subcommittee is selected to draft a proposal that:

- Addresses identified interests of stakeholders.

- Falls within any agreed-upon criteria.

- Incorporates possible solutions developed by the group as a whole.

**The draft proposal is given back to the group for review with the following guidelines:**

- There is no ownership or sponsorship of the draft proposal. It is made of "straw" and criticism cannot hurt it.

- Criticism is sought out, but must be given along with suggestions for how to improve or cure any problems noted in the criticism.

- Input is recorded or submitted in writing.

Those assigned to draft the proposal include the feedback in the next draft. The process is repeated as many times as necessary until a solution is reached. If agreement is not reached, participants should review various methods of "getting unstuck" listed in box 17-3.

## A VISION OF SUCCESS

There is no surefire, cookbook approach to reaching closure. It involves juggling emotions, facts, histories, hopes, fears, and potentials and most of all, relationships. It does help to have an individual to shepherd the process and carry a vision of success for the group. There are as many different styles of reaching closure as there are individuals.[3] What we offer below is a brief description of the process Jim tends to use.

When Jim was mediating complex disputes, as the discussions progressed, he would begin to get a visual image of a settlement that looked like a jumble of puzzle pieces. Each piece of the puzzle was either an individual interest of a party, one of the bits and pieces of their relationship, or some outside pressure. A puzzle piece might be something that one person needed to say to another person. Maybe it was a specific interest that needed to be met. Perhaps it was an issue that needed more resolution. Sometimes it was an image of an outside pressure such as a local politician or other visible leader holding a press conference to set a tone of reconciliation or threaten government intervention.

In his mind, he would create visual images of the various puzzle pieces fitting together. Some pieces would not fit and they would have to be reshaped. Maybe someone wasn't yet ready to let go of a past hurt, so that would require reshaping that piece of the puzzle, perhaps by orchestrating an apology or by helping someone let go of the issue through their own personal growth, or through the power of forgiveness. Sometimes puzzle pieces could be reshaped by helping a voice be heard or a truth be spoken that had been kept silent for too long. Sometimes pieces didn't fit because they lacked fairness or a sense of justice, so that's where time and energy needed to be focused. More often that not, it simply took creativity and a lot of perseverance to help parties sculpt pieces that met their needs and brought resolution to the problem and reconciliation to their relationship.

As the puzzle started to take shape in his mind, he would try to gain preliminary acceptance, piece by piece, of the solution he envisioned. He would ask questions like "If we could figure out a way to solve the problem of X, would that make your claim to Y moot?" As small pieces fit together and larger sections of the puzzle started to materialize, Jim would encourage the parties to visualize a final solution. Once parties started imagining success, it was usually just a matter of time until the optimal solution appeared to everyone. Then it was a process of articulating the solution and documenting it so that everyone had the same understanding of the agreement and commitment to it.

## A DOZEN WAYS TO GET "UNSTUCK"

No methodology guarantees success. Sometimes in spite of everyone's best efforts the parties get stuck and reach an impasse. That can be because the interests are incompatible and it's time to consider letting go of a possible agreement and instead implementing contingency plans. Before you reach that point of giving up and moving on, however, it is worthwhile making every effort to break the impasse. Here are twelve helpful tools and processes to help you break an impasse and get back on the track to an agreement:

1. *Jointly review the interests of all parties and any shared vision of success.* Sometimes simply reminding parties of their interests and what success would look like and feel like is enough to get things moving again.

2. *Look for undiscovered interests.* It may seem as if the proposed solution is doing a good job of meeting all the interests that have been expressed, yet someone is still reluctant to agree to the proposal. This is a sure sign that undisclosed or undiscovered interests are not being met. Sometimes that is because the party may not be aware of the interests. Probing questions such as "Why doesn't this proposal meet your needs?" or "What need is not being met by this proposal?" can help reveal the interests that are not being met.

   Other times, a party may be unwilling to be open about the undisclosed interest. This is a more difficult situation and it raises a Red Zone flag. We suggest that it be dealt with in a straightforward way, from the Green Zone, without shaming or blaming, but with directness. Something like "We seem to have met all of your interests, yet you are still unwilling to agree to this proposal. That leads us to conclude that there are some other interests that you are not sharing with us. Before we start making up our own stories about this, can you tell us what that's about?"

3. *Seek more clarity of the task by reviewing and reaffirming the nature of the problem.* It's easy to get off task and start trying to solve additional

issues that may not have been included in the original problem statement. Just as often, parties find that as they work, the nature of the problem changes. Sometimes parties gain a different understanding of the problem as they start trying to solve it. It can be helpful to check to make sure everyone is still trying to solve the same problem.

4. *Review the problem-solving process being used.* Parties are often tempted to skip steps in the process and prematurely rush directly to inventing solutions. Skipped steps will haunt negotiators when they are trying to reach closure. Make sure you've taken the time to fully complete each step before moving on.

5. *Review your contingency plan and/or discuss the consequences of a failure to reach agreement.* Are you passing up a potential agreement because you do not have a clear understanding of your contingency plan? If contingencies are strong, they can provide good information about how the settlement proposal must be improved to make it acceptable. A review of contingency plans can bring parties back to the reality that they are better off reaching agreement if the contingencies are poor. A discussion of the consequences of a failure to reach an agreement can be sobering. People often underestimate the impact of failure in negotiations. It makes potential implementation of contingency plans much more real, and in many cases that can bring parties back to the table with a renewed sense of purpose.

6. *Review where you have been successful and unsuccessful so far, paying particular attention to patterns that may become evident.* Sometimes patterns emerge that reveal information. For example: "All our successful collaborative efforts involve our manufacturing plants in Denver, Santa Fe, and Stockton. Let's take a look at what we're doing there that we may not be doing in our other locations."

Patterns of failures can also be rich with information: "I notice that every single proposal that includes a joint committee review of the design engineering specs has failed. Maybe we ought to find a better way of doing that."

7. *Do a force-field analysis about getting an agreement.* A force-field analysis looks at the forces that are both helping you move toward a goal or an agreement and hindering your movement in that direction. We usually make two lists, one of the hindering forces

and one of the helping forces. Then we review what we can do to increase the impact of the helping forces and decrease the impact of the hindering forces. See box 17-2 for an example.

---

**BOX 17-2**

**Goal: To improve communications between the front office and shipping**

| Things That Hinder Our Success | | | Things That Help Our Success |
|---|---|---|---|
| We don't know each other's schedule | ⬇ D E C R E A S E  I M P A C T | ⬆ I N C R E A S E  I M P A C T | We hold meetings |
| When people fail to return phone calls | | | When people return phone calls promptly |
| We don't have a good way of leaving messages in the shipping department | | | We get minutes from our regular meetings |
| Orders change every few hours | | | We prioritize projects weekly |

---

This group decided they couldn't do anything about orders changing hourly, but that they could increase their regular meetings from once a week to twice weekly, and someone would take notes that would be sent to everyone that same day. They also had a discussion about their failure to return phone calls promptly. Once several people realized the impact of their not returning calls, they made commitments to be more conscientious about that. They also ordered a new message machine for the shipping department to replace the old one, which was broken.

8. *Take time out (a cooling-off period)*. When people are tired and frustrated, they are not good problem solvers. A little time off for some rest and reflection can bring the mood back to the Green Zone.

9. *Return to inventing solutions using new techniques.* Maybe you just haven't been creative enough in inventing solutions. You haven't yet found the gold nugget. Return to the solution-building stage of the process and in a structured way use different tools to generate many more possibilities. First return to chapter 16 on inventing creative solutions to review the list of guidelines and possible methods of generating ideas. Then pick out two or three methods that you haven't yet tried and lead the group in a new creative process.

10. *Try a pilot project.* Pilot projects can be a wonderful way to experiment with solutions that might be too risky to adopt permanently. They provide an opportunity to try out something new and see how it actually works without having to make a long-term commitment. An important factor in any agreement for a pilot project is having clarity about what happens at the end of the agreed-upon trial period.

    We've seen some parties enter into agreements that lack clarity regarding what happens at the end of the trial, and chaos ensues. One party thought that they would return to the old status quo at the end of the trial period unless the parties specifically agreed to continue the new process. The other party thought the new process would automatically continue at the end of the trial period unless the parties specifically agreed to end it and return to the old status quo. Both sides felt betrayed.

11. *Restructure the group.* Adding new people to the problem-solving team can help generate new energy and enthusiasm in the process. New people can also look at things afresh and add a new perspective. If some people are particularly good at building bridges and problem solving, you may want to create a subcommittee and let those individuals work in a way that is less hampered by the larger group.

    Sometimes some people in groups simply disrupt reaching a solution. Get rid of those people. We want to be clear, however, that we are not suggesting that someone be replaced simply because they disagree with your proposed solution. We are talking about the few individuals who really have more fun fighting than they do getting along. If someone offers no positive energy working toward a solution and does little else than sow the seeds of discontent, you will be doing everyone a disservice to keep him or her involved.

12. *Seek a third party for either process or content assistance.* Groups can get stuck in a couple of ways. They may not have process skills to

create an agreement. Perhaps they have poor communication skills or lack experience with group facilitation or effective meeting protocols. Perhaps they're not inventing good solutions because nobody has ever run a brainstorming session before. A facilitator, mediator, or meeting planner can enrich the group's problem-solving ability by giving them more structure or more effective processes to reach agreement.

Other groups have good process skills but lack experience or expertise with the nature of the problem they are trying to solve. Here it is helpful to bring in an outsider with subject matter expertise: maybe bring in an IT consultant to help set up better communications systems for an alliance. In the school district labor strikes Jim has mediated, negotiators would almost always bring in budget experts because the California school funding process is so bewildering that nobody at the bargaining table (including Jim) had a clear understanding of how much money the district would actually receive the following year.

---

**BOX 17-3**

**Getting Unstuck**

1. Jointly review the interests of all parties and any shared vision of success.

2. Look for undiscovered interests.

3. Seek more clarity of the task by reviewing and reaffirming the nature of the problem.

4. Review the problem-solving process being used.

5. Review your contingency plan.

6. Review where you have been successful and unsuccessful so far, paying particular attention to patterns that may become evident.

7. Do a force-field analysis about getting an agreement.

8. Take time out (a cooling-off period).

9. Return to inventing solutions using new techniques.

10. Try a pilot project.

11. Restructure the group.

12. Seek a third party for either process or content assistance.

## CLARITY AND COMMITMENT

What you want to end up with is a compliance-prone agreement: an agreement that people voluntarily, proactively, and wholeheartedly support because they think it is fair. It must reflect both clarity and commitment. It must meet the interests, at least reasonably so, of everyone who has the ability to undermine the agreement.

We see lots of examples where one party to a dispute forces an agreement onto the other side through sheer power. This is not an agreement that will withstand the test of time. A labor-management agreement where that has occurred (i.e., it was forced upon a weaker party with little consideration for the interests of that party) will have many more grievances filed over the life of the agreement. It builds resentment rather than relationships and is a breeding ground of passive-aggressive behaviors and sabotage. It will be devoid of the discretionary emotional energy it takes to be wildly successful.

Agreements that lack clarity will also breed disruption. This is why, whenever possible, we avoid around-the-clock crisis negotiation. Agreements reached in a hallway at 4 a.m. after thirty-six straight hours of mediation tend to be as bleary as the negotiators.

Always take the time to review the details of your agreements. Be sure you have a common understanding of all the details as well as a common understanding of what will happen to resolve any disputes that should arise later. Time spent gaining clarity at this stage will speed up your implementation down the road.

---

**BOX 17-4**

Compliance-prone agreements require both *clarity* and *commitment.*

---

Commitment should be reflected in some obvious and/or symbolic manner. Shaking hands after clearly restating the agreement is a common and effective method. People remember the gesture and it means something important to most people. If we're working in a group and are seeking agreement of all the group members, we usually go around the group after agreement is reached and ask for a symbolic indication of their commitment. Usually it is simply asking everyone to say out loud "Yes, I agree." If anyone says anything other than "Yes, I agree," such as "Yeah, it's all right" or "I can go along with that," we take that as a "No" and have more discussion about that person's hesitancy to fully commit to the agreement.[4]

## COMMUNICATING TO CONSTITUENCIES

Most people have constituencies, whether they are teammates, stockholders, business partners, managers, union members, voters, family members, or their own internal judges. In communicating agreements to their constituencies they should have two goals in mind. The first is to communicate the substance of the agreement. The second is to communicate it in a manner that cultivates the relationship with the other party, making it easier to resolve future conflicts. Positive communication also increases constituency buy-in, not only to the agreement, but to the long-term relationship as well.

It is an appropriate time to indicate appreciation for the other party and the hard work of all the participants. Hopes for the future of the relations also can set a nice tone, supporting future collaborative efforts.

---

**BOX 17-5**

If handled well, every conflict is an opportunity to strengthen the relationship and make it less likely you will have similar conflict in the future.

---

We've had many experiences where one party to a conflict believes it dominated the other side. Most exhibit the good sense not to flaunt their perceived victory. Others can't resist and brag to their constituencies that they kicked the other side's butt. If one side publicly brags about "winning" a dispute, and in doing so humiliates the other leadership, how easy will it be to resolve their next conflict? People too often forget that in any long-term relationship there are an awful lot of next times.

Remembering that everything we say or do will send a message, it is better to say something like "We faced many difficult problems and worked together very hard to reach an agreement that meets the interests of both parties as best we could." If handled well, every conflict is an opportunity to strengthen the relationship and make it less likely you will have similar conflict in the future.

---

**BOX 17-6**

You can't predict what will happen because more than one set of expectations and desires is involved. The best you can do is to work from the Green Zone, remaining nondefensive and authentic, listen well and tell your truth in an accountable way, and follow the steps of the Interest-Based method that you have just learned.

---

---------------------------------------------------------------------

Exercise 17-1

## Interest-Based Action Plan

Now that you've learned the Interest-Based method by following along in the book, using it as a planning tool on one of your own real problems or conflicts, it's time to put it into practice with the other parties involved. Once you start the process, it will be difficult to predict and control exactly what will happen. More than one set of expectations and desires will be involved that will influence the process. The best you can do is to work from the Green Zone, remaining non-defensive and authentic, listen well and tell your truth in an accountable way, and follow the steps of the Interest-Based method that you have just learned. The following points are a few things you should consider as you put the Interest-Based method to work on your real issue:

- Who are the people that need to be involved?

  _____

  _____

- How and when will I contact them?

  _____

  _____

- How can I best explain my intentions about the problem and about the relationship?

  _____

  _____

- What can I do to help the others feel included in the decision making?

  _____

  _____

- Is there anything I can do to help the others feel more significant, competent, and likable?

  _____

  _____

---------------------------------------------------------------------

## A RECAP OF THE INTEREST-BASED APPROACH

Once you start the process, we suggest you follow the steps as closely as possible. Here's a brief recap of the method:

1. *Set the tone and discuss the process.* Be open and direct about your intentions regarding problem solving as well as your intentions about the relationship. Try to reach agreement about what process you will use to resolve the issues.

2. *Define the problem.* Jointly develop a statement of issues that need to be resolved together.

3. *Discuss the interests.* Gain understanding of the underlying interests of all the parties involved in the dispute. Interests are the wants, needs, or desires that underlie the issues that need to be resolved.

4. *Know your contingency plan.* What will you be able to do on your own without the help or permission of the other side if you can't agree on a resolution? Is there any way you can improve your contingency plan?

5. *Invent creative solutions.* Work together to create a large number of potential solutions to meet as many interests of all the parties as possible.

6. *Reach clear commitments and compliance-prone agreements.* Evaluate possible solutions against interests and contingency plans. Narrow the possible solutions and reach closure. Communicate to any constituencies in a manner that builds the relationship.

## CHAPTER SUMMARY

Reaching closure is the final step in the process. No process, including the Interest-Based method, can guarantee success. If, however, the steps have been followed faithfully, your chances of reaching a positive agreement are dramatically increased. Parties have dealt with inclusion issues, been clear about their intentions, and agreed upon process issues. Then they agreed on the problem statement, which is a list of issues to be resolved by the parties. They have developed contingency plans that they can implement on their own if the parties can't reach agreement. They have also worked jointly to generate a large number of possible solutions to solve the problem.

Now the job is to carefully review all the possible solutions and measure them against the interests of the parties and their contingency plans. Any solution will have to be better than the contingency plans of both parties or they shouldn't enter into it. Once the options have been thoroughly discussed, patterns and possibilities for settlement tend to appear.

A party or a subcommittee can review the discussions and try to form a package that is known as a straw design. The group is asked for feedback to improve the straw design and then it is revised. The process is repeated until everyone is happy with the proposal or it is clear that it's as good as it's going to get. Then commitment is sought.

If groups get stuck, box 17-3, "Getting Unstuck," provides a dozen effective tools and processes for helping them break an impasse.

Compliance-prone agreements require both clarity and commitment. When an agreement is reached, it should be reviewed for clarity. Take the time necessary to fully understand the content of any agreement. Once there is clarity, make sure there is commitment. We prefer requiring everyone in the room to indicate their commitment to supporting the agreement.

Finally, any resolution should be communicated in a way that not only gives the substance of any agreement, but also cultivates the relationship. This signals to constituencies the significance of the relationship, increasing buy-in, not only for the particular agreement, but for the relationship as well.

# GETTING REAL AND GETTING ON WITH IT

This final chapter puts a few things in perspective and ends with fifteen things you can do to improve your ability to be in a relationship.

# GET REAL . . . 15 THINGS YOU CAN DO *TODAY* TO IMPROVE YOUR ABILITY TO BE IN A RELATIONSHIP

**"All this self-esteem** mumbo jumbo and collaborative self-awareness stuff might be good at home, but I think it's a bunch of BS here at work. I just expect people to get along and do their job."

Abe, the plant manager, threw down the gauntlet right at the start of the meeting. He wasn't a touchy-feely guy and he wasn't impressed with what he called "California psychobabble." It wasn't the worst start we've had for a big team meeting, but it was pretty clear it was put-up-or-shut-up time for us.

So with Abe's permission we did a little experiment with some of his employees. We asked for six volunteers and separated them into two teams. We gave each team some simple instructions out of earshot of the other team and all the other participants in the meeting. While Ron was giving instructions, Jim was setting up the room so that the front of the room was messy. Jim dumped the wastepaper basket on the floor and scattered the contents. He dropped training materials, pens, pencils, a newspaper, coffee mugs, and books all over the floor. He tipped a couple of chairs over on their side, tossed some jackets in a corner, and even scattered a few dollar bills and some loose change under the table.

Then we announced to the main group of meeting participants that we needed their help today. We explained that we were going to be interviewing work teams from two different cleaning companies. We wanted the meeting participants to help us decide which team we ought to hire to clean our offices. Then we brought in Team 1.

We announced to Team 1 that they were a cleaning team from a company we were considering hiring to clean all our offices and that as part of their interview we wanted them to give us a demonstration of their work. We turned to the mess Jim had created in the front of the room and asked them to clean it up for us.

The cleaning crew just looked at each other for a few minutes without doing anything. First one person, then the other two eventually started picking things up off the floor and putting them into a big pile in the middle of the table. They looked lethargic and were haphazard in their cleaning. They missed a number of things on the floor and hardly straightened anything on the table. One person grabbed the newspaper and started reading it instead of cleaning. That annoyed another cleaner, who made a snide remark. The third cleaner seemed detached and completely uninterested in the squabble between the other two. The team only noticed the money on the ground because they were trying to hide some of the mess out of sight under the table. When they did see the money, two of the cleaners fought over it, pocketing almost half the money they found instead of putting it on the table. They didn't talk much to each other; they didn't look happy and they didn't seem to get along well.

When they finished, the room was better than it had been, but still pretty mediocre. We thanked Team 1 and said we would be in touch with them. Then we re-created the mess in the front of the room and brought in Team 2. We told Team 2 they were a cleaning team from a company we might hire to clean our offices. As part of the interview, we wanted them to give us a demonstration of their work. Again, we asked them to clean the room for us.

Team 2 immediately turned to each other and talked about how they would divide up the work. Then they went to work with an enthusiasm that was visible to everyone at the meeting. When one cleaner finished her assignment, she immediately volunteered to help whoever needed her. They not only cleaned everything off the floor, they straightened everything on the table as well. When they checked under the table, they found the money and were worried about leaving it out on the table. Instead, they put it in an envelope and brought the envelope over to us. They were continuously talking to each other about work issues as well as their weekend plans. They seemed to be having fun as they helped each other and several times looked for ways to do a better job.

The results were clear. Team 2 did twice as good a job in half as much time. They collaborated and seemed to be really happy with what they were doing and enjoyed each other's company. We thanked them and said we would be getting back to them after the group made a decision.

We turned to the meeting participants and asked them to speculate about what instructions we had given to Team 1 and Team 2. The group said it was obvious: we told Team 1 to do a bad job and Team 2 to do a good job. Not true, we responded. Any other ideas? We got many suggestions, but none were correct. Some people thought Team 1 was underpaid and Team 2 was on an incentive plan. Some thought the teams had different training. Others thought we told Team 2 that they had the skills to do good work and told Team 1 that they were untrained. Someone observed that members of Team 1 didn't like each other and Team 2 must have been friends. Another explanation was that we told Team 1 not to be collaborative and Team 2 to be very collaborative. Wrong again.

In fact we had given simple, but different, instructions to both teams. We told Team 1 that we were going to ask them to do a simple task they could easily perform in a few minutes, and that we were specifically not giving them any instructions about how they should do the task. They could do it any way they wanted to. The only instructions we gave them was about how they felt about themselves. We said we want you to feel insignificant, incompetent, and unlikable about yourself. These feelings were not about the task, but only about how they felt about themselves.

We gave the same instructions about the job to Team 2; however, we told Team 2 that we wanted them to feel significant, competent, and likable about themselves.

## SELF-ESTEEM MATTERS

Obviously, both groups had enough training, skills, knowledge, experience, and incentive to clean up a simple mess in the front of the room. The only difference between the two groups was the level of self-esteem they were feeling. What they felt about themselves was the determining factor in their job performance. The employees with higher self-esteem were significantly better employees. They accomplished more in less time and seemed happier and more satisfied in the process.

Abe could see that both these teams were capable of doing the assignment we gave them. Abe could also see the impact of strong self-esteem on job performance and relationships among the team members. It was no longer California psychobabble; we were talking about bottom-line productivity from that point on. It was about the ability to live authentic lives, get beyond fears and defensiveness, and form collaborative relationships. It was about having what it takes to speak your truth and be accountable for any consequences. It was about operating from the Green Zone.

We mentioned in the introduction to this book that our international colleagues in Japan have delivered a course focusing on self-accountability, truthfulness, and self-awareness in over a thousand Japanese companies. That course is called "Self-Esteem Development Seminar." In a recent example, they conducted a survey measuring the self-esteem of four thousand employees in one of Japan's largest international manufacturing companies. Using a FIRO-based questionnaire called Element O (O for "organization"), they focused on certain areas of the business to get an accurate measure of issues of significance, competence, and likability.[1]

The results reflected an almost 100 percent correlation between the departments with high self-esteem and high productivity. The five divisions where employees had the highest self-esteem were also the five divisions with the highest levels of productivity. The five divisions with the lowest self-esteem scores were also the five divisions with the lowest productivity.

Our partners in Japan have shown that by using organizational surveys to identify departments with low self-esteem, and then focusing on the components of self-esteem such as significance, competence, and likability, productivity increases.

Let's review the five essential skills we've been talking about.

## THE FIVE ESSENTIAL SKILLS TO BUILD COLLABORATIVE RELATIONSHIPS

1. **Collaborative intention:** Individuals stay in the Green Zone, maintain an authentic, nondefensive presence, and make a personal commitment to mutual success in their relationships.

2. **Truthfulness:** Individuals commit to both telling the truth and listening to the truth, and to creating a climate of openness that allows people in the relationship to feel safe enough to discuss concerns, solve problems, and deal directly with difficult issues.

3. **Self-accountability:** Individuals take responsibility for the circumstances of their lives and the choices they make, either through action or nonaction, and the intended and unintended or unforeseen consequences of their actions. They would rather find a solution than find someone to blame.

4. **Self-awareness and awareness of others:** Individuals commit to knowing themselves deeply and are willing to explore difficult interpersonal issues. They seek to understand the concerns, intentions, and motivations of others, as well as the culture and context of their circumstances.

5. **Problem-solving and negotiating:** Individuals use problem-solving methods that promote a collaborative atmosphere. They avoid practices that foster subtle or unconscious competition.

We've given you a map of the terrain, five skills, and new insight for navigating your way into more successful collaborative relationships. We hope you practice your new skills along the way. There is no better way to become more skillful at relationships than to jump in and keep practicing. It will take patience and focus, so keep at it. Don't be in a rush to gain perfection.

These five skills are lifelong tasks, but it is possible to start anew each day. Your power is in choosing not to be overwhelmed, but to ask, "How can I take a few little steps on this journey today?" If you do that, then tomorrow will take care of itself.

So we end with action you can take *today* to improve your ability to be in a successful relationship.

## FIFTEEN THINGS YOU CAN DO *TODAY* TO IMPROVE YOUR ABILITY TO BE IN A SUCCESSFUL RELATIONSHIP

1. *Tell your truth.* Don't be afraid to let yourself and others know what your personal truth is.

2. *Realize that* you *choose.* Eagerly accept responsibility for what is happening in your life. Accept that you are responsible for your own happiness, and that only you can make yourself whole.

3. *Seek deeper self-awareness.* Reflect, read, discuss, meditate, or involve yourself in any activity that aids your awareness of your old programs and deeper levels of being.

4. *Respond emotionally.* Allow yourself to "feel." Have your feelings rather than letting your feelings have you, or numbing out. Realize that all emotions are acceptable, but not all actions are acceptable.

5. *Give up blame and postpone judgment.* We're all trying our best to get by. Seek to understand what is happening and how you contributed to that. Attempt to listen to and clarify one another's viewpoints and interests before defending yourself or making others wrong.

6. *Seek not to consciously hurt others.* Living in the Red Zone causes others pain and takes a severe toll on the quality of our own life. Consciously living in the Green Zone daily and respecting others adds richness to our lives.

7. *Take time to envision yourself as you want to be.* Motivate yourself by thinking about your future, rather than letting yourself be shoved through life by your past. Start being whom you want to be . . . today.

8. *Consciously change your limiting beliefs.* Don't wait for experience to change them for you.

9. *Assert yourself.* Be aware of your boundaries and stand up for yourself. If you don't, who will?

10. *Be as sincere and as vulnerable as possible.* Explore being "present" rather than being "right."

11. *Be in touch with your body and its wisdom.* Seek alignment and connection with the head, heart, and belly. They have much to tell you if you listen.

12. *Seek a higher meaning or purpose in your life.* Explore ways to collaborate with others by doing something you are passionate about, in the service of others.

13. *Treat your personal growth with respect, excitement, and patience, rather than judgment.* Personal growth is a lifelong job. It requires commitment and compassion. Focus each day on becoming your best cheerleader rather than your worst critic.

14. *Give to give.* Give yourself away daily to purpose, people, places, and things you love. Stop waiting for others to love first, accept you, or make it safe for you.

15. *Laugh a little.* Some things are much too important to be taken seriously.

# GLOSSARY

**Adversarial:** An attitude of opposition and antagonism where individuals work against each other rather than working together in collaboration.

**Authentic:** A quality of being genuine or real, not a phony. If individuals are authentic, their actions are consistent with what they say. They are congruent and believable.

**Collaboration:** Working together with an attitude of cooperation and mutual success, and supporting each other's interests and goals.

**FIRO Element B:** A psychometrically validated assessment measuring three key relationship behaviors. The FIRO Element B measures an individual's preferences in the areas of Inclusion, Control, and Openness and provides a way to measure satisfaction regarding each behavior. FIRO Element B is Dr. Schutz's substantial revision of the older FIRO B assessment.

**FIRO theory:** FIRO stands for Fundamental Interpersonal Relations Orientation.[1] It is a theory of relationships that was first developed for the U.S. military by Dr. Will Schutz. The theory holds that people in relationships orient themselves to each other based upon three fundamental behaviors: Inclusion, Control, and Openness. Using FIRO theory, Dr. Schutz improved the success rate of combat information centers in battleships by 50 percent.

**Human potential movement:** Beginning in the early 1960s the human potential movement was a wide-ranging social movement that sought to aid individuals in exploring how to be more self-aware, authentic, personal, spontaneous, and open with themselves and others. It used a wide variety of experiential, psychological, spiritual, and body-awareness methods. Dr. Will Schutz was one of the leaders in the movement along with Abraham Maslow, Fritz Perls, Jack Gibb, Carl Rogers, Ida Rolf, Alexander Lowen, Moshe Feldenkrais, Michael Murphy, Eric Berne, Rollo May, Chogyam Trungpa, Ram Dass, Alan Watts, and Claudio Naranjo, among numerous others.

**Intentions:** An individual's thoughts, purpose, or plan that is firmly held and sharply focused. One's intentions reflect resolve over a course of action or an attitude. Collaborative intention is a determination to behave in a way that supports collaboration, making clear and conscious choices, and not being undermined by unconscious fears or adversarial behavior.

**Interest-Based Problem Solving:** A problem-solving and negotiations methodology that is effective in, and supportive of, collaborative relationships. It is a specific, step-by-step approach to negotiating your way through conflict. It is not based on intimidation and manipulation. Rather, it emphasizes a focus on the underlying "interests" of the parties involved in a conflict. In a special pilot project funded by the State of California, and the Hewlett and Stuart Foundations, ninety-four public school districts in California were able to reduce their labor-management conflict by an average rate of 67 percent by using this approach.

**Passive-aggressive:** Defensive behavior that reflects an aggressive attitude expressed in passive ways, such as procrastination, stubbornness, whining, or pouting.

**Positional:** A term used in negotiations that reflects a rigid, inflexible stance on an issue.

**Projection:** The tendency to ascribe one's own feelings, fears, thoughts, and attitudes to other people or the external world in general. For example, if an individual is deceitful, he or she might project that attitude onto others and believe that everyone else is also deceitful, regardless of any evidence to the contrary.

**Red Zone–Green Zone:** A shorthand description for two very different attitudes. A person in the Red Zone is defensive, rigid, reactive, and adversarial. A person in the Green Zone is nondefensive, authentic, collaborative, and open to other points of view.

**Schutz, Will:** Creator of FIRO theory and the Elements of Awareness, and a leader in the human potential movement. Will Schutz received his PhD in psychology in 1951 and went on to become a highly respected academic on the faculties of Harvard University, UC Berkeley, Antioch University–San Francisco, the University of Chicago, Einstein Medical School, and others. During his career, Will wrote eight books, including the best-selling *Joy* in 1967, *Here Comes Everybody* in 1971, *Profound Simplicity* in 1979, *The Truth Option* in 1984, and *The Human Element* in 1994.

# RESEARCH REPORT

**This book has** its roots at the State of California Public Employment Relations Board (PERB), where Jim Tamm was a former regional director and a senior administrative law judge for twenty-five years before he became a vice president at Business Consultants Network, Inc. PERB is the state agency established to oversee dispute resolution and collective bargaining among public employees. In the late 1980s, the staff at PERB noticed that they kept seeing the same parties end up in litigation each time they had a dispute. Other parties, operating under the same statutes, resolved disputes more effectively and rarely ended up in litigation. The dysfunctional relationships were using a disproportional amount of the State's resources. The staff wanted to find out why some relationships were effective and others abysmal.

PERB sent out a massive statewide survey to over six thousand labor-management practitioners to determine the differences between effective and ineffective labor-management relationships. They discovered that those constituents needing greater assistance in resolving disputes primarily lacked skills in *relationship building* and *conflict resolution*.

Armed with that information, PERB assembled a team of experts from all over the country to develop a training program to assist its public sector constituency. Because the initial workshops were targeted for public sector school districts, the task force included experts from all the major representative groups in California public education, as well as consultants from the California State Mediation/Conciliation Service, the Harvard Program on Negotiations, and PERB. Jim was assigned to the project as both a program designer and faculty member because of his mediation experience. He has mediated almost two thousand employment disputes in the private and public sectors, including more school labor strikes than anyone else in the nation.

With funding provided by the State of California, and the Hewlett and Stuart Foundations, an experiential and highly intensive training program was designed by the team. The program, titled Improving the Labor-Management Relationship, focused on both relationship-building skills and problem-solving skills in a labor-management setting.

The team established criteria for acceptance into the program. Only labor-management groups attending the workshop together would be considered. They had to be willing to work with a follow-up consultant during the year after the training. They would have to send the decision makers from both labor and management in order to be accepted into the training. Thus, in a school district setting, participants would typically include school board members, the superintendent, the superintendent's cabinet, the entire management negotiating team, all the elected union leadership, the union's negotiating team, key union stewards, state or national union representatives, and a paid executive director or other full-time union staff member.

Once criteria were established, the team sought out the most dysfunctional, litigious, adversarial labor-management relationships it could find and invited the participants to enroll in the program. Finding dysfunctional relationships proved to be the easiest part of the project. The groups ranged in size from about fifteen up to almost fifty participants from each labor-management relationship. In the first year the project worked with fourteen different labor-management relationships.

During the first year, the team knew from anecdotal reports that the program was having a positive impact on the relationships it had worked with. A number of individuals reported that they had been able to resolve disputes without resorting to litigation or formal complaint processes. The team didn't fully realize until about sixteen months after the program had begun just how wildly successful the program was. At that time the first systematic research on the impact of the program was conducted by independent researchers. The results of the program in reversing unproductive, adversarial patterns were astonishing, particularly because union-management collective bargaining relationships are traditionally some of the most adversarial relationships in existence today.

This first study, published in 1991 by the Institute of Industrial Relations at the University of California, Berkeley,[1] confirmed that transformations from ineffective, adversarial, nontrusting relationships into effective, cooperative, and trusting working relationships were the norm rather than the exception among participants. Some of the significant findings were:

- Prior to the training 70 percent of participants characterized their working relationship as adversarial. After the training, less than 1 percent said it was adversarial.
- Prior to the training 57 percent said their working relationship was unproductive. After the training 87 percent felt their working relationship was productive.
- Prior to the workshop, "a lack of mutual understanding" was the most cited characteristic of their labor-management relationship. After the training, "effective communication" became the most cited characteristic.
- Participants reported improved constituency support, which was characterized as excellent by only 19 percent before the training and 58 percent after the training.
- Participants believed they were now able to focus discussions concerning day-to-day issues on interests and options (78 percent); before the training such discussions were focused on positions (82 percent).
- Improvements were experienced in resolving conflicts and managing differences, with 89 percent of the participants reporting more effectiveness in this area after the training.
- When asked whether techniques learned in the training were used subsequently, high usage was reported in all four areas surveyed (general problem solving, resolving grievances, collective bargaining, and building trust).
- Almost all the participants felt the workshops had a highly positive impact on both the process and the products of their working relationships.
- The study concluded that the beneficial results were not a momentary "honeymoon" response, but rather were sustainable gains.

The project team was, of course, ecstatic over the findings. Publication of the research enabled Janet Walden, the project leader, to obtain additional funding from the State and the Hewlett and Stuart Foundations, and the training continued at a faster pace. Three years after the first pilot program, the team had trained ninety-four labor-management groups. The dramatic positive results were becoming apparent to the educational community in California, and then eventually to other states and Canada.

In 1993 a second study was published on the impact of the training among the first ninety-four relationships.[2] This research, co-authored by Jim and PERB Sacramento regional director Les Chisholm, studied information obtained from the State of California, which kept accurate data about all labor-management conflicts in California's almost twelve hundred public school systems.

The Chisholm-Tamm research documented an astonishing 85 percent reduction in the rate of disputes filed with the State among employers and unions that had participated in the training three years earlier. The reduction in the rate of labor disputes filed with the State of California for all ninety-four labor-management groups averaged sixty-seven percent. Both the degree of the impact and the long-lasting effect of the training were remarkable. Like the earlier University of California study, this research also concluded that the gains were sustainable over a long term by the great majority of relationships.

By this time the California legislature had established a nonprofit foundation to continue the training in the public sector in California.[3]

During the first three years of the relationship training project, in addition to being on its training faculty, Jim had been assigned to conduct much of the follow-up consulting with parties after the training. He found that while most groups he was working with were able to sustain their gains, some were not. Among the small number of groups that had reverted to adversarial ways, most seemed to be having more trouble with the relationship-building skills than with the problem-solving methodologies they had been taught. People became defensive, quit listening, started making incorrect assumptions, and were not giving each other the benefit of the doubt. They often withheld important information, engaged in public name-calling campaigns, and treated the other party as the enemy. These relationships deteriorated quickly into what they had been before the training or sometimes even became worse.

At about this time Jim teamed up with Ron Luyet, vice president of the international consulting, training, and publishing firm Business Consultants Network, Inc.[4] Working together, we (Jim and Ron) strengthened the interpersonal-relationship-building aspects of the training, adding a training theory about relationship compatibility that had been developed to assist the U.S. military increase the effectiveness of battle command teams. The compatibility training was called FIRO theory (Fundamental Interpersonal Relations Orientation). Using FIRO theory, Navy researchers were able to improve the success rate of battle command teams by 50 percent.[5]

We both were convinced that these same techniques that taught labor-management groups and battle command teams to collaborate more effectively could be adapted for the private sector in non-labor-management settings. We modified the training, removing the labor-management aspects of the program, and made it available to the private sector. This broadened the training's application beyond a labor relations setting, making it particularly effective for executive education programs, new or established teams, leadership development programs, customer or supplier relationships, and management teams, or within units historically at odds with each other such as product development and manufacturing or marketing.

The program, as modified, was then offered to a wide array of participants, such as the U.S. Department of Defense, a major international toy manufacturer, pharmaceutical executive teams, and linemen in power companies. The program was offered internationally, where we worked with a large number of human resource consultants and internal trainers.

In 1999, a third study was conducted on the impact of the program. Professor Mayte Barba[6] surveyed participants from nine countries trained over six years after the addition of FIRO theory and the removal of the labor-management aspects of the program. Professor Barba asked participants about their effectiveness before and after the training regarding four areas: (1) reducing their defensiveness in conflict, (2) getting their interests met in conflict, (3) problem-solving effectiveness, and (4) effectiveness at building and maintaining long-term climates of trust. The results supported our belief that a strong relationship exists between the ability to stay nondefensive in conflict and getting your interests met.[7]

Participants reported, on average, the following gains:

- A 49.5 percent increase in effectiveness at reducing their own defensiveness in conflicted situations.
- A 44.8 percent increase in effectiveness at getting their interests met in conflicted situations.
- A 31.5 percent increase in effectiveness at problem solving.
- A 26.4 percent increase in effectiveness at building and maintaining long-term climates of trust.

Like the two earlier studies, this one also concluded that the increases in effectiveness reported by participants were both substantial and sustainable over a long term.

# LIST OF FIRO
# THEORY–RELATED MATERIALS

**Much of this** book, especially chapters 7 and 8, is based upon the success of FIRO theory (Fundamental Interpersonal Relations Orientation) in building compatibility and improving relationships within organizations. Dr. Will Schutz, the creator of FIRO theory, was a leader in the human potential movement of the 1960s and 1970s. Until his death in 2002, Dr Schutz continued to develop other testing and training materials for improving the effectiveness of individuals and organizations.

The following is a list of some of the more popular materials developed by Dr. Schutz after he created FIRO theory. A more complete list can be obtained by contacting info@firo.net.

## INSTRUMENTS

*FIRO Element B: Behavior.* This is a psychometrically validated assessment measuring three key relationship behaviors. The FIRO Element B measures an individual's preferences in the areas of Inclusion, Control, and Openness, and provides a measure of satisfaction regarding each behavior. This new version retains the attractive properties of the old FIRO B and is the result of a revised and greatly expanded FIRO theory. It is short, simple, and self-scoring and can be completed in fifteen to twenty minutes. It also offers new features and clearer interpretations, based on twenty years of research conducted after the creation of the old FIRO B instrument.

*FIRO Element O: Organizational Climate.* This instrument provides measures of satisfaction within an organization in the areas of inclusion, control, openness, significance, competence, and likability.

Each measure is provided for the organization as a whole and for teams, relationships, and individuals. The instrument can also be used to evaluate the effect of any organizational change.

*FIRO Element F: Feelings.* This instrument measures preferences in the areas of significance, competence, and likability in relationships. It is self-scoring and measures satisfaction.

*FIRO Element S: Self-Concept.* This instrument measures feelings about the self in three areas of behavior (aliveness, self-determination, and self-awareness) and three areas of feeling (self-significance, self-competence, and self-liking). It is self-scoring and measures satisfaction.

*FIRO Element J: Job.* This instrument is designed to help users discover how they behave and feel in their current jobs and how they would behave and feel in their ideal jobs. It allows the user to measure job satisfaction on the whole and in specific aspects. It can also be used for job selection and job placement when combined with other instruments.

*FIRO Element W: Work Relations.* This instrument provides a non-threatening framework for assessing and improving two-person work relationships. These include relationships that bring two people together over a prolonged time, where they usually have a common goal. Users may include supervisors and their employees, coworkers, doctors and patients, lawyers and clients, teachers and students, and members of temporary or occasional groups.

*FIRO Element C: Close Relations.* This element helps explore relationships between spouses, lovers, or close friends, using the basic dimensions of inclusion, control, and openness. It provides a framework for discussion and measurement.

## BOOKS BY DR. WILL SCHUTZ

*The Human Element: Productivity, Self-Esteem and the Bottom Line* (1994). The author shows how to enhance our performance and improve our organizations by developing healthier concepts of ourselves and others. A personal development and leadership guide to creating a work environment where self-determination and openness are the rule.

*The Truth Option* (1984). This volume contains the background ideas behind the Human Element workshops. With the book, a pencil, and honest responses to the exercises and activities, the reader can experience both personal and professional transformation. The methods used in the book have been applied successfully in businesses, universities, and personal-growth centers worldwide.

*Joy: Twenty Years Later* (1989). Joy was the "textbook" of the human potential movement that swept the United States in the 1960s and 1970s. Will Schutz then updated his national best seller to reflect the changes that had taken place since its first publication. He examined the growth of (and resistance to) the *Joy* principles over the next two decades.

*Profound Simplicity* (1979; 3rd ed., 1986). As Will Schutz explored himself and the human condition—through encounter groups, body-work methods, energy techniques, and spiritual disciplines—he discovered that each one, if pursued deeply enough, emphasized the same concepts of truth, self-responsibility, and self-awareness. This book weaves these principles into a foundation for a social philosophy.

*FIRO: A Three-Dimensional Theory of Interpersonal Behavior* (1958; 3rd ed., 1989). This book contains the original explanation of Will Schutz's FIRO (Fundamental Interpersonal Relations Orientation) theory. The book introduces the well-known FIRO B measure (updated and renamed FIRO Element B by Dr. Schutz), provides a literature review, and describes the variables. It is heavily focused upon the psychometrics and statistical analysis of FIRO theory.

## TRAINING GUIDES

*Conversion of FIRO B to FIRO Element B.* This booklet provides information about the evolution of FIRO-B to FIRO Element B, covering the developments that have occurred in FIRO theory and their effects on the Schutz instruments. It also presents a description of the advantages of FIRO Element B over FIRO B. A simple method allows users to convert FIRO B scores to FIRO Element B Scores, thereby preserving all the information previously acquired.

*Guide to Element B: Behavior*. This guide includes information contained in *Interpretation of Element B* and *Conversion of FIRO B to FIRO Element B* and provides detailed directions for administering the FIRO Element B.

## APPENDIX 3
# TABLE OF EXERCISES, TOOLS, EXAMPLES, AND LISTS

# NOTES

## PREFACE

1. James Tamm and Les Chisholm, "Does Interest Bargaining Really Work: A Test Using PERB Data," *California Public Employee Relations (CPER) 101,* (August 1993). For additional information see endnote 2 for appendix 1.

2. This study defined "conflict" as the number of cases filed with the California Public Employment Relations Board in the following three areas:

   1. An "unfair practice charge" (i.e., labor-management litigation).
   2. An impasse in contract negotiations where it had been determined that further negotiations would be futile without the appointment of a state mediator.
   3. A failure of the mediation process that led to the creation of a fact-finding panel.

3. "Analysis of Beyond Conflict Post-Workshop Survey," 1999.

4. Clair Brown and Vince Valvano, "Analysis of Post-workshop Evaluation," January 15, 1991, Institute of Industrial Relations, University of California, Berkeley.

5. Until his death in November 2002, Will Schutz was one of the most respected leaders in the field of human relations and organizational development. His FIRO B questionnaire and Elements of Awareness are some of the most widely used psychometric instruments throughout the world. He served on the faculty of Harvard University, the University of California at Berkeley, and the University of Chicago, among others. He created and chaired the graduate department of holistic studies at Antioch University, San Francisco. Schutz is the creator of The Human Element, an integrated series of modules that address organizational development and compatibility, including many of the concepts that we address in this book.

6. *FIRO: A Three-Dimensional Theory of Interpersonal Behavior* (3rd ed., 1989) contains the original explanation of Will Schutz's FIRO theory. The book introduces the well-known FIRO B measure (later significantly revised and updated as the FIRO Element B), provides a literature search, and describes the variables.

7. Roger Fisher is the Samuel Williston Professor of Law, Emeritus, Harvard Law School. Along with William Ury and Bruce Patton, Roger Fisher coauthored *Getting to Yes: Negotiating Agreement Without Giving In* (Penguin Books, 2nd ed., 1991).

## INTRODUCTION: THE FIVE ESSENTIALS

1. This is a composite picture of several districts Jim has worked with as a mediator and consultant. In several examples, identifying facts are changed as well. The substance of the disputes or the points made are, however, accurate reflections of the situations we have encountered.

2. See for example, Robert Kelley and Janet Caplan, "How Bell Labs Creates Star Performers," *Harvard Business Review,* July-August 1993.

3. From Steven Kelner's presentation at the 2004 annual conference of the Association of Internal Management Consultants.

4. Stan Slap is a consultant specializing in branding and strategic implementation. He can be reached at www.slapworld.com.

5. Don White is now a partner in the consulting firm of Barton and White.

6. Shogo Saito, "The Human Element in Japan," in *The Human Element @ Work: A Fieldbook of Projects Transforming People and Organizations Around the World* (BCon WSA International, Inc., 2004).

7. Maxi Trope, "The People Puzzle," *The Human Element @ Work.*

8. Marie Larssen and Anna-Karin Neuman, "Doing a Freys," *The Human Element @ Work.*

## CHAPTER 1: ATTITUDE AND INTENTION

1. Jim Collins, *Good to Great* (HarperCollins Publishers, 2001).

2. Larry Ellison offered the classic example of Red Zone thinking while he was being interviewed by the *San Francisco Chronicle* newspaper, June 10, 2003. The article noted that Ellison frequently paraphrases a thirteenth-century Mongol warlord: "It's not enough that we win; everyone else must lose."

3. Daniel Goleman, *Emotional Intelligence* (Bantam Books, 1995).

4. See also Joseph LeDoux, *The Emotional Brain* (Touchstone/Simon & Schuster, 1996).

5. Deborah Tannen, *The Argument Culture* (Ballantine, 1998).

6. John P. Kotter and James L. Heskett, *Corporate Culture and Performance* (The Free Press, 1992).

## CHAPTER 2: HEY, BUZZ OFF! . . . I AM NOT DEFENSIVE!

1. "Happiness: Proven Ways to Increase Life Satisfaction and Meaningfulness," a preliminary draft of a manuscript in progress by Gary A. Chapin, 2004.

2. Some details of the three Conflict Lifeline examples have been changed to assure the anonymity of workshop participants.

3. In her excellent book *The Tending Instinct*, UCLA psychologist Shelley Taylor makes a strong case that instead of flight, fight, or freeze, some people, particularly women, turn to social instincts to both give and receive comfort. Taylor refers to this alternative approach as "tend and befriend." Shelley Taylor, *The Tending Instinct: How Nurturing Is Essential to Who We Are and How We Live* (Times Books, Henry Holt and Company LLC, 2002).

4. It is possible to cultivate this "witnessing" part of us. Gaining perspective allows us to be more conscious and base our behavior on our deepest values and intentions rather than just being "reactive" in the moment. It is helpful, from time to time, to pull back and observe our patterns, feelings, and behaviors. This does not mean we are always standing outside ourselves watching. Full engagement and the absence of the "observing self," what has been called flow, is a supremely delightful state to be in. For more information about this state of consciousness see Mihaly Csikszentmihalyi, *Flow: The Psychology of Optimal Experience* (Harper & Row, 1990).

## CHAPTER 3: UNHOOKING YOUR BUTTONS

1. This is a modification of a five-step tool created by Will Schutz called the Levels of Openness/Truth. The tool assists individuals in creating greater openness.

## CHAPTER 4: THE GRAND SIMPLIFIER

1. During his years in residence at Esalen Institute, Will Schutz conducted "Endarkenment" workshops where participants explored the shadow side of their personality.

2. Although the concept is not new, Will Schutz first described the tool as First-Truth-First.

3. A. Mehrabian and S. R. Ferris, "Inference of Attitudes from Non-verbal Communication in Two Channels." *Journal of Consulting Psychology* 31 (1967): 248–52; A. Mehrabian and M. Wiener, "Decoding of Inconsistent Communica-

tions," *Journal of Personality and Social Psychology* 6 (1967): 109–14. Mehrabian's research was followed by additional research by Professor Michael Argyle and his colleagues: M. Argyle, F. Alkema, and R. Gilmour, "The Communication of Friendly and Hostile Attitudes by Verbal and Nonverbal Signals." (Unpublished manuscript, Institute of Experimental Psychology, Oxford University, 1971); and M. Argyle, V. Salter, H. Nicholson, M. Williams, and P. Burgess, "The Communication of Inferior and Superior Attitudes by Verbal and Nonverbal Signals," *British Journal of Social and Clinical Psychology* 9 (1970): 222–31.

4. Albert Mehrabian, *Silent Messages* (Wadsworth Publishing Company, 1971), 46–47. In his book, Professor Mehrabian offers an extensive analysis of the impact of nonverbal behavior on communications.

## CHAPTER 6: MAKING CHOICES AND TAKING RESPONSIBILITY FOR THEM

1. Viktor E. Frankl, *Man's Search for Meaning*. First published in 1946 under the title *Ein Psychologe erlebt das Konzentrationslager*. First translation published by Beacon Press in 1959, revised 1962; Washington Square Press, 1995.

2. John Mirowsky and Catherine Ross, *Social Causes of Psychological Distress*, 2nd ed. (Aldine De Gruyter, a Division of Walter de Gruyter, Inc., 2003).

3. We've changed several of the identifying factors to assure the anonymity of the employees.

4. Being trusted is a foundation for being a successful leader. To assist leaders in collecting specific feedback about how they are evaluated by those they lead, Ron has developed a Trustworthy Leader Survey surveying such components of trustworthiness as clear intention, openness, accountability, self-awareness, mutuality, authenticity, and skillful action.

## CHAPTER 7: UNDERSTANDING YOUR OWN BEHAVIOR IN RELATIONSHIPS

1. For a deeper understanding of the FIRO theory we suggest you read Schutz, *The Human Element: Productivity, Self-Esteem and the Bottom Line* (Jossey-Bass, 1994). For individuals particularly interested in the statistical research underlying FIRO theory see Schutz, *FIRO: A Three-Dimensional Theory of Interpersonal Behavior*, 3rd ed. (South San Francisco, CA: 1989). For additional information about FIRO-based instruments, see appendix 2.

2. A comparison of the scores provided by the two instruments created by Dr. Schutz follows.

## FIRO ELEMENT B SCORES COMPARED TO FIRO B SCORES

| FIRO Element B provides | FIRO B provides |
|---|---|

### Inclusion

| | |
|---|---|
| 1. What I do | 1. What I do |
| 2. What I want to do | |
| 3. Measure of satisfaction | |
| 4. What others do toward me | |
| 5. What I want others to do toward me | 2. What I want others to do toward me |
| 6. Measure of satisfaction | |

### Control

| | |
|---|---|
| 7. What I do | 3. What I do |
| 8. What I want to do | |
| 9. Measure of satisfaction | |
| 10. What others do toward me | |
| 11. What I want others to do toward me | 4. What I want others to do toward me |
| 12. Measure of satisfaction | |

### Openness (Firo B scale called Affection)

| | |
|---|---|
| 13. What I do | 5. What I do |
| 14. What I want to do | |
| 15. Measure of satisfaction | |
| 16. What others do toward me | |
| 17. What I want others to do toward me | 6. What I want others to do toward me |
| 18. Measure of satisfaction | |
| **18 total scores including all of the original 6 scores** | **6 total scores** |

3. In the older FIRO B, Schutz used the term *affection* rather than *openness*. When he updated the instrument creating the FIRO Element B, he changed the term to *openness*. Schutz believed that affection was more of a feeling that was reflected by the behavior of openness and that openness was therefore a more accurate term for what he was seeking to measure.

4. Schutz's research determined a slight bow in the midrange scores.

5. While some individuals used this insight into how they were dealing with the dissatisfaction in their lives, many of the men had little institutional or family support to make any changes. A number of them chose to make no changes in spite of such little happiness. Without any support systems, the risk of change was greater than their dissatisfaction.

For examples and additional information about how FIRO theory and the FIRO Element B are being used in culturally diverse coaching programs in Brazil, United Kingdom, Denmark, Mexico, France, and the United States see *Coach: A Partner for Your Success*, Ane Araujo (Marcondes & Consultores Associados, 1999); *The Human Element @ Work: A Fieldbook of Projects Transforming People and Organizations Around the World* (BCon WSA International, Inc., 2004); and *Leadership et Confiance*, Alain Duluc (Dunod, 2003).

6. W. B. Alexander, R. A. Gonzales, J. F. Herminghaus, G. Marwel, and L. Wheeless, "Personality Variables and Predictability of Interaction Patterns in Small Groups," unpublished paper, Massachusetts Institute of Technology. The objective of this study was to explore the interpersonal relations in a fraternity at MIT. The data was made available to Dr. Schutz and he wrote about the study in his books *FIRO: A Three-Dimensional Theory of Interpersonal Behavior* (3rd ed. 1989, WSA) and *The Human Element: Productivity, Self-Esteem and the Bottom Line* (1994, Jossey-Bass).

## CHAPTER 9: BREAKING FREE OF THE PAST ONE THOUGHT AT A TIME

1. The meditations in Stephen Levine's book *Guided Meditations, Explorations and Healings* (Doubleday, 1991) are also very helpful for developing compassion and healing from past trauma, gaining a greater degree of self-acceptance, and learning forgiveness of those who have hurt you.

2. Traditionally, one of the most direct ways of developing an objective observer is through the practice of some form of meditation. We have recently noted an increase in use of meditation practices in many business executive education programs, and we highly recommend you consider exploring a practice or

method that fits you. Many local recreation departments, hospitals, fitness centers, and religious institutions teach meditation methods. One of the most accessible and well-researched forms of meditation is called MBSR (Mindfulness-Based Stress Reduction). The MBSR method was developed by Dr. Jon Kabat-Zinn and his colleagues at the Stress Reduction Clinic of the University of Massachusetts Medical Center. The MBSR program is fully described in Dr. Kabat-Zinn's book, *Full Catastrophe Living: Using the Wisdom of Your Body and Mind to Face Stress, Pain and Illness* (Dell Publishing, 1990).

3. Each January for over thirty years, Jim has been meeting for at least four days with a group of college friends. While they see each other during the year, this time is specifically set aside for personal growth. It has been Jim's single most powerful tool for self-awareness and personal growth.

The success of Jim's group has been enhanced by several factors:

1. *They have continuity.* They've known each other well for over thirty-five years. Together they've been through the birth of children and the death of parents, retirements and career changes, betrayals, relative wealth and financial setbacks, several divorces, even more marriages, and a few infidelities scattered along the way. They've also shared countless mistakes and celebrated even more successes.

2. *They commit to a common purpose.* The January time is set aside for self-awareness and personal growth. It's not time for golf or parties. It's a time for exploration of the ways they are living their lives.

3. *They commit to telling each other the truth.* If they ever adopted a motto for those retreats, it would be "The truth is spoken here." Having the advantage of a thirty-five-year history makes it difficult to BS each other.

4. *They hold each other accountable.* If members commit to working on an issue during the next year, they'd better be ready to report on their progress at the next group. For the past twenty-five years, the last day of each year's meeting is devoted to videotaping. Each member does a review of the previous year and a preview of the upcoming year. Making your commitments on videotape ups the ante.

5. *They keep a long-term perspective.* Most significant change happens slowly over time, rather than in a blinding flash of light. Twenty-five years of videotapes support that belief. No one tries to change the world overnight. Typically everyone is working on one or two issues at a time over the long term. They each, in their own way, seek to build a rich, authentic life in their own style.

## CHAPTER 10: STRATEGIES FOR COLLABORATIVE SUCCESS

1. Neil Bodine, "Interest-Based Aikido: Taming the Positional Tiger," a white paper published by the Center for Collaborative Solutions. Neil Bodine is a partner in the firm of Beeson, Tayer & Bodine, which specializes in the representation of public- and private-sector labor unions. He is also the founder of The Workplace Institute and director of education and training at the Center for Collaborative Solutions. In the paper Mr. Bodine credits the term *interest-based aikido* to Steve Barber.

2. Vance A. Kennedy, *Awareness and Choice: A Workbook in Human Relations* (Belmont, CA: Pea Press, 2000).

3. The Radiant Transit Exercise is available for purchase in English, Spanish, French, or Swedish.

4. The simulation is based upon an old game-theory scenario called Prisoner's Dilemma. In that scenario. two thieves are arrested and kept in separate rooms unable to communicate with each other. If neither prisoner confesses (i.e., collaboration between the prisoners), the police will still have enough evidence to convict both and sentence them to one year in prison. If only one prisoner confesses (defecting from the relationship), it will insure that he does not go to prison, but that his partner goes to prison for a long sentence. If they both confess (they both defect from the relationship), both of them will go to prison for a long sentence. Of course, since they can't communicate with each other, they have to decide on their own whether to collaborate and remain silent or defect by confessing. There are many simulations other than Prisoner's Dilemma for modeling social and business decision making; however, we have found that Prisoner's Dilemma tends to bring out more of the participants' unconscious competitive or collaborative strategies that make for a rich debriefing session when they are related back to the participants' employment environment. For an excellent discussion of some of the implications of this game, we suggest chapters 3 and 4 of Matt Ridley's *The Origins of Virtue: Human Instincts and the Evolution of Cooperation* (Penguin Books, 1996) and Elinor Ostrom's *The Commons* (Cambridge University Press, 1990).

5. Authors vary widely about the wisdom of making the first offer in a negotiation. Some believe that making the first offer provides an opportunity to anchor the expectations of the other side at either a much higher or much lower figure, therefore creating an advantage. Others disagree, believing that it is better to get the other side to make the first offer, thus revealing important information about their expectations and strategy. We believe that using an interest-based approach to negotiations minimizes the advantage or disadvantage (however you look at it) of making the first offer, since any possible options should be thoroughly discussed and measured against your underlying interests.

6. James Tamm and Les Chisholm, "Does Interest Bargaining Really Work: A Test Using PERB Data," *California Public Employee Relations (CPER)* 101 (August 1993). For additional information see endnote 2 for appendix 1.

7. "Analysis of Beyond Conflict Post-Workshop Survey," 1999.

## CHAPTER 11: WE'VE GOT A PROBLEM; NOW WHAT DO WE DO ABOUT IT?

1. Ellen F. Wachtel, *We Love Each Other, But: Simple Secrets to Strengthen Your Relationships and Make Love Last* (St. Martin's Press, 1999).

2. James Tamm and Les Chisholm, "Does Interest Bargaining Really Work: A Test Using PERB Data," *California Public Employee Relations (CPER)* 101 (August 1993). For additional information see endnote 2 for appendix 1.

## CHAPTER 12: HOW DO WE GET STARTED?

1. Dr. Schutz found that as groups develop, the predominant areas of interpersonal behavior begin with inclusion, followed by control, and finally openness. He also found that as groups anticipate termination, they follow the opposite sequence, in that the predominant areas of interpersonal behavior relate first to openness, followed by control and finally by inclusion. Will Schutz, *FIRO: A Three-Dimensional Theory of Interpersonal Behavior*, 3rd ed. 1989, WSA.

## CHAPTER 14: WHAT DOES EVERYBODY REALLY NEED?

1. All the negotiating time was a period to get to know each other and to build the relationship upon which the real business would be conducted. Most of the successful negotiations were completed over banquet dinners, toasting each other's success and the successful venture. It was the friendship between the parties that sealed any deal. It was not the bottom line, because the parties could almost always get as good a deal someplace else.

Dean Teng also encountered strong gender issues during her negotiations. Dean Teng, who is bilingual, bicultural, and biliterate in different Chinese dialects, always found it a challenge to negotiate with male Chinese executives. For example, when she met with top executives of an international airline in China, they always directed their comments to Dean Teng's assistant, a Caucasian male. Any negotiator without Dean Teng's bicultural experience and negotiating savvy could waste months, if not years, just determining who is in charge and who can make decisions. Most Americans want to ride into China like John Wayne, negotiate a contract, and get out of town. Most end up being disappointed because of their lack of awareness of cultural issues and impatience.

## CHAPTER 15: WHAT SHOULD WE DO IF WE CAN'T REACH A SOLUTION?

1. In their popular book *Getting to Yes: Negotiating Agreement Without Giving In* (Penguin Books, 2nd ed., 1991), Roger Fisher, William Ury, and Bruce Patton refer to this as a BATNA, or Best Alternative To a Negotiated Agreement.

## CHAPTER 16: NOW WE GET TO THE FUN PART!

1. The American Arbitration Association (AAA) at www.adr.org is a good source for finding qualified expert arbitrators. Some states, such as California, also have mediation and arbitration services. In California contact the California State Mediation and Conciliation Service (SMCS) at www.dir.ca.gov/csmcs. The Federal Mediation and Conciliation Service also provides similar services at www.fmcs.gov.

2. Steven J. Brams and Alan D. Taylor, *The Win-Win Solution: Guaranteeing Fair Shares to Everybody* (W.W. Norton & Company, 1999).

3. This was reported in the "Other Perspectives" column by reporter Carol Smith of the *Seattle Post-Intelligencer*.

## CHAPTER 17: PUTTING THE PUZZLE TOGETHER

1. Steve Barber is a partner in the Barber & Gonzales Consulting Group. In the article "Multiparty Applications of the Interest Approach" published by Barber & Gonzalez Consulting Group, Barber says he typically works with four types of disputes:

1. *Highly polarized* settings where parties are at "war" but realize that at some point the fighting will cease. They will either run out of ammunition or have an equilibrium of power to continue to stalemate each other.

2. *Simply contentious* situations where the parties act out past win-lose injuries in their current situation.

3. *Strained and suspicious* relationships where the parties are making a conscious effort to succeed with each other but are wary of "those other guys."

4. *Rational and purposeful* relationships that honor the principles of a positive relationship through an effective negotiation process.

2. The Straw Design as a Closure Tool is a derivative of a document developed for and copyrighted by the California Foundation for Improvement of Employer-Employee Relations (CFIER). It is modified and reprinted with permission.

3. A great description of different closure styles is available in the book *When Talk Works: Profiles of Mediators* by Deborah M. Kolb and Associates (Jossey: Bass Publishers, 1994).

4. Will Schutz developed a decision-making process called Concordance, which is like a high-octane version of consensus. Concordance stresses the importance of paying attention to issues of Inclusion, Control, and Openness. The Inclusion criterion states that the decision-making team consists of those who know most about the content of the decision and those who are the most affected by it. The Control criterion states that every person on the decision-making team has equal control or power and that everyone has a veto. The Openness criterion for Concordance, which is what distinguishes it most from consensus, is a requirement that everyone commit to being totally open and honest. Everyone must commit to openly expressing all relevant thoughts and feelings. Openness means not withholding; failing to say something relevant is as much a violation of the openness principle as intentionally lying. It is a "withholding lie." Using Concordance, what is lost in decision-making time is more than gained back when implementing the decision. Schutz used Concordance successfully in such high-profile, controversial decisions as distribution of annual salary bonuses and hospital staffing, as well as more mundane decisions.

## CHAPTER 18: GET REAL

1. The FIRO Element O provides a measure of satisfaction within the organization in the areas of inclusion, control, openness, significance, competence, and likability. The data can be reported for the organization as a whole, and/or for divisions, departments, teams, relationships, and individuals. See appendix 2 for additional information.

## GLOSSARY

1. For a deeper understanding of the theory we suggest you read Will Schutz, *The Human Element: Productivity, Self-Esteem and the Bottom Line* (Jossey Bass, 1994). For individuals particularly interested in the statistical research underlying FIRO theory, see *FIRO: A Three-Dimensional Theory of Interpersonal Behavior*, 3rd ed. (South San Francisco, CA: 1989). For additional information about FIRO-based instruments see chapters 7 and 8 and appendix 2.

## APPENDIX 1: RESEARCH REPORT

1. Clair Brown and Vince Valvano, *Analysis of Post Workshop Evaluation*, January 15, 1991, Institute of Industrial Relations, University of California, Berkeley.

2. James Tamm and Les Chisholm, "Does Interest Bargaining Really Work: A Test Using PERB Data," *California Public Employee Relations (CPER)* 101

(August 1993). This study researched the files of the California Public Employment Relations Board (PERB), which is the state agency with jurisdiction over labor-management disputes in the public sector. PERB keeps accurate data of all public sector unfair-labor-practice cases filed in the state by unions against management, management against unions, and individuals against either unions, or management. PERB also keeps accurate records of any time the parties reach an impasse in bargaining and request a mediator or a fact-finding panel. Thus, Tamm and Chisholm were able to accurately research the dispute history of all the parties attending the Improving the Labor-Management Relationship training program sponsored by the State and the Hewlett and Stuart Foundations.

The study reviewed all the parties attending the training for the first three and one-half years of the project. A total of ninety-four labor-management relationships were included in the study. No parties were included in the study unless they had completed the training at least six months earlier in order to avoid a "honeymoon" effect. The research was organized by the length of time that had elapsed since the parties had experienced the training: thirty-six months or more; twenty-four to thirty-five months; twenty-four months or more (combining the first two categories); seven to twenty-three months; and seven months or more (all relationships). The average rate of PERB cases filed was then calculated for each group (both before and after) and the rates were compared. The reduction in the rate of PERB filings for the 36+ group was 85 percent; for the 24–35 group, 80 percent; for the 24+ group, 82 percent; for the 7–23 group, 44 percent; and the overall reduction was 67 percent. When the relationships with the highest and lowest number of filings were excluded from the calculations to see if the extremes were creating unreliable averages, the total reduction jumped from 67 percent up to 74 percent.

Tamm and Chisholm also considered the impact of any statewide reduction in the number of labor-management disputes. They discovered an across-the-board reduction in the number of labor-management disputes of 23 percent. Hence some of the decline in the rates of filings in the sample relationships may be explained by a trend of unknown origin, such as economic conditions or changes in the law, or a general increase in experience in the bargaining process. But this general reduction in labor disputes during the time of the study by no means explains the exceptionally large reduction among training participants. To a degree, however, the large reduction of the parties included in the study helps explain the general decrease in filings in the state.

At the time of the study Tamm was a senior administrative law judge for PERB in the San Francisco office. Chisholm was the regional director of PERB's Sacramento regional office.

3. In 1990, the California legislature authorized the creation of a nonprofit foundation called CFIER (California Foundation for the Improvement of Employer-Employee Relations) to continue the PERB training. The CFIER pro-

gram was limited to labor-management disputes within public sector constituents. In 2001, CFIER merged with another nonprofit organization, The Workplace Institute, which was focused on building collaborative labor-management relationships in the private sector. The merged organization was renamed the Center for Collaborative Solutions (CCS) and has greatly broadened its scope. CCS is a particularly strong resource in the field of after-school programs. CCS can be contacted at www.ccscenter.org.

4. The company was at that time named Will Schutz Associates (WSA). The company was purchased by WSA's largest international affiliate partner, Business Consultants, Inc. The company was renamed BCon WSA International, Inc., and is now Business Consultants Network, Inc.

5. FIRO theory was created for the U.S. military by Dr. Will Schutz. For a more complete description see chapter 7, "Understanding Your Own Behavior in Relationships," or see Will Schutz, *The Human Element: Productivity, Self-Esteem and the Bottom Line* (Jossey-Bass, 1994). For individuals particularly interested in the statistical research underlying FIRO theory see Will Schutz, *FIRO: A Three-Dimensional Theory of Interpersonal Behavior*, 3rd ed. (South San Francisco, CA: 1989).

6. Professor Barba is currently director of Business Administration Studies at Universidad Tec de Monterrey in Cuernavaca, Mexico. Professor Barba's 1999 study is titled "Analysis of Beyond Conflict Post-Workshop Survey."

7. Because Professor Barba asked participants about their current effectiveness rather than their effectiveness immediately after the workshop, she noted that there may have been other influencing factors that were not measured by her survey. She noted, for example, that other workshops or a general increase in maturity level or additional living experience may also have contributed to an increase in effectiveness in conflicted situations. She also noted, however, that the consistent theme of answers to open-ended questions in the survey strongly suggested that participants viewed the skills learned in the workshop as the single most important factor in their increased effectiveness.

# INDEX

**If you would** like information about how to bring better collaborative skills into your organization or company, or if you have any comments or questions or want more information about the research reported in this book, please contact us at:

JimTamm@radicalcollaboration.com
and
RonLuyet@radicalcollaboration.com

Or call us at 1–800-INCLUSION (1-800-462-5874) (U.S. and Canada) or +650-871-4290 (internationally), or visit our Web site at:

www.radicalcollaboration.com

Or write us at

Business Consultants Network, Inc.
401 Marina Blvd.
South San Francisco, CA 94080

If you would like to receive twelve months of collaborative tips by e-mail, please sign up at:

www.radicalcollaboration.com